Colson Whitehead

Colson Whitehead

The Postracial Voice of Contemporary Literature

Kimberly Fain

ROWMAN & LITTLEFIELD
Lanham • Boulder • New York • London

Published by Rowman & Littlefield
A wholly owned subsidiary of The Rowman & Littlefield Publishing Group, Inc.
4501 Forbes Boulevard, Suite 200, Lanham, Maryland 20706
www.rowman.com

Unit A, Whitacre Mews, 26-34 Stannary Street, London SE11 4AB

British Library Cataloguing in Publication Information Available

Library of Congress Cataloging-in-Publication Data

Fain, Kimberly, 1974–
Colson Whitehead : the postracial voice of contemporary literature / Kimberly Fain.
p. cm.
Includes bibliographical references and index.
ISBN 978-1-4422-5013-0 (cloth : alk. paper) – ISBN 978-1-4422-5014-7 (ebook)
1. Whitehead, Colson, 1969– – Criticism and interpretation. I. Title.
PS3573.H4768Z63 2015
813'.54–dc23
2014049612

∞™ The paper used in this publication meets the minimum requirements of American
National Standard for Information Sciences Permanence of Paper for Printed Library
Materials, ANSI/NISO Z39.48-1992.

Printed in the United States of America

For my husband, Anthony Johnson, who makes life even more beautiful and my parents, Constance and Herbert Fain, for fostering my love of the written word.

Contents

Acknowledgments

My interest in Colson Whitehead emerged when I wrote the *Zone One* chapter in Keenan Norris's *Street Lit: Representing the Urban Landscape*. Norris's editorial guidance was extremely supportive during this process. As I researched Whitehead's zombie-themed book, I became interested in his total body of work. Once I read *The Intuitionist* and *John Henry Days*, I was determined to contribute to his literary legacy. Once I mentioned my proposal idea to Keenan, his enthusiasm was boundless; he was always willing to exchange ideas and consult with me at a moment's notice.

Secondly, I'm thankful for Stephen Ryan's acceptance of my proposal. Immediately, Stephen was open to my ideas and my approach to studying Whitehead. He realized that my scholarship on Whitehead would result in a positive addition to already existing literary criticism. Simultaneously, the book would distinguish itself from past methods of studying Whitehead. Furthermore, when I wanted to revise my literary methods and rearrange chapters, Stephen never hesitated to support my ideas and wishes.

During this process, editor-in-chief Kevin Larimer enthusiastically searched the *Poets & Writers* archives for his 2001 feature article on Colson Whitehead. Additionally, the books and culture editor at *Texas Monthly* and former *Village Voice* television editor, Jeff Salamon, graciously spoke to me about Whitehead. Salamon, Whitehead's former Brooklyn poker buddy, praised Whitehead's writing skills and integrity. Of course, I would like to thank my other editor, Lara Graham. She worked hard to bring this book to fruition. Not to mention, her considerate temperament, patience, and skill made me feel confident that my book was in good, capable, and skilled hands.

Also, I would like to thank my family. Tirelessly, they provided me with space and time to further my scholarship on Whitehead. Instead of sidetracking me from my research, reading, and writing, my husband, Professor Anthony Johnson, was always willing to discuss concepts, themes, and characters. His marketing and advertising background and experience in radio and television deepened my analysis of mass media and consumer culture. And his profound understanding of human nature, popular culture, and the commodification of black culture enhanced my interpretation of Whitehead's characters and motifs.

Lastly, I wish to acknowledge my parents, Professor Herbert and Professor Constance Fain. For without them, I would not have gained my love for history, law, literature, and popular culture. By exposing me to African American and American culture during my upbringing and education, my scholarship on Whitehead benefited immensely from their efforts.

Introduction

In the process of composing my *Zone One* chapter for inclusion in *Street Lit: Representing the Urban Landscape*, the concept of an entire book devoted to Colson Whitehead's literary works seemed paramount. The applicable literary theories and criticism of Whitehead's nonfiction and fiction books contain explicit and implicit themes of individualism, freedom, and equality. Whitehead accomplishes this feat in *The Intuitionist, John Henry Days, Apex Hides the Hurt, The Colossus of New York, Sag Harbor*, and *Zone One* by constructing characters that are racially exceptional and universally accessible. Readers of any diverse background will channel consciously or subconsciously their knowledge of history, pop culture, literature, literary theory, technology, and science fiction to interpret his texts. Therefore, Whitehead's approach to his characters and themes do not fit neatly into the foundations of American literature or African American literature. Whitehead's narrative technique is best described as experimental in nature and progressive in subject matter.

Due to Whitehead's recent presence in the literary scene, there are some challenges presented when consolidating and dissecting his work. *Intuitionist* was published in 1999 to rave reviews comparing Whitehead's debut novel to Ralph Ellison's *Invisible Man*.[1] There are also references to his literary mastery in the vein of Toni Morrison.[2] Although various journals such as *African American Review* and *Callaloo* critiqued *The Intuitionist*, they mainly focused on thematic issues of racial progress and racial passing. Many of these critiques ignored the significance of his book in terms of modern-day race relations, while others singularly focused on racial issues at the expense of focusing on issues of class and educational progress. After winning the PEN/Faulkner Award for *The Intuitionist* (1999), Whitehead's second novel was a finalist for the National Book Critics Award and Pulitzer Prize: *John*

Henry Days (2001).[3] Much of the criticism of this work focuses on an African American folk hero, John Henry, and his physical strength versus technological progress in the Industrial Age. *John Henry Days'* historical characters and modern Digital Age characters deserve readers' attention due to the African American folklore and pop culture elements. Then there is *Colossus of New York* (2003), which is rarely criticized by journals yet reviewed by numerous newspaper and pop culture magazines. Nevertheless, this nonfiction tribute to New York after 9/11 deserves attention because of its connection to the themes of urban spaces, deconstruction, and reconstruction in the postapocalyptic *Zone One* (2011). *Apex Hides the Hurt* (2006) won the PEN/Oakland Award.[4] Since this work receives the least amount of attention from scholars and mixed reviews from critics, I chose to devote only one chapter to its criticism. However, various sections of this book will contain relevant references to *Apex*. The critically acclaimed and autobiographical novel *Sag Harbor* (2009) focuses on a 1980s African American Manhattanite who travels each summer with his family to visit the Hamptons. Consequently, *Sag Harbor* was a finalist for the PEN/Faulkner Award and the Hurston/Wright Legacy Award.[5] Lastly, *Zone One* is a tribute to the dreams and aspirations of those who live and die in Manhattan prior to the zombie plague and those who live postapocalypse. In the process of gathering information, I used new millennium methods of research that some professors and scholars may or may not choose to access. For instance, there are numerous newspapers, magazines, and online literary journals that contain interviews of Colson Whitehead. These sources are extremely enlightening when filling in the blanks of scholarly research. In these New Age mediums, Whitehead makes his themes and authorial intentions clear in the printed interviews and in his numerous online interviews, readings, or speeches.

Although the African diaspora scholarship discusses Whitehead with an intense amount of depth, by means of accessing literary forebears such as W. E. B. Du Bois, Zora Neale Hurston, Ralph Ellison, and Richard Wright, these critics did not always contain information from Whitehead's interviews. Then there are mainstream journals that singularly discuss Whitehead in terms of technological advancement and the horror genre, yet they neglect the issues of marginalization and race that are both subtle and obvious when interpreting universal themes. Herein lies the challenge of compiling this critical study. Due to Colson Whitehead's abilities as a literary writer and tendency to challenge the significance of commercial culture and American canonical texts, there is a vacuous hole in the scholarship on Whitehead that needs to be occupied. Whitehead channels his African American heritage via foreparent texts, yet his work lacks the activism of 1960s protest novels.[6] Sanders I. Bernstein of the *Harvard Crimson* writes that Whitehead's "novels have been faulted for their refusal to directly confront issues of race head-on."[7] Instead, Whitehead uses satire and sarcasm in novels such as *John*

Henry Days and *Apex Hides the Hurt* to exemplify his "comedic command of language and his ability to create interesting conceits that explore race in a post-racial world."[8] Cameron Leader-Picone, a former graduate fellow at Harvard's W. E. B. Du Bois Research Institute, was compelled to write a chapter on Colson Whitehead for his dissertation. Leader-Picone believes that Whitehead "moves [African American literary tradition] forward while also drawing deeply from it."[9] Consequently, Whitehead's subtle style is representative of the new millennial African American tradition of addressing race.

Despite the impact of the African American literary tradition, Colson Whitehead is similarly influenced by the white male writers, as well as one black male writer of his Harvard milieu. Due to his literary achievements, Whitehead joins other fellow Harvard alums such as John Updike, Norman Mailer, e. e. cummings, T. S. Eliot, W. E. B. Du Bois, Henry James, and Ralph Waldo Emerson.[10] Prior to Whitehead's literary presence, the impact of the aforementioned writers is legendary. Each of those writers are instrumental in the construction of American literature and theory. Within this circle of literary giants, Whitehead's writings demonstrate that his forebears have made literary footprints on his authorial journey. John Updike wrote in the *New Yorker*, "The young African-American writer to watch may well be a thirty-one-year-old Harvard graduate with the vivid name of Colson Whitehead."[11] With the presence of racial irony in *The Intutionist*, satirical elements intersect with Norman Mailer's "The White Negro." e. e. cummings's "pity this busy monster, manunkind" epitomizes scientific progress at the expense of nature and humanity. Idol worship of science and technology, which is a prominent theme in *John Henry Days* and *Colossus of New York*, mimics the foreboding tone of T. S. Eliot's *Wasteland*. Both books explore the futility of the sentimental populace and aimless stragglers that roam in *The Colossus of New York* and postapocalyptical *Zone One*. Pompey's "Uncle Tom" demeanor and Lila Mae Watson's racial invisibility and detective prowess in *The Intuitionist* are allusions to W. E. B. Du Bois's theories on double consciousness and racial invisibility in the *Souls of Black Folk*.[12] Henry James's constant discussion of Americanness in terms of European heredity and American identity is widely read in literature programs due to his publication of *The Americans* and *Daisy Miller*. Distinguishing American identity occurs in almost every one of Colson Whitehead's novels, including *Apex Hides the Hurt* where characters are trying to decipher the inextricable links between African and European heritage, which impacts both blacks and whites in the United States.[13] Lastly, Ralph Waldo Emerson's views of individualism, mysticism, and/or self-reliance are echoed in Whitehead's protagonists, such as *The Intuitionist*'s Lila Mae, *John Henry*'s J. Sutter, and *Zone One*'s Mark Spitz. These black and white influences do not make his work inferior or superior to his literary forebears. As Henry Louis Gates once stated in *Signifying Monkey*, "Europeans and Americans neither invented literature and its theory nor have a monopoly on its development."[14] Instead, these European American and African American influences fuel the hybridity that is reiterated in every one of Whitehead's works. Consequently, a thorough and exhaustive study of Whitehead's books should contain a wide range of critical study that is not limited or singularly defined by one culture seizing precedence over another.

   In the process of researching for this critical study, references are made to Du Bois's *Souls of Black Folk*, Larsen's *Pass*, Ellison's *Invisible Man* and *Going to the Territory*, Wright's *Black Boy* and *Native Son*, bell hooks's *Ain't I a Woman* and *Writing Beyond Race*, Gates's *Signifying Monkey*, and Morrison's *Playing in the Dark*. All of Whitehead's works contain applicable elements to the folklore, rhetoric, theories, themes, and vernacular contained in these studies of African American literature, ethnic, and cultural studies. Morrison's study on the construct of blackness and whiteness in American literature forms the basis of black and white symbolism and imagery in early American texts.[15] Simultaneously, this book will examine texts such as Henry David Thoreau's "Civil Disobedience," and Edgar Allan Poe's "Masque of the Red Death," and their method of providing a context for themes of freedom, individualism, and equality within the context of moral ambiguity, class divisions, and the social constructs of blackness and whiteness. According to Morrison, although Poe's and Hawthorne's works are generally devoid of black characters and themes, along with Melville their use of black and white imagery creates the basis of black and white character construction in the nineteenth-century American literature.[16] Furthermore, the discussions of scholars such as Harold Bloom, Jonathan Culler, Terry Eagleton, and Robert Dale Parker, on literary theory and analysis add depth to the carefully threaded themes that are interwoven in Whitehead's books.

   Each chapter in this book combines African, African American, and European influences to interpret the commercialism, mass media, and pop culture elements in all of Whitehead's works. Whitehead speaks to the human condition that is captured in his sincere devotion to movies, music, and artifacts that distinguish the American culture from other cultures outside the United States. Faulknerian-styled sentences, Richard Wright's complexity, Ralph Ellison's eloquence, George A. Romero's cinematic, horror/science-fiction motifs, and Justin Cronin's commercial appeal are also evident in Whitehead's work. Whitehead's literary genius often confounds those who study him. In the literary journal *Callaloo*, Linda Selzer refers to "Whitehead's exhilarating culture, genre, and media-crossing art" as New Eclecticism.[17] In all of Whitehead's books, he reworks "literary traditions that range from folklore, the slave narrative, literary modernism, postmodernism, and black urban fiction, to detective noir, magical realism, image fiction, and post-soul literature."[18] His experimental technique of "new media formats, satiric juxtaposition of generic elements, and artistic play with previous intellectual and artistic traditions also invite comparison to the sampling and mixing techniques of the hip hop music that he has written about in his fiction" and in such magazines such as *Granta*, *Harper's*, *Newsday*, the *New Times*, *New York*, *Salon*, *Spin*, *Vibe*, and the *Village Voice*.[19] Furthermore, he incorporates pop culture artifacts (images, ideas, and trends) of an obsessive mass media and digitized society into his artfully composed historical and science-fiction novels, such as *The Intuitionist*, *John Henry Days*, and *Zone One*. Whitehead's social critique of race, class, and commercial culture proves why he has been honored as a finalist for the following accolades: Hemingway Foundation/Pen Award, Hurston/Wright Legacy Award, the Los Angeles Fiction Times Award, Pen/Faulkner Award, National Book Critics Circle Award, Pulitzer Prize, and so forth. Furthermore, he has won the Cullman Center for Scholars and Writers Fellowship, the Guggenheim Fellowship Award, the MacArthur "Genius" Grant Award, Whiting Writers Award, and Young Lions Award.[20]

For the purposes of adding depth to the themes of freedom, individualism, and equality, I offer my study of law. Although I refrain from making references to legal cases and treatises that would fit more appropriately in a law journal or legal case book, I encourage readers to contemplate the Declaration of Independence and the individual rights mentioned in the Constitution. Concepts of life, liberty, and the pursuit of happiness and freedom of expression are frequently referenced and acted upon in pop culture and literary studies. Ralph Ellison alludes to this legal influence in our literary heritage in his essay "The Novel as a Function of American Democracy."[21] Ellison claims that the "American nation is based upon revolution, dedicated to change through basic conceptions stated in the Bill of Rights and the Constitution."[22] Thus, the multifarious knowledge that classic and contemporary writers have of these texts often supports the foundation for their textual arguments and barriers to a character's motives, goals, and development. Oftentimes, the American ideal and the American reality are in conflict. Thus, the American Dream becomes an elusive, exclusive, and metaphorical myth that infects every tentacle of a character's life in their frustrations and accomplishments. There is the dream realized by some Americans and the *Dream Deferred* that Langston Hughes references in his classic poem. Whitehead frequently challenges notions of American identity and privilege that is determined by race, class, and/or education. Thus, methodical study of cultural, sociopolitical, and historical context is essential to understanding Whitehead's genre-bending works that are not clearly defined like the diverse cultural heritage of many people who inhabit America.

Colson Whitehead's novels are contemporary classics that seek to function in a digital and postracial world of his own creation. Most Americans are still trying to define who and what it means to be an American. Is the

Declaration of Independence's proclamation that "all men are created equal"[23] and the implication that prosperity can be achieved if they work hard evidence of a dream realized or dream deferred? Are American Dreams built on reality or delusion? Are education, materials goods, wealth, and/or fame proof that a person has achieved the American Dream? Whitehead depicts social status and pop culture artifacts as a means to define our aspirational nature, the material trappings of success, and the inevitable void of mass consumption on the spirits of individuals who live in the metropolis. Furthermore, he reconfigures genre tropes and explores themes of detachment, dread, loss, freedom, redemption, and transformation in the New York landscape of the past, present, and future. Whitehead's depiction of New York as a utopian symbol of prosperity and his progressive response to the accessibility of the American Dream is an amazing journey into the mind of a literary genius.

Due to the hybridity of his works, Whitehead's books cannot be limited to one theory of literature. Professors and students can argue a number of various theories when interpreting his works: African American, aesthetics, modernism, postmodernism, Jacques Derrida's deconstructionism, gender and sexuality, structuralism, and poststructuralism. When determining whether to study his works alongside canonical works that have been studied and criticized for centuries, all of those theories have a certain level of application. However, one political philosophy that has application as a theory of examining literature is postracialism. Jonathan Culler asserts that "theory itself intermingles ideas from philosophy, linguistics, history, political theory, and psychoanalysis."[24] Postracialism suggests that America's election of our first African American president is a signifier that racism no longer exists. Even though a number of politicians and everyday people embrace this notion, there are many African American writers and artists who insist that the election of Barack Obama does not speak to the end of racism. Although tempers rise when discussing postracialism in American society and politics, the term *postblackness*, which is a term that is embraced by artists, has gained popularity amongst many African Americans. Touré's book *Who's of Afraid of Post-Blackness: What It Means to Be Black Now* and feminist writers such as bell hooks's *Writing Beyond Race: Living Theory and Practice* approach ways to interpret black art, music, cinema, and/or literature in a postblack or postracial society; both authors acknowledge there is evidence in American culture, politics, and literature that racism is still an issue in America. Thus, an examination of racial passing in *The Intuitionist*, racial exceptionalism in *John Henry Days*, racial and communal identity in *Apex Hides the Hurt*, class and education privilege *Sag Harbor*, and racial invisibility in *Zone One* qualify postracialism as a valid method for studying literature.

In all of Whitehead's works, there is the notion that racism exists, yet a character or society can attain the quality of racial irrelevance due to their talents, passing, education, economics, and/or color blindness of characters toward one another. Ultimately, a society may attain a level where race does not or should not matter. Although it is evident from Whitehead's interviews and writings, he is not under the impression that racism is irrelevant. Whitehead once said that "he writes about race because as 'a black writer, that's my business.'"[25] However, he does flirt with the idea of postracial characters such as James Fulton in *The Intuitionist*, John Henry in *John Henry Days*, the unnamed narrator in *Apex Hides the Hurt*, Benji Cooper in *Sag Harbor*, and *Zone One*'s Mark Spitz who live in racially unconscious or conscious societies. As a self-proclaimed postracial czar or secretary of postracial affairs, Colson Whitehead's sarcastic declaration designates him as the unofficial leader of this theoretical literary movement that challenges racial assumptions of readers by oftentimes neglecting opportunities to mention his protagonists' cultural heritage.[26] Race is inferred by the other characters' attitudes or responses to the protagonist, yet ethnicity remains an ancillary factor, which is superseded only by the universal themes of class and commercial culture. These are characters, such as Lila Mae Watson, who are not limited by society's misnomers about them or their racial heritage; J. Sutter and Benji Cooper, who are widely accepted by their white peers; and Mark Spitz, who are defined by more than their race. These characters succeed by their notions of self-determination and intelligence. Thus, when they are individualistic in nature and self-reliant, some critics consider this as evidence of their alienation from the African American community and their marginalization from the mainstream culture.

Although the Declaration of Independence and the US Constitution suggest elements of an aspirational society, readers must remember that the drafters of these documents were white, male property owners of land and/or people.[27] Founding Fathers such as James Madison, George Mason, and George Washington shaped the geographical, economic, and individual destinies of Americans.[28] Leaders who negotiated our independence and liberation from Europe in essence gained even more political, legal, and economic control over the land and the people in the New World. Herein lies the conflict and the irony of the Founding Fathers' ideals, intentions, and reality.

Whitehead's literary footprint reflects the sociocultural and sociopolitical struggles that remain from this duplicitous, complex, and unresolved history. William Faulkner speaks of this ever-present history that plagues Southern society. Yet, this book argues that this multifarious past frustrates not only Southern racial relations but Northern racial relations as well. The Southern hierarchal structure during slavery, the Reconstruction era, and the Jim Crow era is a symbol of the complex capitalistic structure of American society. In Jonathan Levy's *Freaks of Fortune*, he states, "For men who were masters of households, the ownership of physical forms of capital and wealth—slaves and above all land—anchored economic security."[29] Thus, economic security in America is rooted in land ownership and subservience of groups with no liberty or legal status.

However, postracialism is a perspective born in the new millennium. Postracialism has elements of the aspirational nature of Americans presented as a modern truth and possibly an attainable reality in the future. Could the concepts of freedom, individuality, and equality truly exist in American society despite our troubled history? If any society has a chance to achieve this, it would be America first because of our diversity and interracial interdependence. Colson Whitehead broaches this concept so brilliantly in *Zone One*. Therefore, I was compelled to read all of his works through the lens of the American Dream or the American nightmare. For an author who appears to have achieved a certain level of postracial success, Whitehead's literary work creates the opportunity to combine my graduate studies in American literature with my sociocultural and sociopolitical knowledge gained from my legal studies. In the process of studying the double-consciousness and the racial-invisibility-laced narratives of Ellison, Hurston, Wright, Morrison, and now Whitehead, it's impossible to disregard laws and government structures, such as plutocracy, meritocracy, and democracy, that facilitate or inhibit the American Dream. Undoubtedly, the depth of Whitehead's articles and books indicate that he is well versed in the fragmented identity of African Americans within our American culture. In 2008, Whitehead wrote as a contributor for the *New York Times* an article entitled "Visible Man," which is a satirical piece on race, economic, and political privilege.[30] Naturally, Whitehead's "privileged childhood on Manhattan's Upper West Side, [as] the third of four children" whose parents "owned an executive recruiting firm"; his attendance at a "private school and summer[s] in the Hamptons"; and his Ivy League education influence his historical perceptions and authorial intent of his literary pursuits.[31] One must wonder if this privileged educational background could lead Colson Whitehead to write an ironical/satirical article entitled "The Year of Living Postracially."[32] Is it possible for a postracial society or postracial individual to exist in literature but not in the real world?

Perhaps, due to Whitehead's upper-middle-class rearing, attendance at America's number one prep school Trinity,[33] and a Harvard education, his intention as a writer is to deconstruct race as a factor in the achievement of the American Dream. Instead, Whitehead's books attribute struggles to the individual, and the conflicts faced by his characters are symptomatic of the human condition. By continuing to broaden the scope of who is considered an American, Whitehead reconstructs the American identity to be inclusive rather than exclusive. He achieves this feat by including African Americans amongst the class of people who may achieve the American Dream, assuming they are hardworking, educated, and/or upwardly mobile. Although many critics disagree with the notion that the American Dream is equally accessible, Whitehead's novels consistently demonstrate that despite racial segregation and past discrimination, in the future, class will be the main factor in determining opportunity and accessibility instead of race. For an African American author, Whitehead's postracial or postblack attitude that cultural distinctions are passé in a global society or at least in literature is unique and relevant in a transformative society.

NOTES

1. Bob Minzesheimer, "'Intuitionist' Lifts Novelist to New Heights," *USA Today*, December 1999, accessed December 31, 2013, http://www.usatoday.com/.
2. Ibid.
3. "Colson Whitehead: 2013—US and Canada Competition Creative Arts—Fiction Bio," John Guggenheim Memorial Foundation: Fellowships to Assist Research and Artist Creation, accessed December 31, 2013, http://www.gf.org/.
4. Ibid.
5. Ibid.
6. Sanders I. Bernstein, "Colson Whitehead '91: One of Harvard's Recent Authors Keeps It Real," *Harvard Crimson*, April 16, 2009, accessed January 1, 2014, http://www.thecrimson.com/.
7. Ibid.
8. Ibid.
9. Ibid.
10. "Notable Graduates," Harvard University, 2013, accessed January 1, 2014, http://www.harvard.edu/.
11. John Updike, "Tote That Ephemera: An Ambitious New Novel from a Gifted Writer," *New Yorker*, May 7, 2001, accessed January 1, 2014, http://www.newyorker.com/.
12. W. E. B. Du Bois, *The Souls of Black Folk* (New York: Barnes & Noble Classics, 2003), 7–15.
13. Colson Whitehead, *Apex Hides the Hurt* (New York: Doubleday, 2006).
14. Henry Louis Gates, *The Signifying Monkey: A Theory of African-American Literary Criticism* (New York: Oxford University Press, 1989), xiv.
15. Toni Morrison, *Playing in the Dark: Whiteness and the Literary Imagination* (New York: Vintage, 1993), 51–54.
16. Ibid.
17. Linda Selzer, "New Eclecticism: An Interview with Colson Whitehead," *Callaloo* 31, no. 2 (spring 2008): 393.
18. Ibid.
19. Ibid.
20. "Colson Whitehead . . . Bio."
21. Ralph Ellison, "The Novel as a Function of American Democracy," in *Going to the Territory* (New York: Vintage, 1995), 311.
22. Ibid.
23. "The Declaration of Independence," *A New World Is at Hand "The Charters of Freedom,"* US National Archives and Records Administration, accessed January 2, 2014, http://www.archives.gov/.
24. Jonathan Culler, *Literary Theory: A Very Short Introduction* (Oxford: Oxford University Press, 2011), 19.
25. Minzesheimer, "Intuitionist."

26. Colson Whitehead, "The Year of Living Postracially," *New York Times*, November 3, 2009, accessed January 1, 2014, http://www.nytimes.com/.

27. "Biographical Index of America's Founding Fathers," *A New World Is at Hand "The Charters of Freedom,"* US National Archives and Records Administration, accessed January 2, 2014, http://www.archives.gov/.

28. Ibid.

29. Jonathan Levy, *Freaks of Fortune: The Emerging World of Capitalism and Risk in America* (Boston: Harvard University Press, 2014), 3–4.

30. Colson Whitehead, "Visible Man," *New York Times*, April 24, 2008, accessed January 1, 2014, http://www.nytimes.com/.

31. Rohan Preston, "Colson Whitehead's Zombie Dream," *Star Tribune* Books, October 29, 2011, accessed January 2, 2014, http://www.startribune.com/.

32. Whitehead, "Year of Living Postracially."

33. "No. 1: Trinity School," *Forbes*, last updated April 29, 2010, accessed January 2, 2014, http://www.forbes.com/.

Part I

The Intuitionist

Chapter One

Verticality

Allegorical Symbols of Racial and National Uplift

When Colson Whitehead sauntered onto the literary scene, *Esquire*'s Sven Birkerts fondly declared that "a young black novelist—had stepped into a literary power vacuum."[1] Whitehead's subtle yet intelligent candor discussed the "ever-thorny issue of race," according to Birkerts, in a lively and innovative way.[2] Amid the metaphorical and literal darkness of the metropolis live the mysterious and sometimes comical characters of *The Intuitionist*. In the evening, the city light is "the secondhand gray of ghetto twilight, a dull mercury color."[3] Jay Thratchenberg, a book critic for the *Austin Chronicle*, describes the early to mid-1950s New York metropolis as "an impersonal, intimidating presence unto itself with a grimy, dark, moody foreboding."[4] Meanwhile, the citizens who live in the outskirts of the metropolis travel at an exhaustive pace. With so much frenzied hustle and bustle, their memory of their initial purpose of their urban quest fails them.[5] The one-way streets are designed to inhibit U-turns, making flight a complex initiative.[6] The streets are paved in a politically active city that is continuously transforming.[7] Whitehead specifically states that this is "not a Southern city . . . but the most famous city in the world."[8] Yet, Whitehead resists critics' assumptions that the narrative transpires in New York. When book critic Valerie Boyd compared this ironic novel to Ralph Ellison's classic *Invisible Man*, she insisted that Whitehead's choices are intentionally ambiguous. Like Ellison, Whitehead "never names the city or the year in which the story takes place."[9] Whitehead asserts, "*The Intuitionist* takes place in a kind of detective novel Gotham that is like an essential city, not necessarily New York."[10] Gary Krist of the *New York Times* describes this big city as a "New York where money and power—those twin engines of all modern societies—are inextricably associated with the politics of vertical transport."[11] By not appointing New York as the narrative locale, *The Intuitionist* becomes an allegorical tale that represents industrialization and technological advancement in almost any major Midwest or Northern city: Boston, Chicago, Detroit, Philadelphia, Pittsburgh, St. Louis, or New York. In this allegorical, satirical, and symbolic narrative about "social progress, racial struggle and elevator inspectors," the infrastructure represents the structural iniquities and privileges of an innovative metropolis on the cusp of cultural, economic, and political transformation.[12]

LILA MAE WATSON: THE FIRST "COLORED" FEMALE ELEVATOR INSPECTOR

Lila Mae Watson, the first black woman elevator inspector, has an impeccable service record until an elevator crash tarnishes her reputation. In this hardboiled detective fiction and satirical novel, Lila Mae becomes the unwilling subject of an intense "political battle between the Intuitionists and the Empiricists."[13] Lila Mae is a proud Intuitionist who uses "professional magic inasmuch as she relies on her perceptions to cure the elevator of its sickness in the primitive yet sophisticated urban society."[14] The Intuitionists are categorized as "freaks and misfits" by the Empiricists.[15] Due to their practice of diagnosing the condition of an elevator with their feelings, Intuitionists are viewed as "voodoo inspectors" and "witchdoctors."[16] In "Recalibrating the Past: Colson Whitehead's *The Intuitionist*," Alison Russell asserts that "the Empiricists' racially inflected terminology for Intuitionists characterizes their competing belief systems as a cultural, as well as epistemological, conflict."[17] Meanwhile, the Empiricists utilize more traditional methods for inspecting elevators. In an issue of *Science Fiction Studies*, Isiah Lavender III contends that the "Empiricists depend on cold hard facts of physical measurement to rigorously check the structural and mechanical details of the elevators."[18] Thus, they are considered pragmatists and conservative. Despite the Empiricists' drive for innovation, they are also regressive minimalists who are distressed by the "growing numbers of women and colored people in the Guild."[19] Lila Mae, a symbol of colored progress, threatens the leadership of the Elevator Guild. When the Fanny Briggs Memorial Building elevator crashes after Lila Mae inspects it, the timing of the disaster is suspicious since Intuitionists and the Empiricists are vying for the guild chair position in a heated political battle. To determine whether the elevator accident is an act of sabotage, Lila Mae goes underground to prove her innocence.[20]

In the process of clearing of her name, Lila Mae learns information about the deceased founder of Intuitionism—James Fulton. Fulton was a forerunner in elevator technology. Prior to his death, he was working on "the black box" that would ultimately revolutionize vertical transport in terms of elevator travel. Ultimately, this "second elevation, unlocking the sky" is both a literal and figurative transformative state for those who seek the black box.[21] Lavender asserts that "the concept of verticality, both architectural and cultural governs the action of both camps as they vie to find the black box."[22] Thus, the "social, political, and cultural possibilities of race in other place and times" speaks to the possibility of improved race relations in society.[23] However, the potential setback of Lila Mae's career is proof that everyone is not ready for "colored progress" in this segregated metropolis. In an attempt to avoid the reoccurrence of last summer's riots, the mayor refuses to address a reporter's questions on the issue of "colored progress."[24] Thus, the reader knows that the social implications of Lila Mae's vindication are not only personal but communal as well. The community has a collective interest in the success of individuals who are pioneers in their fields. Ultimately, Lila Mae's success or failure will determine the progress or the regression of an entire race.

EMPIRICISM VERSUS INTUITIONISM: THE WARRING FACTIONS OF THE ELEVATOR DEPARTMENT

Whitehead's *Intuitionist* speaks to the disturbing tendency of technological progress advancing far beyond the pace of social progress.[25] On the issues of race, class, and gender, the department rivalry between these two factions is satirical due to its mockery of the political strife between traditionalists and progressives. There is a sense that the Empiricism represents conservative thought, and the Intuitionism represents liberal thought. However, Lila Mae's underground journey proves that there is reason to distrust individuals on both sides of the political spectrum. Personal, professional, and political alliances in this "book drenched in allegory" do not always reveal their actual loyalties.[26] As Lila Mae attempts to erase her tarnished name, she realizes that Intuitionism is not without scandal.[27] She encounters ransacking "thugs [and] political crossfire between municipal factions" that threaten the progress of a city on the rise and its inhabitants who live therein.[28] Both parties are subject to extreme behavior in acquiring the elevator guild position. Whoever holds the chair position will be the head of the Elevator Department and the possible master of Fulton's black box technology, which will result in urban domination. Gary Krist writes in the *New York Times* that the "second elevation," according to Whitehead, is a "new stage in the evolution of African American social identity."[29] Elevation serves the dual purpose of "architectural and social" levity.[30] Thus, Lila Mae's presence in this "established hierarchy" manifests the upward mobility and racial uplift of African Americans.[31] But for the reigning social hierarchy, that is exclusive rather than inclusive; levity means continued and expanding supremacy of the elite. Empiricists and Intuitionists desire the black box technology for the purposes of "verticality, both architectural and cultural."[32] Neither group appears to have a sincere interest in deconstructing the social hierarchy that bars disenfranchised groups from enjoying technological and economic progress. Thus, from a utopian perspective, this new elevator technology signifies the second elevation from the racial strife and tension that pervades the city landscape. But in terms of the warring factions, control of the black box means ensured domination for elite members who reside at the top of the social hierarchy. The stakes are high for those who seek supremacy or equality; therefore, the search for the black box becomes a mystery that must serve the greater good of humanity. Lavender claims "ascension of humanity, particularly the black race, from the city as we know it, from the cramped spaces of inequality."[33] Ideally, black box elevator technology, in the right hands, creates the possibility of cross-cultural connection, equality, and social integration despite the resistance and fears of the power structure.

THE MECHANICS: THE UNDERGROUND MEN OF THE ELEVATOR DEPARTMENT

The concept of elevation is an abstract symbol that pervades the narrative. Implicit in the phrase *upward mobility* is the possibility to rise above the circumstances of an individual's current state, race, or economic status. When the audience meets the "colored men" of the underground garage, dichotomous divisions exist between high and low. The physical and economic segregation between whites who work aboveground and the black workers who work underground is evidence of racial invisibility. The "colored men" of the novel are working-class mechanics who toil beneath the surface where "there are no windows permitting the sky."[34] The dimly lit environment does not prevent them from taking agency over this enclosed and subpar space. In the midst of this gloom, the men have found comical ways to address their low-wage status and disapproval of leadership. They scrawl "horns, boiling cysts, [and] the occasional cussword" across Frank Chancre's teeth, all of which demonstrate how they don't take Chancre and his promises seriously. Although the African American men's actions may demonstrate "myriad tiny insurrections," their passive rebellion is nearly invisible due to their low-wage status.[35] Since the men's doodling exists below the surface and their labor is not valued by the department, their actions are not noticeable to the power structure.

But Whitehead insists that although their minor insurrections go unnoticed, they somehow "count for something."[36] How can these minor violations of company policy, barring campaign posters near headquarters, amount to something if they are invisible to the ruling factions? For a novel, in which every word bears consequence and every object or place represents a concept grander than itself, the underground men and their symbols of insurrection bear immense significance. Whitehead's use of the terms *underground* and *invisible* is an allusion to Ralph Ellison's *Invisible Man*. Thus, the mechanics' dark locale is literally below the surface and figuratively suggestive of the second-class citizenry of African Americans regardless of their designative jobs. Thus, defacing the posters of the current guild chair, Chancre, is an act of rebellion proving that the mechanics and African Americans as a whole are not satisfied with their inferior working conditions and their overall progress in American society. In this instance, campaign posters transform into a makeshift satirical cartoon depicting the black male mechanics' disenfranchisement. Although Whitehead's subtle political statement lacks the overt articulation present in protest novels of the twentieth century, such as Richard Wright's *Native Son*, Ellison's *Invisible Man*, and Ann Petry's *The Street*, Whitehead exposes his segregated characters' racial reality as a writer who is living in an integrated society.

Since Whitehead articulates the cultural and socioeconomic experiences of African Americans and Caucasian Americans in the metropolis, the subtlety of his narrative is unobtrusive yet political. According to Thomas C. Foster, author of *New York Times* best seller *How to Read Like a Professor*, all writing is political on some level; realist writing that explores "human problems, including those in the social and political realm, that addresses the rights of persons and the wrongs of those in power—can be not only interesting but hugely compelling."[37] In one terse scene, Whitehead exposes the social stratification experienced by black males in a segregated working place and the unequal treatment maintained by leaders like Chancre. Lavender asserts that "white racists like Chancre" cause the "immobility of black uplift."[38] Due to leaders like Chancre, blacks are barred from ascending the economic hierarchy.[39] Admittedly, Chancre says that he believes in colored progress at a moderate pace because he fears anarchy.[40] If the mechanics felt acknowledged and appreciated for their service, they would not have depicted the guild chair as a buffoon. Even some white characters have contempt for Chancre because he is perceived as a ruthless bully.[41] Thus, Whitehead uses satire as a way to communicate issues of disenfranchisement that is humorous in nature. Since *The Intuitionist* addresses "power structures, relations among classes, issues of justice and rights, interactions between the sexes and among various racial and ethnic constituencies," Foster would consider this literary work political.[42] Even though Whitehead and the men operate under a guise that appears nonpolitical, their actions buck the power structure and speak to the social injustice of their times.

THE FANNY BRIGGS "FUGITIVE SLAVE" MEMORIAL BUILDING

From an outward glance, Lila Mae may also appear apolitical. However, her status as the first black female elevator inspector positions her as a political representation of racial uplift. Early in the narrative, Lila Mae is assigned by Chancre to inspect the Fanny Briggs Memorial Building "in an attempt to draw votes from his more liberal opponent."[43] The Briggs building epitomizes uplift ideology because Fanny Briggs is a hero to African Americans.[44] Linda Selzer states in "Instruments More Perfect than Bodies: Romancing Uplift in Colson Whitehead's *The Intuitionist*," "As a slave woman who taught herself to read, Fanny Briggs provides what appears to be an originary model of black uplift through education and self-reliance."[45] Since Lila Mae is associated with Fanny Briggs's legacy, Briggs's "status as a marker of apparently authentic black empowerment" is paramount to the narrative.[46] As the first colored woman inspector, Lila Mae is a pioneer in her field. When the reader learns that Lila Mae wrote an oral report on Fanny Briggs, this deepens the significant connection between Lila Mae and Fanny Briggs. Thus, the individual's progress narrative transforms into a communal progress narrative signifying uplift ideology. Even though Lila Mae conducts herself as a reluctant face of "colored progress" because after all she is just doing her job, the Briggs building has historical significance for the populace. Now, the mayor suffers from fewer complaints by disgruntled citizens that lead to embarrassing demonstrations with flying tomatoes and spoiled cabbages.[47] The mayor's conciliatory appeasement "illustrates the manner in which narratives of self-reliance can be used to circumscribe more collective forms of social action."[48] Therefore, the mayor does not have to make authentic structural changes because he is reinforcing the narrative of self-reliance. Pull yourself up from your bootstraps? Fanny Mae taught herself to read, and she was an escaped slave. Consequently, the Briggs-elevator free-fall after Lila Mae's inspection reminds us that the infrastructure is still plagued by structural inequities that are symbolized by the monuments we build.

Lauren Berlant says that "the scene of a catastrophe that reveals the machinery of white supremacy as at the heart of not only politics and corporate ideology, but engineering itself."[49] And the timing of this accident, immediately before the mayor plans to ride the elevator, is a suspicious "high-profile mess-up."[50] Lila Mae eventually discovers that she has been sabotaged by the Empiricists, Intuitionists, or the elevator companies United or Arbo who vie for the guild chair's support. What is supposed to be a career-making case morphs into an impending employment termination for Lila Mae. Despite Lila Mae's apolitical nature, she is at the center of a mystery that has political, socioeconomic, and racial implications. Whitehead utilizes elevator technology, an African American female pioneer, and the frayed infrastructure to articulate his elevation or progress narrative. The elevator is a symbolic representation for upward mobility and the transcendence beyond human limitations. One escalator specialist, Chuck, discusses how the desire to elevate is biological and goes beyond the physics of a building.[51] Surveying the landscape below is a celestial experience that Chuck likens to becoming a "sky king."[52] Thus, the eighteen-floor Fanny Briggs building represents racial inclusion, for African Americans will now see an emblem of racial progress in the urban skyline. By choosing to name a municipal building after a fugitive slave who learns to read, the citizens have concrete proof that equality is attainable despite historical tensions and transgressions. Thus, Selzer asserts that "uplift ideology constitutes a literacy, or shared set of signifiers through which individuals, communities, and nations seek to read or to define themselves."[53] For the African American community, the Briggs building embodies redemptive power of literacy and education.

However, the Briggs building is a symbol that has multiple meanings. According to Richard Chase, author of *The American Novel and Its Tradition*, a symbol means an autonomous linguistic fusion of meanings.[54] Therefore, the Briggs building may also stand as political appeasement that serves the mayor's reelection bid more than the residents of the metropolis. With regard to Lila Mae, the Fanny Briggs building represents an elevator freefall that threatens to end her career. Like most symbolic representations in America, the Fanny Briggs building has different meanings for various people. Yet, the Fanny Briggs building contributes to the allegorical structure of the narrative. However, *The Intuitionist* is not pure allegory because the symbols do not have fixed meanings. Chase argues that "pure allegory (if it can ever be isolated as such) assumes two fixed discourses—a language of static signs and a set of truths to which they refer."[55] Elevators and the buildings they serve have multiple meanings in this narrative; there is no fixed or static meaning confining the reader to a singular interpretation. Another interpretation of the Briggs elevator crash would signify that racial progress theory is a flawed narrative. The Fanny Briggs elevator freefall is Lila Mae's downfall if she does not prevail in uncovering the conspiracy. If the racial progress narrative is flawed, for every rise that occurs in the African American community, there will be a conspiratorial catastrophe orchestrated by the social hierarchy that fears equality, inclusion, and the upward mobility of those formerly deemed as inferior.

Ultimately, *The Intuitionist* is a symbolic sociocultural act in terms of analyzing the African American novel.[56] Bernard W. Bell, author of *The Afro-American Novel and Its Tradition*, argues that the African American novel is a hybrid of "social and cultural forces that shape the author's attitude."[57] Thus, the symbolic objects such as the elevators and campaign posters, symbolic institutions such as the Briggs building, and terms such as *underground* and *invisibility* are not contradictory signs. These symbols have multiple meanings that are a culmination of Whitehead's educational, economic, and historical background that shape his tone toward his authorial subjects. In Ellison's essay "The Novel as a Function of American Democracy," he says that the novel functions as a vehicle for a writer to "express his own vision of reality."[58] Furthermore, the novelist is permitted "to write out of his own group background and his own individual background."[59] Whitehead's novel, like other African American novels, have "borrowed from western culture and adapted in their quest for status, power, and identity in a racist, capitalist, patriarchal American social arena" their elevation narrative and/or African American progress narrative.[60] In essence, *The Intuitionist* utilizes Western cultural notions of elevation and progress while intermeshing African American cultural signs of achievement. Consequently, the symbols in *The Intuitionist* have a hybrid allegorical structure that incorporates the multifarious meanings of classic American and African American narratives.

THE URBAN POLITICS OF VERTICALITY: ARCHITECTURAL, CULTURAL, AND ECONOMIC PROGRESS

Whitehead's *Intuitionist* promises to discuss the theory of elevators and the relevance of innovative technology. But this elevator narrative essentially examines upward mobility in a segregated society. As many of Whitehead's books suggest, technology is the great equalizer in an unequal world. Technology provides stability and comfort; it improves life by potentially serving all of humanity in a universal manner. But technology tends to isolate geographically, alienate socially, or dislocate physically those who desire to shield themselves from the everyday human or the real world. Consequently, those who are disadvantaged and thus barred from accessing technology suffer from estrangement as well. Berlant expresses the significance of the black box:

> The black box is a reimagining of white flight, but instead of outward to the suburbs it goes upward. Rather than being locked in an inner city with blacks and other minorities, the whites (like *Blade Runner*'s Tyrell) move upward to display their superiority and to separate themselves from contact with blacks who are permanently locked, motionless, in the lower class. After all, suburban whites still have to come into the inner city to work, but if whites are elevated, they can leave the "ghetto" behind permanently.[61]

The politics of verticality is about architectural, structural, institutional, economic, and cultural progress. According to the architectural hierarchy, upward expansion uplifts an individual's living arrangements and the imminent space to look down on the world below. The further the elevator rises toward the sky, the higher you reside on the power structure or the social hierarchy. Fulton's papers on the black box technology is a gateway to the second elevation, which equates to a superior lifestyle for the populous instead of a privilege for an elect or select few. As the narrator tells us, "It is important to let the citizens know it is coming. To let them prepare themselves for the second elevation."[62] Thus, this second elevation of the future, which is set in a prior era, is a reimagining of our historical past. In novels such as *The Intuitionist* the "historical pasts and the phantasmatic futures are the heuristics that bring us back to what is affectively charged and experienced in, but what can only be intuited as, the historical present."[63] Whitehead's experimental style elevates elevator pioneers and revolutionary black box technology into iconic status by compelling us to experience America's racial past via an authentic yet satirical lens. Consequently, we as the reader internalize these dual perspectives of Whitehead's literary milieu, futuristic technology set in the past, as the historical present.

NOTES

1. Sven Birkerts, "Carry That Weight," *Esquire*, May 2001, 30, http://search.ebscohost.com/.

2. Ibid.

3. Colson Whitehead, *The Intuitionist* (New York: Anchor, 1999), 1.

4. Jay Trachtenberg, "The Intuitionist," *Austin Chronicle*, March 24, 2000, accessed January 3, 2014, http://austinchronicle.com/.

5. Whitehead, *Intuitionist*, 17.

6. Ibid.

7. Ibid., 12.

8. Ibid., 13.

9. Valerie Boyd, "The Intuitionist," *Star Tribune*, May 1, 1999, accessed January 3, 2014, http://www.startribune.com/.

10. Gary Krist, "The Ascent of Man," *New York Times*, February 7, 1999, accessed January 3, 2014, http://www.nytimes.com/.

11. Ibid., 1.

12. Ibid.

13. Isiah Lavender III "Ethnoscapes: Environment and Language in Ismael Reed's *Mumbo Jumbo*, Colson Whitehead's *The Intuitionist*, and Samuel R. Delany's *Babel-17*," *Science Fiction Studies* 34 (2007): 191.

14. Ibid., 192.

15. Whitehead, *Intuitionist*, 24.

16. Ibid., 7.

17. Alison Russell, "Recalibrating the Past: Colson Whitehead's *The Intuitionist*," *Critique* 49, no. 1 (2007): 50.

18. Lavender, "Ethnoscapes," 192.

19. Whitehead, *Intuitionist*, 20.

20. Lavender, "Ethnoscapes," 191.

21. Ibid.

22. Ibid., 192.

23. Ibid., 191.

24. Whitehead, *Intuitionist*, 22–23.

25. Jeffrey Allen Tucker, "'Verticality Is Such a Risky Enterprise': The Literary and Paraliterary Antecedents of Colson Whitehead's *The Intuitionist*,'" *A Forum on Fiction* 43, no. 1 (2010): 149.

26. Trachtenberg, "Intuitionist," 1.

27. "The Intuitionist," *Publishers Weekly*, December 1, 1998, accessed January 3, 2014, http://www.publishersweekly.com/.

28. Ibid., 1.

29. Krist, "Ascent of Man," 2.

30. Laura Bonds, "The Intuitionist," *Memphis Reads* (blog), June 6, 2007, accessed January 3, 2014, http://memphisreads.blogspot.com/.

31. Ibid.

32. Lavender, "Ethnoscapes," 192.

33. Ibid., 193.

34. Whitehead, *Intuitionist*, 18.

35. Ibid.

36. Ibid.

37. Thomas C. Foster, *How to Read Literature Like a Professor* (New York: Harper, 2003), 110.

38. Lavender, "Ethnoscapes," 194.

39. Ibid.

40. Whitehead, *Intuitionist*, 115.

41. Ibid., 111.

42. Ibid., 115.

43. Linda Selzer, "Instruments More Perfect than Bodies: Romancing Uplift in Colson Whitehead's *The Intuitionist*," *African American Review* 43, no. 4 (winter 2009): 685.

44. Ibid.

45. Ibid.

46. Ibid.

47. Whitehead, *Intuitionist*, 12.

48. Selzer, "Instruments More Perfect," 685.

49. Lauren Berlant, "Intuitionists: History and the Affective Event," *American Literary History* 20, no. 4 (winter 2008): 8, accessed January 5, 2014, http://alh.oxfordjournals.org/.

50. Whitehead, *Intuitionist*, 109.

51. Ibid., 106.

52. Ibid.

53. Selzer, "Instruments More Perfect," 685.

54. Richard Chase, *The American Novel and Its Tradition* (Baltimore: Johns Hopkins University Press, 1957), 80.

55. Ibid., 81.

56. Bernard W. Bell, *The Afro-American Novel and Its Tradition* (Amherst: University of Massachusetts Press, 1989), 339.

57. Ibid.

58. Ralph Ellison, "The Novel as a Function of American Democracy," in *Going to the Territory* (New York: Vintage, 1995), 318.

59. Ibid.

60. Bell, *Afro-American Novel*, 339.

61. Lavender, "Ethnoscapes," 194.

62. Whitehead, *Intuitionist*, 255.

63. Berlant, "Intuitionists," 14.

Chapter Two

Lila Mae, the Invisible Woman of *The Intuitionist*

Time magazine's contributor Walter Kirn famously describes *The Intuitionist* as the "freshest racial allegory since Ralph Ellison's *Invisible Man* and Toni Morrison's *The Bluest Eye*."[1] Alison Russell agrees with Kirn's assertion; however, she adds that this "postmodern antidetective story" explores "the process of perception and the nature of learning."[2] Instead of anguishing over her ambivalent existence within the elevator department, Lila Mae utilizes her invisibility as a black woman to uncover clues and learn the truth about Empiricism and Intuitionism. In the process of perceiving the possibilities of elevation, she must deconstruct the texts of James Fulton, the father of Intuitionism. Fulton is a trickster as much as he is a genius, rendering his writings "cryptic as any canonical religious text."[3] Yet, behind the white veil of a black male who denies his heritage, Fulton's text may return a sense of equilibrium to an unbalanced and unequal world. Russell argues that "this is a novel that requires rereading, re-vision, as pieces of the puzzle emerge."[4] Thus, *The Intuitionist* is an enigma within an enigma. As the audience witnesses Lila Mae masquerade as a maid at a minstrel show, she dupes those who underestimate her intelligence. Thus, Lila Mae is the perfect disciple of an Intuitionist god. Ultimately, Lila Mae deconstructs Fulton's texts, unlocking verticality of the future. The cryptic puzzle of the novel is not hindered by the "unspecified time and setting of the novel," which is fragmented and nonchronological.[5] This is due in part because the fragmented nature of the narrative represents the fragmented identity of the African American story in America. Saundra Liggins writes in "The Urban Gothic Vision of Colson Whitehead's *The Intuitionist* (1999)," "The past still influences the present and future, and issues of identity still create conflicts within the individual."[6] Historically, in the 1800s, the North is portrayed in literature as an African

American promise land of hope and opportunity.[7] Ralph Ellison's *Invisible Man* and Richard Wright's *Black Boy* shatter the mythology of the North. Once the protagonists realize the region is not absolved from "racism or other forms of oppression," they are filled with disillusion and acrimony.[8] Whitehead symbolically uses "elevators and racial conflict as structural features of a twentieth-century America built on nineteenth-century foundations."[9] Consequently, capitalism masks the invisible engines or unseen human labor necessary for the elevation of the privileged class and veils the double consciousness of Lila Mae due to her race, class, and gender, which often function as social impediments in a technosocial world.

LILA MAE, THE INVISIBLE WOMAN OF THE UNDERGROUND

Before Lila Mae existed as the Invisible Woman of the underground, Ralph Ellison's *Invisible Man* spoke authentically in terms of the African American experience. Ellison implored his audience to introspectively examine the American story and the darker side of the romanticized notion of the American Dream. Ellison focuses his classic tale on the social alienation of an unnamed, young, black male whose life experiences are orchestrated by forces beyond his control.[10] As the protagonist gains painful acceptance of his human condition, he attempts "to define a meaningful identity for himself" in the midst of his marginality as the Invisible Man.[11] When the young man discovers the American plight of blacks and whites, he is disillusioned and "takes up residence in an abandoned basement." He faults the color of his skin for his blighted existence until he discovers "that everyone, black and white alike, lives in "lawless, amoral, chaotic world, where honorable intentions and high moral standards have little absolute value."[12] Ellison's eloquent depiction of the American experience exemplifies the interconnectedness of blacks and whites. This contentious yet interdependent relationship makes the marginality of the Invisible Man hypervisible in a racially conscious society. Furthermore, this interconnectedness theory of the American experience that binds both blacks and whites is essential to Ellison's theories as an artist. Ellison's goal was to imitate men such as "Page and Lawrence in mastering and synthesizing the conventions of the Euro-American and Afro-American classical traditions."[13] Despite Ellison's intentions to study Euro-American classical music at Tuskegee, he turned to literature when he discovered T. S. Eliot's *Waste Land*. He then traveled to New York, experienced the Harlem Renaissance, met Richard Wright and began to study the "literary theory and technique of Eliot, Joyce, Dostoyevsky, James, Pound, Stein, Hemingway, Malraux, Faulkner, Hughes, and Wright."[14] Ellison truly believed that as an artist he was forced to confront his "mixed background as American, as Negro American, and as a Negro from . . . a pioneer background."[15] Like Ellison, the hybridity of black and white culture as fused in Whitehead's *Intuitionist* is an embodiment of African American social heritage and the universal conflicts of the American experience. The study of blackness must be inevitably paired with the study of whiteness in our American milieu; thus, *The Intuitionist* is a universal American text.

Whitehead blends metaphors and borrows from his literary heritage to introduce Lila Mae, who retreats to the underground like the Invisible Man. In "Ralph Ellison, Race, and American Culture," Morris Dickstein states that the *Invisible Man* is really about "unshaping of illusions" and entering into "a new awareness" of your identity and the human potential that exists therein.[16] Like Ellison, Whitehead mocks the corporate and government structures and the class system that pervades American society. Lila Mae is linked to the Invisible Man because, like he, she "is an unshakable innocent, immature, eager to get ahead, trained in the habits of deference and humility."[17] Despite her desire to follow the rules of a society that is exclusive rather than inclusive, she is the sacrificial lamb for corporate, government, and elite interests. Jeffrey Allen Tucker writes in "Verticality Is Such a Risky Enterprise," "Lila Mae had to live in the equivalent of a janitor's closet because separate dormitories had yet to be constructed for African Americans, who are referred to not as 'African Americans' but as 'colored' or 'Negro.'"[18] What is the implication here for African Americans who desire progress in a segregated or disenfranchised society? Ellison says that the "price we pay for progress is terrible, but that we cannot afford to close our eyes and stop."[19] Although Ellison is referring to America's pioneering heritage, this declaration is distinctly applicable to the African American experience. After all, during the Jim Crow era, traveling North for a black Southerner was a new frontier. There was a dreaded sense of the unknown intermingled with the promise of a better life. Lila Mae's opportunity to attend the elevator school is also her denigration as a second-class citizen. Thus, her progress is evidence of the regressive nature of those who claim enlightenment. She is hypervisible at her school because she is the only black female. Yet, she is invisible because she is socially and physically alienated from intermingling with other whites who attend the school. Under the guise of inclusion lies the reinforcement of her perceived inferiority and the anxiety caused by the presence of black skin. Liggins states that "race relations at the school were characterized not only by whites' disregard for blacks, but by a blatant fear and hostility towards blacks."[20] Consequently, there is an implication that black skin is impure and has the moral authority to corrupt the other students, thereby poisoning the system at large.

When Lila Mae must descend underground, this is a metaphorical state of undercover detective work that she must engage to salvage her identity and personal well-being. Liggins claims that "Whitehead thus depicts the black female figure in white society rendered invisible and 'naturalized' as a maid;

thus, he illustrates the narrow-mindedness and racism within the Department and indeed within the larger US society."[21] Both Ellison and Whitehead's protagonists live in a segregated society, but Whitehead's protagonist is subverted further underground because she is a woman of color. According to Liggins, "If race and gender erase Lila Mae, race distinguishes as hypervisible a blackface duo, 'Mr. Gizzard and Hambone,' actually two white elevator inspectors, who perform at the banquet."[22] Although the white audience celebrates the white performers that mimic black folk culture in their dress, manner, jokes, and dialect, the colored maids are appalled. Although Lila Mae is equally offended by this spectacle, feeling "mutual disbelief, shame, and anger," she does not speak to the other women about the foolish display.[23] She justifies her treatment of the women as the nature of her undercover work. But Lila Mae chooses an act of silent yet passive resistance to cope with her shared destiny with the other women. Prior to giving one of the attendees a fork, "she drags it through grease and the contents of the garbage can."[24] Thus, Lila Mae links her destiny with the underground men who work in the garage. Both the black mechanics and Lila Mae defy and condemn a culture that subverts their very existence into invisible nonexistence by engaging in passive resistance.

INVISIBILITY IN POE'S "MASQUE OF THE RED DEATH"

In the midst of the invisible and mask motif, Edgar Allan Poe penned a macabre tale in 1842 entitled "The Masque of the Red Death," where death himself moves with impunity.[25] In this morbid pre–Civil War tale, Poe lends a decadent and foundational gaze at the historical and literary background of a gothic grim reaper and the cryptic allusions to race and class. As the black plague ravishes the countryside, Prince Prospero's response is to engage in revelry with his elite guests.[26] In an attempt to shield themselves from the deadly pestilence, the courtiers bolted everyone in the castle; therefore, nobody was allowed exit or enter.[27] The exclusive party guests danced at the masked ball and feasted on the endless beauty of the colorful chambers.[28] Initially, the upper-class partygoers are unaware of his presence despite his mask that "resemble[d] the countenance of a stiffened corpse" and his clothing that is "besprinkled with the scarlet horror" of the Red Death or Black Plague.[29] In this allegorical tale, as the Black Plague travels amongst the decadent celebrators, the prince is the first to recognize his menacing threat. After the prince confronts Death with maddening rage, the greatest threat to immortality, he then succumbs to the dreaded disease. Once the guests notice the supernatural presence, they don't muster courage until their prince is dead. In the next moments, their confrontation with mortality comes at the price of their demise.[30] In the "Masque of the Red Death," death is an archetypal symbol representing finality. Death, whose dark mask is menacing, portrays darkness as something or someone to be feared or dreaded. In other words, the death of the elite epitomizes the expiration of a way of life or a society in transition. Typically, this text is studied in terms of fear, mortality, and disease. However, the Red Death serves as retribution to the upper class due their disregard for the poor. Although the symbolic imagery is an archetype for fractures in the class structure, I would like to extend the symbolic imagery to the ominous presence of darkness or the color black. By extending the archetypal reference of darkness or blackness, the reader realizes this threat to social order is more than a fear of industrial progress. This fear may be interpreted as a reluctance to accept racial changes in social order. Perhaps there is a fear of social intermingling between blacks and whites or the possibility of miscegenation caused by racially mixing with the other. Nevertheless, blackness not only means disease and death in Poe's dark tale. The omnipotence of blackness in this tale equates to the impending end of white dominance or supremacy over all peoples deemed as the societal other.

After Tucker makes reference to Whitehead's exposure of structural deficiencies in nineteenth-century foundations, she analyzes Poe's "Tales of Ratiocination," "The Murders in the Rue Morgue," and the "Purloined Letter."[31] Detective Auguste Dupin uses his powers of "observations and inferences" like Lila Mae to solve mysteries.[32] Tucker states that "Lila Mae describes Fulton, in effect, as another descendant of Dupin."[33] When Whitehead refers to the limits of logic, Tucker suggests that *The Intuitionist* is "paying homage to Poe and the paraliterary genre he created."[34] Yet, Tucker synchronously reexamines her former assertion. Prior to this analysis, most available research lacks racial interpretations of "The Masque of the Red Death"; however, in *Romancing the Shadow: Poe and Race*, authors Elise Lemire and Lindon Barrett offer Poe's "Tales of Ratiocination" as confirmation of how racial history "directly impinges on the narrative."[35] Since the perpetrator is an orangutan and their species is considered to be more "closely related to blacks than whites, 'the offending orangutan represents . . . signifiers of race: linguistic, anatomical, physiognomic, geographic.'"[36] Therefore, there is definitely implicit commentary on "whiteness in opposition to a debased notion of 'blackness.'"[37] Furthermore, fears of racial mixing are alluded to when the "placement of one [orangutan] 'in the bedroom of two white woman' played on the phobic attitudes of anti-abolitionists toward miscegenation."[38] By examining the faulty relationship of "cultural logic" caused by the consummate fears of miscegenation and the loss of racial preeminence in the 1800s, readers realize Whitehead's allusions to Poe as "critical commentary on racial representation in Poe's detective fiction."[39] Thus, critical claims by Toni Morrison, claiming that Poe is essential to "the context of the racial discourse of his day," are substantiated by Whitehead's "African American detective story."[40]

Allegorically, regardless of Poe's intentions, the subconscious or conscious fear of blackness extends to the fear of the "darky" or African Americans themselves. Morrison argues in *Playing in the Dark: Whiteness in the Literary Imagination* that Americans discussed themselves in "allegorical, sometimes metaphorical, but always choked representation of an Africanist presence."[41] Although Poe was raised in the South, Richmond and Baltimore, an American scholar said in 1936 that "Poe has little to say about the darky."[42] Morrison cringes at the use of the term "darky" because it is "more acceptable than [the word] 'nigger.'"[43] Nevertheless, Morrison insists that "no early American writer is more important to the concept of American Africanism than Poe."[44] Morrison refers to the resolution of Poe's novel *The Narrative of Arthur Gordon Pym* to reiterate how, when darkness is encountered, "impenetrable whiteness" follows.[45] In Poe's 1938 novella, the darkness only subsides when the white curtain deflects onto the water.[46] Humongous white birds fly from "beyond the veil."[47] Then, the men's pathway is obstructed when a "shrouded human figure" is "the perfect whiteness of the snow."[48] Thus, whiteness reigns supreme in *Gordon Pym*. However, six years later when the "The Masque of the Red Death" is published, blackness appears to win by holding "illimitable dominion over all."[49] Poe's ambivalence over class and racial matters is evident. In these contrasting narratives, white dominates as a symbol of enlightenment and goodness, functioning as salvation of humankind. Meanwhile, black dominates as a symbol of disease and decay, functioning as an annihilator of whiteness. Despite whites' attempts to shield themselves from the darkness that stains white homogeneity, this classic tale suggests an insurmountable and historical fear of black dominance that seeps into every aspect of American culture.

LILA MAE'S MASK OF INVISIBILITY

Lila Mae wears a mask for protection, to shield her feelings, motivations, and intentions. The narrator tells us that Lila practices on making "such a sad face hard" because her facial expression must operate as a veil.[50] After she's dressed, she is then "armed. She puts her face on."[51] And like Poe's "Masque of the Red Death," she represents death, danger, and disruption to the social order of American establishment. Although there is no royalty in America, as in the case with Prince Prospero, Southern planters were considered Southern aristocracy in American society. Perhaps, since Poe was adopted by planters, who would eventually experience the end of the Southern aristocracy due to the Civil War, he was conscious of the ruling class's fears. Lila Mae's investigation into the elevator accident subverts beliefs, power, and social order with the black box technology for the perfect elevator. Undoubtedly, on the surface the mask represents death, disease, and plague. But for the Southern hegemony, blackness represents evil and inferiority and the culmination of their reign. Although Poe doesn't speak explicitly on black and white relations through his use of satire, each colorful and decorative room represents the stages from birth to death. Each floor the perfect elevator travels through represents freedom from social order and restraints based on race, class, and gender. As a person elevates beyond the known world, their existence becomes more celestial. With each room in the castle, the guests draw closer and closer to death, disease, and/or hell. In *The Intuitionist*, elevation is a heavenly freedom. In Poe's "Masque," the final room represents a hopeless end. The "corpse-like mask" of the uninvited guest is literal yet illusory and supernatural because he has no "tangible form."[52] Poe defines darkness as evil, undesirable, and horrific. Poe's commentary on death not only represents the human condition but also symbolizes a death of status, social restrictions, and the severance of a way of life by the entrance and spread of blackness, darkness, or the other.

Whitehead counters Poe's depiction of blackness with *The Intuitionist*'s minstrel show, while subverting the trepidation of the black mask in "The Masque of the Red Death." In *The Intuitionist*, Lila Mae's black mask is omnipotent as it brings forth truth and clarity to a blackface spectacle. When Lila Mae dresses as a maid, she is able to mask her true intentions at the minstrel show. However, this blackface spectacle represents the assumptions and stereotypes of blackness in a white-dominated society, and audience members at the performance and readers of the narrative would be in error if they assume they are authentically experiencing black culture. Instead, blackface presents a mockery and misappropriation of black culture for farcical laughs. Therefore, Morrison suggests that minstrelsy provided freedom to explore taboo subject matter that is forbidden in American culture.[53] In conjunction with the analysis of Morrison, the minstrel show reinforces stereotypes and fears of integration. Thus, Whitehead reveals the majority's attempt to maintain an exclusive hierarchal structure threatened by the presence of blackness, in particular, by black masculinity, which is evidenced by subjugation of black males to inferior working conditions away from the other employees. They work inside the invisible cocoon of the garage. As symptomatic of that social hierarchy, Whitehead exposes the systematic indoctrination and tomfoolery in American society.

As the blackface performers attempt to demean their black subjects, by depicting black men as alcoholic, oversexed, lazy bums who fear white authority, Whitehead writes that "their faces are smeared black with burnt cork, and white greasepaint circles their mouths in ridiculous lips."[54] For the purpose of entertainment, offensive and monolithic black masks on white skin perpetuate a denigrating image of blackness that comforts those in power.

Therefore, low expectations cause exceptional blacks such as Lila Mae to move laterally or rise without warning. In *The Signifying Monkey: A Theory of African-American Literary Criticism*, Henry Louis Gates believes that as early as 1828, the minstrel show is "signifying black difference—Afro-American spoken vernacular discourse—could be the object and the mechanism of parody. The black English vernacular, as early as this, was a sign of black difference, blackness of tongue."[55] Consequently, the minstrel show mockingly distinguishes differences in views, values, language, and black and white culture.

By assuming that blackness or Africanist presence is negative, Lila Mae is able to navigate herself in the crowd behind the protection of the stereotypical mask of the black maid. Due to their service work, maids were considered insignificant because whites saw "domestic service jobs performed by black women as being merely an extension of the 'natural' female role and considered such jobs valueless."[56] Thus, pretending to work as a maid is a perfect disguise because it upholds the power structure's assumption of black women's role. Therefore, her coworkers don't even recognize her—not even Pompey, who must wipe the tears of laughter "from his eyes." His black mask of respectability blinds him to seeing Lila Mae as well. The people only "see colored skin and a servant's uniform."[57] Nobody suspects that she is intelligent enough to pull off such a heist. Their presumed intellectual governance makes them oblivious to Lila Mae's prowess in the scenario. This ability to trick those in power is an invisible mask that functions as armor from intrepid white gazes. Thus, racial invisibility serves as a veil of protection while simultaneously subverting the person's individuality as a human being.

DOUBLE CONSCIOUSNESS, INVISIBILITY, AND MASKS

Within this notion of double consciousness are the underlying intentions of the African American novelist. Bernard Bell states that from the inception of the African American, the black American experience is of primary concern. Yet, there is a "corresponding ambivalence toward the literary traditions of the day."[58] For instance, he states that the impact of "popular fiction and a predominantly white audience" caused most early novelists to include a minstrel character in their narrative. However, minstrelsy is portrayed not only from the white perspective but from the black perspective as well. Both Ellison and Whitehead employ caricatures for farcical purposes. In the *Invisible Man*, there is the battle royale, which mocks black culture and black masculinity "to reinforce caste lines and perpetuate the myth of white supremacy."[59] In *The Intuitionist*, the minstrel show is performed by two white men in blackface. This incorporation of white culture motifs, such as the minstrel show, into the black narrative reflects the double consciousness felt not only by black characters but also by black novelists. Ellison explores double consciousness by reconciliation of his dual identity "as a Negro and as an American."[60] Few contemporary artists embody Ellison's effortless blend of "high and low, classical and vernacular, eastern and western, northern and southern . . . braided together into an authentic American creativity."[61] Whitehead also incorporates opposing lifestyles and perspectives to emphasize the conflict of invisibility on the African American mind and spirit. Dickstein argues that *The Invisible Man* is a test of "his grandfather's double message of humility and enmity, seeming accommodation and inner resistance."[62] Whitehead parrots these interactions with Lila Mae and her father. Although Lila Mae insists that she attend this all-white elevator school, he reminds her not to socialize or trust white society. Initially, Lila Mae buys into the idea that "the keys to freedom, literacy, and fulfillment in a puritan, capitalistic system" are engaging in "sobriety, piety, thrift, honesty, hard work, property ownership, and education."[63] Even though Lila Mae rents her apartment and claims to be an atheist, she has pious loyalty to her profession and believes that a dedication to the aforementioned ideals will gain her entry into the middle class. However, Lila Mae's journey of disillusionment is symbolic of the conflicts faced by early African American writers. Meanwhile, other African American novelists believed wealth acquisition and supporting black businesses would eradicate racial discrimination.[64]

Nevertheless, the ambivalent and incongruence of capitalism achieved by the exploitation of others are mirrored in black narratives due to an "unfilled promise of the nation and the unrelenting desire of black Americans for economic, political, and cultural self-determination."[65] Both Ellison and Whitehead understand the Du Boisian notion of double consciousness that frustrates the African Americans' quest for equal access and opportunity. W. E. B. Du Bois stated in *The Souls of Black Folk*, "One ever feels his twoness—an American, a Negro; two souls, two thoughts, two unreconciled strivings; two warring ideals in one dark body, whose dogged strength alone keeps it from being torn asunder."[66] Hence, the African American is always conscious of his dual identity as both a black person and an American. Furthermore, Du Bois states that the African American does not seek to Africanize America or "bleach his Negro soul in a flood of white Americanism."[67] Consequently, there is only a desire to discover one's own individuality and walk through the "doors of Opportunity" without the reality of doors closing "roughly in his face."[68]

As an African American woman, does Lila Mae suffer from a sense of triple consciousness that is not experienced by Ellison's anonymous narrator? Whitehead places Lila Mae in a pre–civil rights era milieu, while adopting the conventions of early African American writers with a focus on black femaleness instead of black male masculinity. Lila Mae Watson's last name alludes to another Watson in the Sherlock Holmes adventures. [69] Yet, Whitehead simultaneously engages in "revision of the genre undermin[ing] the ethnocentric perspective of Western science." [70] Russell makes reference to *The Blues Detective: A Study of African American Detective Fiction*, by Stephen F. Soitos. Soitos asserts that "African American writers have revised the formulas of classical and hard-boiled detective fiction to present their 'social and political viewpoints and worldviews' by infusing their texts with four black detective tropes: 'alteration of detective persona, double-consciousness detection, black vernaculars, and hoodoo.'" [71] Lila Mae masks her vulnerability as a woman throughout the novel. She wears her suits, and she is always conscious of her father's warnings about white society. Russell asserts that "in keeping with the double-voicing of the text, *The Intuitionist* also foregrounds Lila Mae's double consciousness, a trope that Soitos, acknowledging Gates, associates with the trickster figure, disguises, and the 'doubling aspects of masks.'" [72] Russell says that "in stark contrast to the white performers dressed in blackface, Lila Mae wears a different kind of mask." [73] Thus, as previously stated, by adhering to stereotypical notions of black womanhood, Lila Mae's successful facade as a maid fools white society. Her invisibility transforms her into a trickster figure because the audience views blackness as a monolithic prototype instead of a fully actualized human being named Lila Mae. Thus, double consciousness, masks, and invisibility are inextinguishable literary motifs that Whitehead borrows from his literary predecessors. Within those tropes, Lila Mae's individuality and status as a literary character of note is accomplished and elevated by Whitehead.

Evidently, progress is stalled when groups are denied their equal rights as individuals. Due in part to the mask of invisibility experienced by both narrators, Whitehead is aware of comparisons to Ellison. In an interview for the *New York Times Book Review*, Whitehead says that "anytime an African-American writes an unconventional novel, the writer gets compared to Ellison. . . . But that's O.K. I am working in the African-American literary tradition. That's my aim and what I see as my mission." [74] Apparently, Whitehead's authorial intent navigates within the African American literary tradition. Nevertheless, there is a conscious attempt to distinguish himself from Ellison, which emulates his subversion of detective motifs from classic writers such as Poe. Although Whitehead is flattered by comparisons to Ellison, he dismisses the commonalities. Under the intrepid gaze of double consciousness, invisibility, and masks, the stark similarities between the themes of *Invisible Man* and *The Intuitionist* is an intentional linkage between two narratives of racial progress. *The Intuitionist* provides a female perspective to the notion of invisibility and offers an enlightened perspective of elevation from an artist who has the unique skill to benefit from Ellison and Poe's footprints. In the tradition of great artists before him, Whitehead takes the skeletal bones buried underground by the masters and fleshes out a unique, not derivative, narrative, erecting new interpretations into the literary motifs of classic authorial artifacts.

NOTES

1. Walter Kirn, "Books: The Promise of Verticality," *Time*, January 25, 1999, accessed January 26, 2014, http://content.time.com/.

2. Alison Russell, "Recalibrating the Past: Colson Whitehead's *The Intuitionist*," *Critique* 49, no. 1 (2007): 46.

3. Ibid., 49.

4. Ibid.

5. Ibid.

6. Saundra Liggins, "The Urban Gothic Vision of Colson Whitehead's *The Intuitionist* (1999)," *African American Review* 40, no. 2 (summer 2006): 359.

7. Ibid., 360.

8. Ibid.

9. Jeffrey Allen Tucker, "'Verticality Is Such a Risky Enterprise': The Literary and Paraliterary Antecedents of Colson Whitehead's *The Intuitionist*," *A Forum on Fiction* 43, no. 1 (2010): 152.

10. Claudia Tate, "Notes on the Invisible Women in Ralph Ellison's *Invisible Man*," in *Ralph Ellison's* Invisible Man*: A Casebook*, ed. John F. Callahan (New York: Oxford University Press, 2004), 254.

11. Ibid.

12. Ibid.

13. Bernard W. Bell, *The Afro-American Novel and Its Tradition* (Amherst: University of Massachusetts Press, 1989), 193.

14. Ibid., 194.

15. Ibid.

16. Morris Dickstein, "Ralph Ellison, Race, and American Culture," in *Ralph Ellison's* Invisible Man*: A Casebook*, ed. John F. Callahan (New York: Oxford University Press, 2004), 136.

17. Ibid., 135.

18. Tucker, "Verticality," 151.

19. Ralph Ellison, "The Novel as a Function of American Democracy," in *Going to the Territory* (New York: Vintage, 1995), 312.

20. Liggins, "The Urban Gothic Vision," 362.

21. Ibid., 363.

22. Ibid.

23. Ibid.

24. Ibid.

25. Edgar Allan Poe, "The Masque of the Red Death," in *The Complete Tales of Edgar Allan Poe* (New York: Barnes & Noble, 1999).

26. Ibid., 292.

27. Ibid.

28. Ibid., 293.

29. Ibid., 295.

30. Ibid., 296.

31. Tucker, "Verticality," 152–53.

32. Ibid., 152 (133).

33. Ibid., 152–53.

34. Ibid., 153.

35. Ibid.

36. Ibid. (Barrett, 172).

37. Ibid.

38. Ibid., 153 (Lemire, 178).

39. Ibid., 153–54.

40. Ibid.

41. Toni Morrison, *Playing in the Dark: Whiteness and the Literary Imagination* (New York: Vintage, 1993), 17.

42. Ibid., 10.

43. Ibid.

44. Ibid., 32.

45. Ibid.

46. Edgar Allan Poe, *The Narrative of Arthur Gordon Pym of Nantucket*, in *The Complete Tales of Edgar Allan Poe* (New York: Barnes & Noble, 1999), 760.

47. Ibid.

48. Ibid.

49. Poe, "Masque of the Red Death," 296.

50. Colson Whitehead, *The Intuitionist* (New York: Vantage, 1999), 57.

51. Ibid.

52. Poe, "Masque of the Red Death," 296.

53. Morrison, *Playing in the Dark*, 66.

54. Whitehead, *Intuitionist*, 154.

55. Henry Louis Gates, *The Signifying Monkey: A Theory of African-American Literary Criticism* (New York: Oxford University Press, 1989), 92.

56. bell hooks, *Ain't I a Woman: Black Women and Feminism* (Boston: South End Press, 1981), 91.

57. Whitehead, *Intuitionist*, 153.

58. Bernard W. Bell, *The Afro-American Novel and Its Tradition* (Amherst: University of Massachusetts Press, 1989), 35.

59. Ibid., 197.

60. Dickstein, "Ralph Ellison," 128.

61. Ibid., 129.

62. Ibid., 135.

63. Bell, *Afro-American Novel*, 35.

64. Ibid.

65. Ibid.

66. W. E. B. Du Bois, *The Souls of Black Folk* (New York: Barnes & Noble Classics, 2003), 9.

67. Ibid.

68. Ibid.

69. Russell, "Recalibrating the Past," 50.

70. Ibid.

71. Ibid., 50–51.

72. Ibid., 51.

73. Ibid.

74. Daniel Zalewski, "An Interview with Colson Whitehead: Tunnel Vision," *New York Times Book Review*, May 13, 2001, accessed February 8, 2014, http://www.nytimes.com/.

Chapter Three

Piercing the Veil

Passing, Color Blindness, and Postracialism

In essence, the perfect elevator is a metaphor for the perfect society, in which race and ethnicity are irrelevant factors. Perhaps, in a color blind or postracial society, the white world that James Fulton passes into would accept "the white-appearing son of a black woman in the South."[1] Due to segregation, Fulton's conflicted youth causes him to envision a new world that is devoid of "racist social codes." Thus, Fulton's uplift ideology is not centered on race or ethnicity. Instead, Fulton's "concern for purity is translated into a quest for mechanical perfection that ultimately seems to pathologize humanity." Nevertheless, his followers, such as Lila Mae, have a religious devotion to uplift that is deeply connected to the "motivations, aspirations, and writings of James Fulton." Lila Mae refers to Fulton's first volume of *Theoretical Elevators* as "holy verses." Thus, Lila Mae concurs with her Intuitionist colleagues who equate the second elevation to the "the second coming of Christ." However, Fulton's intentional masking of his mixed-raced background causes Lila Mae to question her fidelity to him. Furthermore, Fulton's writings reveal "troubling indications that his quest for the perfect elevator entails a rejection of . . . the natural world, speech, communal relations, and the physical body itself."[2] Consequently, Fulton's artificial white mask operates as his subconscious call for a color-blind or postracial society, which are essential components to the satirical realm of *The Intuitionist*. James Fulton, the father of Intuitionism, ironically achieves an unparalleled level of success. Since Fulton's mixed racial heritage as an African American ascertains privileges associated with white skin, he transcends racial, regional, and social boundaries by passing as a white man. Furthermore, he exhibits racial exceptionalism with his black box technology.

Therefore, passing and color blindness are tools of postracial progress, signifiers of social advancement by obtaining white privilege.

POSTRACIALISM: POSTMILLENNIAL REALITY OR MYTHOLOGICAL FALLACY?

Depending on the advocate, the term *postracial* substantiates or discounts the existence of racial signifiers in academic, media, political, and social realms. Despite the popular use of the term, the "Urban Dictionary" is the first vocabulary source to define "postracial" as "a term used to describe a society or time period in which discussions around race and racism have been deemed no longer relevant to current social dynamics."[3] The term *postracial* was "popularized after the election of Barack Obama to the presidency of the United States of America in 2009."[4] For some Americans, the presidential election of an African American and his ascension into the upper echelon of society, such as the coveted White House, is proof that racial exclusion and discrimination are buried relics of a bygone and archaic age. Therefore, the question remains, how is postracialism relevant to the satirical themes of *The Intuitionist*? Since Fulton racially passes as a white man, into a world where his race is an invisible nonfactor, he lives a postracial existence in a pre–civil rights era society. Due to Fulton's futuristic desire to transcend society beyond its metaphysical limits, Whitehead positions the context of postracialism as a relevant postmillennial discussion. Moreover, Fulton's scientific genius has the potential, in the right hands, to create a postracial utopian society where metaphysical elevation is boundless in the future.

Ultimately, Fulton's technology will transform the cities and the nation beyond the average citizens' imagination. But given the problematic history of America, is such advancement possible in the absence of racial oppression? According to the philosopher Kwame Anthony Appiah, in America, race and nationalism has been inextricably linked.[5] Literary production and literary study will continue to focus on race as long as racism is an issue. Therefore, authors such as Whitehead will methodically discover innovative ways to dissemble a racially plagued past. Although Americans are generally repulsed by various global terrors, racism is not over because "racialism in our own century has produced lynchings in the American South, sustained the racist South African state, and led to the still unthinkable horrors of the Nazi holocaust."[6] Reasonably speaking, there are infrastructures, artifacts, ideologies, policies, and individuals who are culturally dependent on these atrocities to sustain their existence. Some political parties frame their status quo mentality as a cultural preservation of values. Thus, contemporary artists such as Whitehead position their texts in the past to illuminate the present state of racial injustice. Whitehead opposes racism by threading satire into

The Intuitionist. He characterizes Fulton as a trickster figure who cajoles everyone into believing he is white. Since Fulton's fair skin blinds whites as to his African American identity, Fulton's success does not signify that a postracial society exists. Although *The Intuitionist* is a historical narrative rooted in detective fiction, the story has a satirical bend serving as "a kind of protest, a sublimation and refinement of anger and indignation."[7] Whitehead utilizes the racial motifs of passing and postracialism as tools of satire, operating "with humor and wit for the purpose of improving institutions or humanity."[8] Although Whitehead's style is subtle yet direct, his poignant use of wit, humor, and trickery "inspires a remodeling" of America's urban landscape and America's institutions.[9] Thus, the second elevation will potentially transform the cities into a postracial milieu of the future. But until then, everyone is awaiting the second coming.

POSTRACIALISM IS THE NEW PASSING OF THE MILLENNIUM

In 2009, Whitehead declares in the *New York Times* article entitled "The Year of Living Postracially," "ONE year ago today, we officially became a postracial society. Fifty-three percent of the voters opted for the candidate who would be the first president of African descent, and in doing so eradicated racism forever."[10] In this satirical editorial, Whitehead admits that naysayers "believe that we can't erase centuries of entrenched prejudice, cultivated hatred and institutionalized dehumanization overnight." Nevertheless, he would like to offer his solutions in the supposed postracial era. Therefore, when Whitehead announces his desired position as the "secretary of postracial affairs . . . [or] postracial czar," the sarcastic tone is clear and the atmospheric tension is broken. As the satirical article continues and the inaudible laughter mounts, Whitehead jokes about the transition from the terms "Colored" to "Negro" to "African-American." Then, Whitehead suggests the term "People Whose Bodies Just Happen to Produce More Melanin, and That's O.K.," or "PWBJHTPMMATOK." Finally, as the postracial czar, he will change the names of television shows; novel titles, with the exception of Toni Morrison's *Beloved* because it's "invitingly post-racial"; characters in novels; and the heated racial plots of movies such as *Do the Right Thing.* This will decrease a hostile atmosphere and offer less threatening racial overtones.[11] Although Whitehead disputes the idea of a postracial society, he extrapolates a word from its political application into a mock government position that gives him mock authority over the entertainment industry. Effectually, Whitehead is acting as "self-appointed guardian of standards, ideals and truth; of moral as well as aesthetic values . . . to correct, censure and ridicule the follies and vices of society and thus to bring [a] . . . civilized norm."[12] Thus, borrowing the postracial ideology from the sociopolitical domain and its application into the sociocultural milieu of literature is quite a compelling theoretical method.

However, in 2010, Tim Wise offers sociopolitical and cultural insight into postracialism in the origins of *Colorblind: The Rise of Post-Racial Politics and the Retreat from Racial Equity*.[13] In contrast to Whitehead's satirical mockery of the mythic notion of postracialism, Wise has a decidedly serious and foreboding tone. According to Wise, postracial politics was born when President Barack Obama proudly proclaimed, "There is not a liberal America and a conservative America—there is not a Black America and a White America and Latino America and Asian, there's the United States of America," in his 2004 keynote address.[14] For most Americans, this speech resonated a sense of unity and racial angst from oppression associated with past transgressions. By Obama's mixed-racial heritage and presence on the stage, there was a subliminal message that racism was passé.[15] Furthermore, Wise claims society erroneously assumed that an Obama presidency would eradicate all traces of racism. Simultaneously, acknowledging the history and dangers of modern-day racism, Wise criticizes conservative individualism and postracial liberalism for the postracial politics. And Wise states that postracial rhetoric of racial transcendence does not result in a race-neutral practices. Instead, this idea of racial exceptionalism or transcendence results in color-blind universalism that deepens the racial divide.[16] Although I neither denounce nor endorse Wise's perception of Obama's positive and/or negative role in postracial political thought, Wise presents a compelling argument that has deep roots in the passing literary motifs of the past and contemporary era in such novels as Weldon Johnson's *Autobiography of an Ex-Coloured Man* (1912), Nella Larsen's *Passing* (1929), Fannie Hurst's *Imitation of Life* (1933), Whitehead's *Intuitionist* (1999), and Philip Roth's *Human Stain* (2000), all of which delve into postracial characters and/or societies before that term was in use or popularized in 2009.

Although *The Intuitionist* was published in 1999, Whitehead's mixed-race character, Fulton, forces his readers to reimagine a society where race lacks relevance after achieving a certain level of success. Natchez, the romantic and duplicitous interest of Lila Mae, says to her, "His color doesn't matter once it gets to that level. The level of commerce."[17] Although these postracial statements may or may not congeal with Whitehead's ironical status as the postracial czar, the socioeconomic politics of color-blind or postracial ideology is evident. Ironically, even as people evaluate the mythology or reality behind postracialism, Appiah profoundly speaks on the irony of the term race. Although many people identify themselves as belonging to a potential race, "there is a fairly widespread consensus in the sciences of biology and anthropology that the word 'race,' at least as it is used in most unscientific discussions, refers to nothing that science should recognize as real."[18] Appiah asserts that scientists refute the notion of "racial essence" as an explanation for "a person's moral, intellectual, or literary aptitudes."[19] Thus, race is a social construct that has sociopolitical and cultural importance because of the legacy and the economic systems imported to its relevance. Consequently, the terms *color blind* and *postracial* are social constructs and mythical notions that serve the interests of the term's proponents.

Even bell hooks asserts in *Writing Beyond Race: Living Theory and Practice*, "Even though race is not a taboo topic in today's culture, many folks are unable to talk race without perpetuating racist thoughts and actions."[20] Although hooks has written and published "more than twenty books," she is often classified narrowly, in a way that decreases her readership. Narrow classifications and the lack of acknowledgment received for "writing beyond race" essentially bars the public from realizing the "complexity of [hooks's] being and becoming."[21] Thus, hooks is admittedly a feminist theorist and cultural critic, yet she believes, despite her privileged position as a successful writer, that America is not living in a postracial or postblack era.

Hooks is not the only cultural critic who perceives postracialism as nonexistent. However, if we are not living in a postracial society, are we in an era of postblackness?

According to the cultural critic Touré, the author of *Who's Afraid of Post-Blackness*, the terms *postblack* or *postblackness* have enlightened connotations associated with the expansion of the term *black*. In the foreword to *Who's Afraid of Post-Blackness*, social critic Michael Eric Dyson supports Touré's assertions when he states that more blacks should give themselves "permission to divide into subgroups, or out-groups, organized around what [they] like and dislike," which does not make them any less black.[22] In essence, blackness should not be defined by a liberal or conservative view of life. Instead, blacks should be able to have a "different take on Blackness and race."[23] In other words, blackness is not a monolithic culture that is complex or simplistic in nature. Touré introduces his notion of postblackness by speaking of a skydiving experience. Thus, Dyson and Touré, like Whitehead, are constantly in the midst of reconstructing black identity and expanding the singular views of black activities, interests, and identity within and beyond the black community. Touré suggests that "to experience the full possibilities of Blackness, you must break free of the strictures sometimes placed on Blackness from outside the African-American culture and also from within it."[24] Some may argue that Whitehead, hooks, and Touré's view of blackness is tempered by their postmillennial viewpoint. African American artists who refuse to allow race to inhibit their American experience is not a revolutionary concept. But the term *postblack* is becoming more relevant in a supposed postracial society. In reality, how does postblackness compare to postracialism? I would argue that postblackness is the unintentional or intentional performance of existing outside of the prescribed black identity that has manifested from past exclusion and systematic racism. Meanwhile, the political origins of postracialism serve economic interests, manifest social angst, and fuel literary argument by asserting that racism is dead, which is symptomatic of ahistorical blindness.

THE POSTRACIAL FULTON

Since postracialism has a political and social presence, the concept as a literary method or movement within African American literature, ethnic, or cultural studies is relevant. Although the term *postracialism* is not invented by Whitehead, this literary forerunner perfects and modifies postracialism in his novels. I speak to postracialism as a social, political, and literary theory that is ideal yet dangerous because of the elements of racial invisibility. Postracialism has existed for centuries in American novels that undervalue or ignore racial differences and claim indifference to historical achievements, social transgressions, and racist infrastructure that perpetuate class as the culprit of inequity and exclusion as opposed to race. Thus, novels that mention the racial makeup of characters as an afterthought are postracial. Whitehead's literary angst or ambivalence is evident by arguing against this movement in "The Year of Living Postracially." Yet, Whitehead's novels continuously flirt with the possibility of postracial characters or postracial societies that exist beyond the confines of race.

In American novels, characters exhibiting the power of whiteness and its actualized and/or perceived privileges are at issue in the characterization, conflict, and resolution of their obstacles. With regard to themes of individuality, freedom, and opportunity, fears of African Americanness bar recognition as fully realized citizens in America. However, Whitehead's postracialism must exist within poststructuralism and postmodernism because it is a rejection and refusal to submit characters identities, choices, or fates to a racial hierarchy that presumes inferiority based on racial classification and economic status. The everyday or common humans identify themselves by race. But if this character is exceptional, like Fulton, he does not rely on his racial history and forefathers' experiences for inspiration, identification, or the natural solution to his problems. Thus, how can Fulton be an authentic mythical hero or salvation for African Americans? In this satirical narrative, Fulton is an inspiration for all Americans—everyday Americans. By creating a postracial character such as Fulton or a postracial utopia in literature, does Whitehead absolve himself or African Americans of their personal and communal identity by ignoring or not speaking emphatically to race? Whitehead does not confront racial issues forthright. Thus, some may argue that *The Intuitionist* falls short of its literary goals. However, I beg to differ; the notion that one novelist, particularly an African American novelist, holds the burden of resolving hundreds of years of racial turmoil in one novel is an overreaching assumption. Instead, Michele Elam suggests in "Passing in the Post-Race Era: Danzy Senna, Philip Roth, and Colson Whitehead" that the postracial elements of *The Intuitionist* function in a distinct and effective manner:

> Indeed, Whitehead's is a passing novel in both form and content. *The Intuitionist* passes as a dystopic naturalistic novel, replete with grotesque one-dimensional characters who seem socially and genetically overdetermined, only to transmogrify into a realist novel with characters of psychological depth, qualified agency, and unpredictable futures. It passes as detective fiction—opening with a catastrophic accident that we are initially led to believe is the result of worldly political intrigue and sabotage. In fact, we discover, the inexplicable Briggs's fall is a sign of *the* Fall, a glimpse into a postlapsarian world in which the social and racial order will suddenly and utterly collapse. The detective novel's epistemological requirement—that the world can be known—dissolves into science fiction's conceit—that worlds can be imagined. Thus, revelation and discovery of the "answer" that Fulton is passing too is not the climax but only a complication in *The Intuitionist*.[25]

In essence, Whitehead's passing novel is a hybridity of a dystopic naturalistic novel, realist novel, detective vision, and science-fiction narrative that does not seek to resolve the racial problems of the new millennial generation. Instead, the racial complexities of the novel, such as Fulton's passing, "fragment the novel into Faulknerian" proportions.[26] Through the mythological writings of Fulton, Whitehead questions passing as a historical method of postracial transcendence. However, the reader must determine if passing is a necessary method of survival in the new cities. If Fulton's elevator dreams manifest, racial implications will not transcend into the future. Therefore, Whitehead's genre-bending narrative satisfies its literary intentions by mimicking and mirroring the complex, racial, and multiracial identities of an enslaved past while reimagining a color-blind and postracial utopia of the future.

SCHUYLER'S *BLACK NO MORE*: THE PERILS OF COLOR BLINDNESS AND POSTRACIALISM

Although Whitehead positions Fulton as a postracial character living in a racially divided society, George S. Schuyler presents the character of Max Disher in a race-conscious society that speaks to ahistorical blindness. In *Black No More* (1931), Schuyler reimagines black bodies as white people. Schuyler not only eradicates the black race, but he ignores the rich cultural history of black people. Meanwhile, *The Intuitionist* suggests "destroy[ing] this city" and rebuilding a new society because "all the people are [now] gone."[27] In other words, for an enlightened society, Whitehead does not

suggest the eradication of any one race. However, Schuyler maintains white
dominance by metaphorically bleaching and scientifically removing the pig-
ment from black people's skin. Thanks to a physician named Dr. Junius
Crookman, the solution to America's racial problems is surmounted on
blacks: "To either get out, get white, or get along."[28] After being called a
"nigger" by a white woman, Disher is the first black man to subject himself
to the scientific and social experiment. Therefore, Dr. Crookman's bleaching
techniques aid blacks in acquiring their supreme desire of white skin and the
privilege of whiteness.

According to Robert Dale Parker, in *How to Interpret Literature: Critical
Theory for Literary and Cultural Studies*, the process of experiencing whiteness occurs when one can look down on those who are deemed inferior
because they are not white.[29] While Whitehead uses satire to remodel or
reconstruct faulty institutions, Schuyler utilizes satire invectively to express
"dislike, disgust, contempt, or even hatred" toward a person, "class or
group," institution, or society.[30] Thus, Dr. Crookman and Disher place the
blame of racism not on the oppressor but on the oppressed. However, this
mindset is fortuitous because it demonizes black people for not being born
with white skin. According to Schuyler's satirical methodology, all problems
would evaporate if there was one uniform skin color—white. In *Black No
More*'s postracial society, if white dominant culture is maintained, will the
eradication of the black race aid the white privileged class with an opportunity to prosper?

Black No More parodies the performance of whiteness and blackness by
enlisting stereotypes, such as describing the protagonist, Disher, as a "coffee
brown" man whose "negroid features had a slightly satanic cast."[31] Subsequently, Disher's girlfriend Minnie is characterized as a "yallah" woman
who is spoiled, uppity, and "stuck on her color."[32] Therefore, Minnie is
unappreciative of the money Max spends on her because her light skin is the
cause of her superiority complex. Schuyler's novel is a precursor to *The
Intuitionist* because scientific technology creates a postracial society or Afro-
futurist existence where race is a nonfactor.

Black No More also presumes that blacks, such as Fulton, who are able to
pass due to their European features, are at a social and economic advantage.
Thus, Schuyler's postracial society is also about mischaracterization of black
identity and blacks' desire to absolve their own presence from American
society. The disappearance or annihilation of black identity is suggestive of a
black-culture wipeout that reeks of black genocidal undertones. In the essay
"The Negro-Art Hokum," Schuyler states that "Negro art 'made in America'
is . . . nonexistent."[33] Evidently, this is no surprise that Schuyler disavows
the importance of black culture. Moreover, he effactually distances himself
from his own African Americanness during most of the novel. Schuyler also
claims in his essay on "Negro Art" that black "literature, painting, and sculp-

ture of Aframericans" is derivative and identical to the works of white Americans.[34] Schuyler clearly perceives no value in the artifacts or relics of blacks' contribution to American culture. However, by emphasizing the economic deprivation of blacks' absence, he does place value on economic structure. Evidently, a contemporary postracial discussion of *Black No More* must discuss one of the earliest, if not the first, depiction of postracial blindness, masquerading as a satirical criticism of white hegemony.

Generally, Schuyler's satire is perceived as an artistic achievement. Yet, Schuyler fails to acknowledge the degrading politics of laws and policies, created and maintained in the Jim Crow era. Furthermore, his satire is rooted from the mythological premise that all blacks desire white skin. Consequently, *Black No More* reinforces dreaded black skin as the potential cause of racism. Instead of depicting white culture as transformative in nature and capable of enlightenment, Schuyler chooses to whitewash or bleach black people with a chemical formula. Consequently, black culture resonates as valueless and insignificant. Even though *The Intuitionist* has a minor character that sells skin-whitening cream and other products for the purpose of racial assimilation, there is not an attempt to erase a people. *Black No More* is a black holocaust of sorts, ripping the raggedy bandage off the vestiges of slavery: invisibility, alienation, and dislocation. James Miller writes that the "helter skelter rush" to become white "literally devastates the black community's economy and social structure."[35] Since Schuyler ends his narrative with a backlash against whiteness, partially due to the discovery that violence and corruption exists in white culture as well, there is a clear rejection of a postracial society. In essence, blacks return to their bleak and segregated lives. Thus, Schuyler's narrative, due in part to the stock characters, is more minstrel in nature than a successful satirical tool lifting the veil of postracial blindness and racial ignorance. Schuyler's postracial society is a milieu that ignores black culture, while promoting the values, traditions, and social mores of the dominant culture—that is, until the resolution of the novel takes a dramatic turn. *Black No More* criticizes the irony of racism. When one character is discovered to be white, he is hung by a KKK-like figure. Within this novel, there is no acknowledgment of a black identity worth sustaining. Nor is there a sincere criticism of racial segregation and discrimination. Schuyler offers only a cynical condemnation of both black and white culture in terms of economic aspirations and achievements.

WHITEHEAD'S POSTRACIAL AMERICA

Whitehead dismantles American infrastructure in a Derridean manner. For Jacques Derrida, deconstruction is a "*political* practice, an attempt to dismantle the logic which a particular system of thought, and behind that a whole system of political structures and social institutions, maintains its force."[36] Therefore, Derrida does not deny that these structures or institutions exist in society. Instead, he is asserting that they are a result of a "deeper history—of language, of the unconscious, of social institutions and practices."[37] Hence, Whitehead positions African American identity as an interior monologue of an American structure and social institutions. African Americanness is not portrayed as a subpar or subset of Americanness. Instead, Whitehead presents a people who will shed their mask of invisibility after Fulton's elevation occurs. African Americans' authentic nature and individuality should exist outside the parameters of double consciousness, caused by systematic emotional and physical displacement. Consequently, if a postracial society is ever to occur, *The Intuitionist* acknowledges our racially plagued past yet seeks societal transformation and suggests a mental cleansing of antiquated ideologies and the tearing down of our past infrastructure to seek meaningful rebirth. Thus, Whitehead's satirical method of postracialism as a functional theory, movement, or discussion within the literary community is necessary. Literature is a place where the darkness is unveiled and an idealized view of humanity may emerge. In essence, Whitehead strives to deconstruct institutional thought and the use of race as a barometer of future success. Instead, Whitehead contributes to the reinterpretation and reconstruction of African American identity within the generalized concept of American identity, while fully realizing that America may aspire but has not reached a postracial existence.

Postracialism may have positive or negative intentions depending on the political, cultural, or literary advocate. Nevertheless, postracialism is evidence of our aspirational nature as a society. However it is broached in the literary world of imminent possibilities, postracialism is most definitely not a sociopolitical or cultural reality. Perhaps postracialism should not manifest itself empirically if it promotes the maintenance of racism while eliminating the history, lifestyles, and celebration of ethnic cultures. In *The Intuitionist*, there is a potential for a postracial society that is inclusive of everyone despite racial distinctions. However, in the wrong hands, Fulton's technology would cause a further economic, social, and racial divide for the new cities on the American horizon.

NOTES

1. Linda Selzer, "Instruments More Perfect Than Bodies: Romancing Uplift in Colson Whitehead's *The Intuitionist*," *African American Review* 43, no. 4 (winter 2009): 692.

2. Ibid.

3. "Post-racial," Urban Dictionary, 2014, accessed January 1, 2014, http://www.urbandictionary.com/.

4. Ibid.

5. Kwame Anthony Appiah, "Race," in *Critical Terms for Literary Study*, ed. Frank Lentricchia and Thomas McLaughlin, 274–87 (Chicago: University of Chicago Press, 1995), 287.

6. Ibid.

7. J. A. Cuddon, "Satire," in *Dictionary of Literary Terms and Literary Theory*, 780–84 (New York: Penguin, 1998), 780.

8. C. Hugh Holman, "Satire," in *A Handbook to Literature*, by C. Hugh Holman and William Harmon, 4th ed., 398–99 (Indianapolis: Bobbs-Merrill, 1981), 398.

9. Ibid.

10. Colson Whitehead, "The Year of Living Postracially," *New York Times*, November 3, 2009, accessed January 1, 2014, http://www.nytimes.com/.

11. Ibid.

12. Cuddon, "Satire," 780.

13. Tim Wise, *Colorblind: The Rise of Post-Racial Politics and the Retreat from Racial Equity* (San Francisco: City Lights Publisher, 2010).

14. "Barack Obama: 2004 Democratic Convention Keynote Address," American Rhetoric, 2012, accessed January 3, 2014, http://www.americanrhetoric.com/.

15. Wise, *Colorblind*.

16. Ibid., 17.

17. Colson Whitehead, *The Intuitionist* (New York: Anchor, 1999), 250.

18. Appiah, "Race," 277.

19. Ibid.

20. bell hooks, *Writing Beyond Race: Living Theory and Practice* (New York: Routledge, 2013), 190.

21. Ibid.

22. Michael Eric Dyson, foreword, in *Who's Afraid of Post-Blackness?* by Touré (New York: Simon & Schuster, 2012), xvii.

23. Ibid.

24. Touré, *Who's Afraid of Post-Blackness?* (New York: Simon & Schuster, 2012), 4.

25. Michele Elam, "Passing in the Post-Race Era: Danzy Senna, Philip Roth, and Colson Whitehead," *African American Review* 41, no. 4 (2007): 749–68.

26. Ibid., 762–63.

27. Whitehead, *Intuitionist*, 198–99.

28. James Miller, foreword, in *Black No More: Being an Account of the Strange and Wonderful Working of Science in the Land of the Free, A.D. 1933–1940*, by George S. Schuyler (Lebanon, NH: Northeastern University Press, 1989), 7.

29. Robert Dale Parker, *How to Interpret Literature: Critical Theory for Literary and Cultural Studies* (New York: Oxford University Press, 2011).

30. J. A. Cuddon, "Invective," in *Dictionary of Literary Terms and Literary Theory*, 425–26 (New York: Penguin, 1998), 425.

31. George S. Schuyler, *Black No More: Being an Account of the Strange and Wonderful Working of Science in the Land of the Free, A.D. 1933–1940* (Lebanon, NH: Northeastern University Press, 1989), [1].

32. Ibid.

33. George S. Schuyler, "The Negro-Art Hokum," in *African American Literary Theory: A Reader*, ed. Winston Napier, 24–27 (New York: New York University Press, 2000), 24.

34. Ibid., 25.

35. Miller, foreword, 7.

36. Terry Eagleton, *Literary Theory: An Introduction* (Minneapolis: University of Minnesota Press, 2008), 128.

37. Ibid.

Part II

John Henry Days and
Apex Hides the Hurt

Chapter Four

The American Spirit

John Henry's Legendary and Epic Stature amongst Folk Heroes Such as Pecos Bill and Paul Bunyan

In the midst of American idealism lies the image of the American cowboy as a frontier folk hero. Although real cowboys existed, their symbol is mythologized within America's faith in "personal guts, integrity, and ingenuity."[1] The cowboy represents our aspirational nature as a society that insists "that in the end right will triumph, virtue will go unmolested, and the forces of darkness will get their due."[2] Marshall Fishwick, author of "The Cowboy: America's Contribution to the World's Mythology," insists that the cowboy perpetuates the method of glamorizing and "selling the American landscape and personality to the rest of the world." The knight errant who travels and mediates the injustices of the unbalanced world is the predecessor of the cowboy morality tale.[3] Bravado and masculinity lies within this myth that has roots in Europe. However, there are other frontier heroes such as the Pecos "Cowboy" Bill and the Paul "Lumberjack" Bunyan. Due to the "exaggeration and the hyperbole that characterizes the American tall tale," chances are slim that these heroes existed in history.[4] Nevertheless, their participation in defining America's character and their innate ingenuity in terms of survival assist in forming America's identity. John "Steel Driver" Henry and Uncle "Storyteller" Remus are African American folk heroes who offer an alternative aspect of the American identity. Consequently, John Henry exemplifies the American spirit, but both he and Uncle Remus present a fracture in the American Dream creed. Uncle Remus is not embraced as much as Pecos Bill, Paul Bunyan, and John Henry because those "folk heroes share such peculiarly American characteristics that all Americans" appreciate and internalize as their own.[5] As a society, we attribute American ideals of freedom, independence, and individualism to our folk heroes; however, those legends represent the aspirational nature of a society that is in a constant state of reinventing American identity.

THE CONSTRUCTION OF THE MYTHOLOGIZED COWBOY IN THE AMERICAN IMAGINATION

America's fascination with the mythologized cowboy coincides with the images of Pecos Bill, Paul Bunyan, and John Henry. Since all three of those legends represent the American ideals of freedom, independence, and individualism, they operate alongside the cowboy archetype. For the average American, the rugged cowboy is capable of conquering nature and the open frontier. Thus, he is a hero for males and an object of romantic fantasy for women. Nevertheless, this enduring cowboy figure has been elevated from a historical reality to a stock image. The constructed legend of the American cowboy derives from cowboy history.[6] According to Fishwick, "The two symbolic figures, the hunter and cowboy, made identical appeals to the trait traditionally valued above all others in the United States: freedom." There was a popular cowboy song attributed to this image of a cowboy's freedom entitled "Don't Fence Me In." The cowboy had the freedom to roam the terrain with no interference.[7] The American GI is an extension of this mythological freedom. Within American society, GIs represent heroes because they "went to all corners of the globe during World War II." Fishwick attributes the construction of the cowboy motif to publishing presses and Hollywood movies. He asserts that "the cowboy legend preceded the American army around the world." Ironically, the open ranges of the West had dissipated by the turn of the century. Nevertheless, this cowboy ideal encompasses the world's fascination with cowboys and freedom quests throughout all regions of America. Initially, the term *cowboy* was used to disparage Tories who raided Whigs' cattle during the revolution. Eventually, the cowboy transformed into a term of endearment for men who drove stray cattle across territories.[8]

In April 1861, the cattle business suffered from the blockade of President Lincoln that prohibited all commercial dealing with the South.[9] Therefore, many "young Texans who had mastered the art of rounding up cattle went off to round up Yankees." Ironically, the number of cowboys was small at the outbreak of the war, and "most of the early men on the range had been Mexican." After the decline of cowboys during the Civil War, there was a boom in the cattle business in the next two decades.[10] Eventually, economic, physical, and social factors nearly decimated the cattle industry. Fishwick claims that despite this collapse, the saga of the American cowboy gripped the American imagination, and achieved a place in that world of legend where rust does not corrode, thieves do not break through and steal, and every bone is construed as a relic. An army of writers, executives, and directors have dedicated themselves to the remunerative principle that old cowboy tales and deeds shall not die, nor even slightly fade away. If anything, they have added to the glamour, glory, and guts of the historical cowboys; they have made him into what Omar Barker calls a "fictidious hero [sic]," a guitar-strumming, holier-than-thou movie set outdoorsman, a pale imitation of the cowboy who was once content to ride the range. [11]

This mythological image of the cowboy is fictitious because his life is romanticized. Within the idealized image, there is no space for the emotional or physical hardships faced by these frontiersmen. Oftentimes, people don't consider the obstacles caused by the wild terrain, animals, or weather incurred on their journeys. Even though there were cowboys of African American and Mexican descent, Hollywood and literature rarely included this image of the nonwhite cowboy in the public's imagination. Essential to American mythology is the image of the cowboy and his horse that is almost as intelligent as a human being. Physically this stereotype is "tall, tanned, [and] sinewy, a man quite at home in the great outdoors. Weather-beaten and rough, this child of nature is innately handsome, despite eyes squinted from the work in the glaring sun and legs bowed from a life in the saddle." Although America is highly mechanized and digitized, the cowboy and horse "form the most enduring team in American mythology." The cowboy's freedom is his own sovereign nation. Since he's a traveling man, he doesn't have a permanent home. Thus, he is not bound by the customs or the laws of any local county or region. The arbiter of his conflicts is his fists or his gun. His "trustworthy revolver" will solve any conflict with a "hostile critter, man or beast." [12] In reality, some of these men shot up towns and then enjoyed the "fallen women" of society. In the past and even today, tourists' dollars are spent encouraging "authentic western hell-raising, no holds barred, out west." Fishwick claims that Las Vegas, Tombstone, and Reno have thrived on this American mythology for years. The western plains were billed as a place where men imagined they could "let off a little steam without ending up in police court." [13] Despite the criminal and sexual exploits of some cowboys, the romanticized ideal of their core values is central to society's identification as Americans.

PECOS BILL, PAUL BUNYAN, AND JOHN HENRY'S CONTRIBUTION TO AMERICAN IDENTITY AND POPULAR CULTURE

According to Ernest W. Baughman who writes in "Folklore to the Fore," Big Man narratives that feature characters such as Paul Bunyan, Pecos Bill, and John Henry connect the reader to common folk heroes.[14] He believes that these stories aid in the traditional heritage of "nourishing a national consciousness and appreciation for it, its institutions, its growth and development, and its national and regional characteristics."[15] He insists that the legends, ballads, and superstitions of a country capture the spirit of the nation and its inhabitants. Young people are taught these stories by their teachers because they define the meaning of America and how America developed as a nation. Oftentimes, these stories portray "violently active strides in settlement, growth, and development." Davy Crockett and other folk heroes represent the fighting spirit of "hardy braggarts" who will fight against any man from anywhere and win. Another folk figure who captures the Wild West cowboy mythology is Johnnie Appleseed. Appleseed is a "wanderer, half-real, half-legendary, [who] becomes a truly great and appealing figure against the background of the ever moving settling and Indian fighting of the Middle West." However, he is a beloved and deified figure because he is a moral man. Appleseed plants apple orchards, takes care of the ailing, warns people of Indian attacks, and fixes household appliances for married women as he roams the countryside. Ultimately, the folk hero is a flawless and aspiring epitome of the American identity. And lastly, Baughman reminds the audience that the "legends of the pirates, canebrakes, lumber camps, work gangs, railroads, cow country, oil fields, whaling ships, clipper ships, and canal boats" exemplify the American spirit and the folk history of America's formation.[16]

PECOS "COWBOY" BILL

According to Brent Ashabranner, men such as Davy Crockett, Sam Houston, Big-Foot Wallace, and Captain Aylett C. Buckner fall into the category of "men who have a factual place in the history of the region but who have been elevated to legendary positions through folk tradition."[17] Those legends are indigenous to southwestern folk culture. However, some southwestern tall-tale heroes have been transplanted from their origins, for example, Paul Bunyan, the Northern timberlands lumberjack, and Gil Morgan, who was a "one-man drilling crew of the Pennsylvania oil fields."[18] Pecos Bill is a construction of an American writer.[19] Ashabranner describes Pecos as a "superlative cowboy, originator of the cattle business and everything connected with it, even to such questionable cowboy pastimes as stagecoach robbing and three-card monte." Pecos Bill is one of the "comic supermen" who benefits from chroniclers that maintain and exaggerate the "true folk basis for their characters."[20] The Pecos Bill legend originates in 1923 with Edward J. O'Reilly's article in *Century Magazine*.[21] Ashabranner attributes the foundational myth of the supercowboy to O'Reilly's article. Supposedly, Pecos Bill lost contact with his "emigrant father" while riding their wagon across the Pecos River in Texas. Since Pecos was only three years old, he grew to adulthood while living with a pack of coyotes. The following events are attributed to Pecos: "invention of the open range cattle industry, his rip-roaring ride on an Oklahoma tornado . . . [and] his digging of the Rio Grande one morning in order to irrigate his private ranch" in what is now known as New Mexico. Most chroniclers such as Leigh Peck, Irving Fiske, and James Cloyd Bowman stay close to O'Reilly's original Pecos Bill myth by adding only a few new events to the saga.[22]

Pecos Bill is a significant figure in the mythological cowboy archetype. Pecos becomes in tune with nature because he is raised amongst coyotes. Although the name Pecos reflects a connection to the river where he lost contact with his family, Pecos is portrayed in cartoons as a blond Texan with no connection to Spanish culture. Pecos exhibits American values because he demands authority over the land and by "assuming leadership of a particularly tough bunch of cowboys." Also, he reaffirms the American ideals of freedom, independence, and individuality because he irrigates his own ditches and conquers a tornado without the help of his fellow countrymen. Pecos solidifies his manhood by falling in love with Slue-Foot Sue or Sweet Sue. Naturally, Pecos becomes smitten when he witnesses Slue-Foot Sue riding catfish, bigger than whales, in the Rio Grande River.[23] Thus, his Americanness is substantiated by retaining his loyalty to his native land, his close proximity to nature, and ingenuity when faced with the impossible. Pecos Bill reiterates the idea that authentic American identity is maintained and/or gained by taming the land and the people, and contributing to the formation of America's future.

PAUL "LUMBERJACK" BUNYAN

For many Americans, Paul Bunyan's folk hero status stands taller than Pecos Bill. Dan G. Hoffman writes in "Folk Tales of Paul Bunyan: Themes, Structure, Style, Sources" that "Paul Bunyan is our last demigod, the self-projection of the woodsmen on our final frontier."[24] He is a gargantuan figure in popular culture because he stands as "a symbol of American size, strength, and ingenuity."[25] In an effort to appeal to the masses, Bunyan "has become a miner, a railroader, an oil driller, a rancher, a farmer, a construction boss, and an entrepreneur in still other industries. The original occupational hero is all but lost in the newer national portrait."[26]

Since 1914, Bunyan folk stories have appeared in print.[27] Although Pecos is featured in a Walt Disney cartoon sequence and in song lyrics, and his likeness was advertised for an insurance company in the *Saturday Evening Post* and *Time*, he never reached the iconic status of Bunyan. Whereas, Bunyan "became a subject for sculpture, ballet, lyric opera, painting, pageantry, and woodcarving."[28] Thus, Bunyan is a central figure in popular culture's deification of folk heroes. According to MacEdward Leach in "Folklore in American Regional Literature," when Bunyan stories transcended from folk culture into fifty tales by regionalist writers, Bunyan became a folk hero in popular literature. Award-winning poets such as "Robert Frost accepted Bunyan as a genuine folk hero." Elevating a folk hero into the popular culture participated in the formation of American identity. Yet, Leach states that inventing stories with characters speaking in a folksy manner and poking fun at folk is similar to "hillbilly cartoons."[29] Early stories feature "Paul Bunyan strapping hams to his feet and skating over the stove to grease it for pancakes, and Pecos Bill getting so damn mad at his wife that he grabs her by the leg and throws her up into the sky so high that she starves to death before she falls to earth."[30] Leach deems pseudo-folklore as dreadful because it profits from falsehoods. Authentic folklore enters popular regional literature and culture when "folk customs, beliefs, rituals, story-plots, characters, and songs" are carefully adapted.[31] Nevertheless, pseudo folk literature and genuine folk literature elevated Paul Bunyan from a regional folk hero into a national folk hero.

Paul Bunyan epitomizes the significance of folk heroes. American writers continue to reinvent the Bunyan tales for the average American's imagination. According to Gladys J. Haney, "The Paul of old was a giant in stature, a super-lumberjack, and a recognized leader of men in the woods. Today, he is credited with digging Puget Sound, being an oil man in the Southwest, building the Panama Canal, and being in service overseas with the A.E.F."[32] In other words, depending on the era or Americans' interests, writers transform Bunyan's historical role in popular culture. However, his larger-than-life persona has some writers depicting him as the spirit of America. Every culture has their heroes. Therefore, it is no surprise that some writers equate his legendary status with Thor or Hercules. Some people believe that Bunyan's importance is evidenced by the "epic scope of the tales and the essential American quality of the theme."[33] Perhaps the epic scale of Bunyan's stories have multiplied and continue to reinvent themselves to appeal to more and more Americans. In America, ideally speaking, people are not bound by rigid stratification of classes. Therefore, Bunyan can dig the Puget Sound as a workman, become an oil man in the burgeoning Southwest, or serve overseas in the military. Bunyan represents how Americans can change jobs or professions or live anywhere they choose. Also, Bunyan, like Pecos, means something different depending on the region or environment of the listener. Reinvention of one's personal identity and relocating one's life from region to region is an essential characteristic of Americanness. By altering Bunyan's heroic exploits based on the listeners' interests, the folktale resonates and remains relevant in the public's imagination. Bunyan provides hope that life's circumstances are not static or unconquerable. Consequently, there are those who believe that Bunyan is the most American of all folktales. [34]

JOHN "STEEL DRIVING" HENRY

W. Nikola-Lisa states in "John Henry: Then and Now" that Henry "has withstood the test of time as a popular American legend with near-universal appeal."[35] Most Americans learn of Henry during their childhood. Ezra Jack Keats's *John Henry: An American Legend* (1965) is the most dominant picture book despite more recent depictions of him. Nikola-Lisa claims that "for Keats, John Henry is the personification of the medieval Everyman who struggles against insurmountable odds and wins." Yet, Keats fails to examine Henry's struggles within the context of his African American heritage during a postslavery and Jim Crow–era world. Julius Lester's (1994) and Terry Small's (1994) accounts "position themselves firmly within the black community, dealing more honestly and squarely with John Henry's African American heritage."[36] Since Henry embodies American identity as the quintessential "Everyman," his appeal to Colson Whitehead is evident. Protagonists such as *Intuitionist*'s Lila Mae and *Zone One*'s Mark Spitz are everyday heroes in mystical worlds. In essence, there is a supernatural quality to the everyman archetype that is a consistent characterization in all of Whitehead's novels. At birth Henry is "unnaturally strong, strong enough, in fact, at birth to wave a hammer (Keats) or hold his cradle high over his head (Lester)."[37]

Most tales claim that Henry was born a slave. Some tales present him with superhuman strength while others reiterate that he was a really strong man. Like Paul Bunyan, various jobs are attributed to John: fieldhand, riverboat work, and drilling.[38] Also, he repairs things like Johnny Appleseed. However, Lester modernizes Henry's skills by having him repair his parents' porch and constructs another wing with a pool and Jacuzzi.[39] In one tale, John Henry saves his crew by "single-handedly paving a new road" to avoid "an untimely explosion." Nevertheless, Henry's fate remains the same in the majority of tales. After Henry "beats the steam drill, [he] emerges into the light of day, and then falls dead from sheer exhaustion."[40] In the battle of wills, man against the machine, man prevailed. However, Lester's account adds an epilogue to the legend. Lester writes that Henry's remains are located on the Whitehouse lawn. Keats, Lester, and Small's versions magnify the importance of Henry's life, accomplishments, and his kind, good-natured identity as a person.[41] Keats is effective at confirming Henry's identity as a universal American folk hero. However, Lester incorporates Henry's African American identity into the realm of American popular culture. Henry's "diction is folksy, filled with regional idioms, colorful expressions, and natural imagery."[42] In Whitehead's account, the audience has a sense of Henry's African American heritage and his American identity as a native Virginian. While Keats's account lacks the double consciousness of black peoples' dual identity as both African and American, Lester's and Small's account also demonstrates John Henry's universal appeal to American values and ideals. Even nature pays homage to Henry. Lester utilizes anthropomorphic images to emphasize Henry's connection with nature. In contrast, Keats follows the folk tradition of Pecos and Bunyan by making nature "visually and textually—subservient to man" because nature is conquerable. Also, Keats transplants Henry to the "arid West, rather than the lush mountains of West Virginia" and celebrates Henry's might as he hammers "through the mountainside."[43] Lester, Small, and Keats all emphasize the "quest for justice, equality, and freedom."[44]

But what does Uncle Remus, as another African American folk hero, offer the audience? Uncle Remus is a manifestation of the preservation of Southern folklore and the plantation. Why is Remus relevant? Remus is a foil for Henry. He subverts the image of Henry. Henry's legendary status is in the tradition of Pecos Bill and Paul Bunyan; they are independent men of strength who refuse to be conquered by nature or man. Joel Chandler Harris, who was fourteen or fifteen at the time the Confederacy fell, was responsible for fusing together various people for the Uncle Remus tales.[45] Although Remus is a "composite of several historical characters . . . a teamster named Uncle Bob Capters, a storyteller named Uncle George Terrell, and a gardener who seems actually to have been called Uncle Remus," Henry differs from Remus because "Remus is a venerable, noble patriarch of eighty: the Aesop of the plantation world."[46] Both Henry and Remus are moral men. However, "Uncle Remus symbolize[s] the Negro who accepts life rather than revolt against it."[47] Henry dies challenging the mechanized world that seeks to reduce and/or replace the laboring men with machines. Remus operates as a trickster figure who is cunning, yet he is complacent with his rural circumstances. Fishwick asserts that "John Henry refused to demur; he defied. He did not depend on cunning but strength to win his battles. And he died with a hammer in his hand."[48] People who are living in a post–civil rights and an aspiring postracial world may relate better to Henry's "bass voice like a preacher, shoulders like a roustabout" or proud labor man. Folk heroes, strong laborers like John Henry—not plantation pacifists such as Uncle Remus—were used to galvanize Americans into entering World War II against Germany and Japan.[49]

In the twentieth century, John Henry and Uncle Remus are black leaders, yet Fishwick equates Remus to Booker T. Washington and Henry to William E. B. Du Bois.[50] Henry symbolizes the limitless possibilities of black manhood in a segregated society. Remus symbolizes the placation of white fears of strong black men. However, Remus is a product of his author's post–Civil War environment. Since Harris was a young man when the Confederacy faltered against the Union Army, Remus reflects nostalgia for a time when blacks understood their subsequent place as second-class citizens or noncitizens. Uncle Remus is not a hero within the cowboy, frontier, or Big Men narratives. Sterling Brown, a literature professor of poetry and folklore,[51] criticized Uncle Remus's folk status. Brown viewed "the old Negro as a walking apologist for slavery."[52] Thus, Remus's propagandized image is culturally appropriated for American audiences and remains an overbroad generalization of elder black men and blacks in general supposed acceptance of an unjust patriarchal society.

Ultimately, the cowboy as a frontier hero is an American image that is relied upon for a sense of nationalistic pride. Since the American cowboy symbolizes "freedom, individuality and closeness to nature," he represents nostalgic hope for our culture.[53] If life seemed too difficult, the public seeks refuge at the movie theater, they read a novel with a cowboy protagonist, or travel the terrain. There is refuge in "the cowboy legend, a tangible safety valve for mechanized and urbanized America."[54] The indelible cowboy image will remain because during the 1950s one in four Hollywood movies dealt with the American West.[55] Quite honestly, it's hard not to admire a folk hero who can tame one of Texas' biggest threats—tornadoes—or a folk hero who transformed his identity from a lumberjack man to an oil man and then to a military man. Furthermore, John Henry has universal appeal because he is a "spokesman for the 'natural man,'" despite his brute strength.[56] There are those who debate his authenticity and/or his integrity. Was he a descent steel-driving man who lived in West Virginia? Or was he really named "John Hardy (a Negro murderer and outlaw)?" Nevertheless, mountains and people acknowledge John Henry was a force to be reckoned with, a true power-house.[57] Meanwhile, Uncle Remus represents the plantation mentality that has a lessened appeal for contemporary audiences. Due to writers, American folk heroes have transformed themselves from the tales spoken in folk tradition into characters in popular literature, television, movies, plays, artwork, and advertisements over the years. When Americans are constantly inundated with these images, they are reminded of the strength, bravery, ingenuity, and resilience of these men. Therefore, the images of Pecos Bill, Paul Bunyan, and John Henry serve the same purpose as real-life heroes. They represent that innate belief that self-imaging or reinvention is not impossible or limited in America. Folk heroes reflect the societal transitions from rural to urban, industrial to mechanized, and East Coast to West Coast; thus, they are inspirations and torchbearers of progress. Elements of freedom, independence, and individualism are constant themes in Whitehead's *John Henry Days*. In the next two chapters, I examine how these themes are challenged in an American society that frustrates the ideas of masculinity and is in constant transition from industrialization to mechanization, and then to a digital and global society.

NOTES

1. Marshall W. Fishwick, "The Cowboy: America's Contribution to the World's Mythology," *Western Folklore* 11, no. 2 (April 1952): 92.
2. Ibid.
3. Ibid.
4. Charles B. Willard, "Our American Folk Tradition: A Unit in American Literature," *English Journal* 42, no. 2 (February 1953): 86.
5. Ibid., 84.
6. Fishwick, "Cowboy," 78.
7. Ibid., 77.
8. Ibid., 78.
9. Ibid.
10. Ibid., 79.
11. Ibid., 81.
12. Ibid.
13. Ibid., 82.
14. Ernest W. Baughman, "Folklore to the Fore," *English Journal* 32, no. 4 (April 1943): 206.
15. Ibid., 207.
16. Ibid., 207–8.
17. Brent Ashabranner, "Pecos Bill: An Appraisal," *Western Folklore* 11, no. 1 (January 1952): 20.
18. Ibid.
19. Ibid., 21.
20. Ibid., 20.
21. Ibid., 21.
22. Ibid., 22.
23. Ibid.
24. Dan G. Hoffman, "Folk Tales of Paul Bunyan: Themes, Structure, Style, Sources," *Western Folklore* 9, no. 4 (October 1950): 302.
25. Ibid.
26. Ibid., 303.
27. Ashabranner, "Pecos Bill," 22.
28. Ibid., 24.
29. MacEdward Leach, "Folklore in American Regional Literature," *Journal of the Folklore Institute* 3, no. 3 (December 1966): 387.
30. Ibid., 387–88.
31. Ibid., 388.
32. Gladys J. Haney, "Paul Bunyan Twenty-Five Years After," *Journal of American Folklore* 55, no. 217 (July–September 1942): 155.
33. Ibid., 157.
34. Ibid.
35. W. Nikola-Lisa, "John Henry: Then and Now," *African American Review* 32, no. 1 (spring 1998): 51.
36. Ibid.

37. Ibid.

38. Ibid.

39. Ibid., 53.

40. Ibid., 52.

41. Ibid., 51.

42. Ibid., 52.

43. Ibid., 53.

44. Ibid., 55.

45. Marshall W. Fishwick, "Uncle Remus vs. John Henry: Folk Tension," *Western Folklore* 20, no. 2 (April 1961): 77.

46. Ibid., 77–78.

47. Ibid., 79.

48. Ibid., 80.

49. Scott Reynolds Nelson, *Steel Drivin' Man: John Henry, the Untold Story of an American Legend* (New York: Oxford University Press, 2008), 163.

50. Fishwick, "Uncle Remus," 82.

51. "Sterling A. Brown," John Simon Guggenheim Memorial Foundation, accessed January 6, 2015, http://www.gf.org/fellows/1904-sterling-a-brown.

52. Fishwick, "Uncle Remus," 84.

53. Fishwick, "The Cowboy," 91.

54. Ibid., 91–92.

55. Ibid., 92.

56. Fishwick, "Uncle Remus," 80.

57. Ibid.

Chapter Five

Heroism and Masculinity in the Industrial Age and the Digital Age

John Henry's appeal, as the everyman or supernatural hero, is inseparable from America's perception of masculinity. In the prologue of Colson White-head's *John Henry Days*, black and white individuals provide the *Chicago Defender* with more information pertaining to the legendary folk hero. John Henry was a powerful man who lived and died in the 1880s, after he proved he could beat the steam drill in a competition.[1] For instance, one letter writer refers to Henry as a "magnificent specimen of genus homo." Another person describes him as the ideal man: "Six feet two, and weighed two hundred and twenty-five or thirty pounds . . . straight . . . one of the handsomest men in the country." Furthermore, most of the respondents emphasize Henry's sexual prowess with women. All over the country, Henry is rumored to have been "the greatest ever," and "he was admired and beloved by all the negro women from the southern West Virginia line to the C & O [Railroad]."[2] At the inception of the novel, there are heteronormative expectations placed upon the folk hero. As a society, with a patriarchal heritage and nostalgia for the cowboy days, the societal expectations associated with manhood are not surprising. J. Sutter, the protagonist of the novel, is a freelance journalist. Jonathan Franzen, in an article entitled "Freeloading Man," praises White-head for delving into the "interior crisis of manhood in present-day America."[3] Whitehead offers a contemporary view or alternate version of typical manhood. At the center of this parallel narrative is the twentysomething Sutter. He is a black male who is raised in an "upwardly striving Manhattan family." Yet, he is the antithesis of Henry because he is not physically strong and he lacks "exemplary character." When Sutter has the opportunity to attend the unveiling of the John Henry stamp at the John Henry Days festival, he does not attend to learn more about the African American folk culture heritage. Instead, he mainly heads to West Virginia for the free events, "prime rib and free drinks." Basically, he accepts writing assignments for the purpose of overindulging in alcohol and food. Also, Sutter has an uncommitted sexual relationship with a publicist named Monica. [4]

When examining preconceived notions of manhood, engaging in sexual interludes is the only gender connection between J. Sutter and John Henry. Therefore, this chapter will discuss how Henry and Sutter are representative of the human condition, the transformative definition of masculinity, and the social complexities of African American manhood in an industrialized age and a Digital Age.

JOHN HENRY: A SYMBOL OF PROPAGANDA AND POP-CULTURE DEITY

The masculine representation of a muscular black man banging his hammer is a provocative image. There are researchers and writers who believe that John Henry may have actually lived. Some even argue that Henry may have labored as a prisoner on the West Virginia railroads. Nevertheless, Henry's image was used to galvanize people to join World War II. [5] Since Henry was a black labor man, loved by both blacks and whites, the government believed that he was the perfect image to unite a nation divided by race. Henry's story would ideally assist "black and white soldiers, sailors, nurses, and merchant seamen [to] find a common American nationalism that transcended race." The Library of Congress housed stories and songs written by folklorists who performed them nationally and overseas to the military. [6] The songs reminded the soldiers of home, and the legend of Henry grew for those who had never heard a John Henry song before. American folklore and folk songs projected the image abroad that America is "diverse and democratic." [7]

After the war effort, Communists used Henry's image to promote their labor principles over capitalism. Playwrights used his image to protest the segregationist Jim Crow South. Eventually, Henry appeared in comic books and on a Burl Ives record in Sunday school. Henry now symbolized America itself. During the segregation era in the South, elementary and secondary schools learned lesson plans devoted to John Henry and other famous African Americans. Scott Reynolds Nelson, author of *Steel Drivin' Man: John Henry*, claims that one history teacher in Cleveland spent the "entire year" teaching her class about Henry. This anecdote sounds doubtful and almost comical, especially when Nelson offers supposed dialogue by the teacher, a former Black Panther activist, who stated that Henry's ruin occurred when he "ended up 'workin for the man' and died an early death." [8] Although Nelson's anecdote buffers the historical impact of the legendary folk hero, many "African American storytellers, schoolteachers, and political activists" used his image to instill black pride and teach black history to their listeners.[9]

Ed Cabbell is a scholar, performer, and founder of the John Henry Memorial Festival in West Virginia.[10] Since 1974, when he started this event as a Black Student Union leader, this jazz and blues festival still occurs each year.[11] But the festival of *John Henry Days* presents a different historical origin within the Appalachian region.

Historian John C. Inscoe writes in "Race and Remembrance in West Virginia: John Henry for a Post-Modern Age" that he was astonished by the lack of response from the "Appalachian literary critics and historians" to the Pulitzer finalist's *John Henry Days*.[12] *John Henry Days* assists the reader in comprehending "the region, its image, and its hold on the rest of the country." According to Inscoe, "In 1996, the U.S. Post Office issued a commemorative series of four stamps focused on American folk heroes: Paul Bunyan, Pecos Bill, Casey at the Bat, and John Henry." Talcott, West Virginia, was the site of the postage unveiling and the subsequent John Henry Days festival. The historical context of these events inspires Whitehead to write his novel. Talcott is "a mile east of the Big Ben Tunnel of the Chesapeake & Ohio Railroad." At the time of its construction, most of the estimated one thousand workers were African American. Unfortunately, due to the egregious conditions, hundreds of the labor men died in the process of erecting the tunnel. Between the years of 1870 and 1872, at the location of the mile-and-a-quarter tunnel, worked the former slave and steel driver John Henry. In most versions of the legend, Henry drops dead after he wins his contest with the steam drill.[13] There are those who wonder why Henry would subject his body to such a contest of wills with an indomitable machine. Inscoe offers a plausible answer: "Whitehead provides a poignant and complex portrait of a man who seems to know that he is doomed and of multiple pressures he faces—from his bosses, from racist Irish workers, and from his fellow black workers."[14] During the Industrial Age, in which Henry lived, masculinity was measured by physical strength. Henry was not only trying to save his job; he was trying to assert and preserve his manhood in a competitive and racist environment that dehumanized his very existence.

POSTMODERN MASCULINITY: TECHNOLOGY, NOT FEMINISTS, IS A THREAT TO MANHOOD AND MALE DOMINATION

In 2008, James Wolcott wrote an article entitled "Men Evolving Badly" for *Vanity Fair*. Wolcott's tone is caustic yet satirical as he expresses fears of men in crisis. He declares that men are in crisis because they have slumped into "pathos, self-recrimination and pathological dysfunction."[15] In other words, there is an endless cycle of men blaming themselves for their perceived inadequacies. How does this pathological dysfunction manifest itself? Now, due to men's feelings of self-loathing, they are committing suicide at a rate that is four times more likely than women. Also, men's testosterone levels are low. Who is to blame for men's feelings of "frustration, festering anger, and doubt, the misery?"[16] Of course, the feminist movement is to blame for this epidemic among men. Now, men are in a state of limbo. Gender roles are changing in America. Unfortunately, this postmodern transformation has some men feeling "devitalized, stigmatized, and cast adrift."[17] How do they respond in world that presents a "kinder, gentler masculinity"? Feminist scholar and writer Camille Paglia has a dumbfounding answer for America's men in crises.

In a *Wall Street Journal* interview by Bari Weiss, "Camille Paglia: A Feminist Defense of Masculine Virtues," Paglia says that America is committing suicide and laments that the primary offenders are feminists and feminine values. Although Paglia refers to herself as "self-described 'notorious Amazon feminist,'" she has numerous indictments against society.[18] She claims that "the military is out of fashion, Americans undervalue manual labor, schools neuter male students, opinion makers deny the biological differences between men and women, and sexiness is dead." Even though Paglia places herself in a class with such provocateurs as Rush Limbaugh and Howard Stern, her scholarly "dissertation adviser at Yale was Harold Bloom." What is the nexus between the "collapse of Western civilization" and the movement to ignore biological differences between males and females? Paglia claims that primary schools are oppressing boys' excessive energy because they are cutting recess out of the school day. Then, there are the "tacit elevation of 'female values'—such as sensitivity, socialization and cooperation . . . rather than fostering creative energy and teaching hard geographical and historical facts." In terms of college, gender politics is taught in a "very anti-male way, it's all about neutralization of maleness." Basically, upper-middle-class men don't know how to talk to women because they are afraid they will offend them. Paglia laments that there are "no models of manhood" and men are forced to emulate masculine values from the movies.

Paglia insists that she is not expressing "nostalgia for the socially prescribed roles for men and women before the 1960s."[19] However, the majority of her arguments are archaically disagreeable. Her traditional views pertaining to gender roles sound as if they are derived more from the Industrial Age than our postmodern digital world. As we evolve into this digital world, America is in a transformative state. When America transitioned from an agrarian society to an industrialized, then a mechanized, and now a digital society, the gender roles of men and women changed. Reasonable minds should rationalize that educational institutions and the workplace is impacted by the easy and affordable access to technology. However, even if one disagrees with Paglia, she offers insight into a segment of American society that misses the days of open ranges, the freedom possessed by cowboys, and masculine folk heroes. Actually, there are men and women who insist that the state of manhood is in crisis; gender roles are being debunked; and men are victims of the feminization caused by women. Based on gender roles, men in the past defined themselves by their physical strength and/or labor jobs. As in the era of John Henry, the mechanized world threatened jobs and compromised America's concept of male domination over nature and machine. Now, if a man sits behind a computer all day, does this action compromise his manhood? Some readers may reason that J. Sutter's intellectual strength as a hero does not match the physical strength of Henry. Perhaps, even though the definition of hero is now dynamic rather than static, there are those who still associate heroism with brawn. Unfortunately, those who blame feminism for men's self-perceived internal and external deficiencies are basing their interpretation of gender roles on a mythologized view of manhood. Society's superhero expectations of men have always been aspirational, not a reality. Perhaps men have always felt the oppressive weight of these societal expectations. Now men feel comfortable expressing their frustrations, and society is listening for the first time. Manhood is about emotional, physical, and social balance, not domination. Qualities such as sensitivity and compromise should not be considered feminine values in a civilized nation. Instead, supposed "feminine values" such as socialization and cooperation should be considered gender-neutral signs of living in a postmodern digital world.

Wolcott argues sardonically on behalf of the emasculated male. Then he debunks the myth of the effeminized males. Based on statistics, males still dominate American society even if they don't realize it. Wolcott states that "the passport privileges of being a man have hardly been revoked."[20] According to David Rothkopf, the author of *Superclass: The Global Power Elite and the World They Are Making*, if a person attends an elite university, becomes wealthy, and is born a male, the individual is more likely to enter the superclass.[21] Although women are at least 51 percent of the people in the world, they comprise 6.3 percent of the superclass. Women are underrepresented in terms of Fortune 500 companies and in Congress. Evidently, men are not in danger of a female-dominated society. Wolcott argues that "the primary threat to the psychological well-being of most men (*and* women) isn't sexual or pop-cultural but economic, the fear that a single swing of the ax could render one destitute and undo everything one has attempted to build."[22] At the center of people's fears over the emasculation of manhood is the fear of losing jobs and a lack of upward mobilization. Since there are men who attach their self-worth to their job status, insecurity in the workforce is the culprit, causing men's insecurities. In a digital society, workload and employees are subject to reduction because technology facilitates efficiency and reduces waste of manpower and time.

If some men feel in crisis, society should empathize with them. According to Claire Caine Miller's article "Technology's Man Problem," women make up 12 percent of engineers at 133 start-up companies.[23] Also, "In 2012, just 18 percent of computer science graduates were women, down from 37 percent in 1985." Ultimately, the lack of women in the tech industry is an issue for society because "the products the tech industry creates are shaping the future for everyone." The low numbers of women's participation in tech fields is attributed partly to the male-dominated environment. At the unveiling of a new tech product, one female tech insider described the crowd as "overwhelming young, white, hoodie-wearing men."[24] Therefore, look past the women and/or feminists for the changes in the workforce and American society. Instead, concentrate on the technology that surrounds us in the workforce and at home. If there is an epidemic of manhood, look no further than the technology humans create to make their jobs easier. As a society, we are consuming the creations of a mostly male tech workforce. Ironically, we are grooming those products to replace us. Soon robots, instead of teachers, will communicate with students via their laptops. Perhaps robots will help a single mother or father raise their children. Or maybe robots will operate most machinery at construction sites instead of laborers.

In comparison to John Henry's laborious strength of might and depth of character, J. Sutter may seem like a weak hero to some critics. After all, he lacks Henry's integrity and sense of purpose. Sutter earns money with his intellect, and he is selfish, unlike Henry. But these are changing times; a man can survive in the world by intellect alone. A man does not cease being a man because he cannot metaphorically beat a steam drill in a competition. Self-worth should not be determined by a person's ability to fight in the military or shoot a weapon like a gunslinger of yesteryear. Ironically, the threat to manhood, as Henry finds out, is the technological ingenuity of our own making. Whether Whitehead acknowledges it or not, *John Henry Days* is arguing that the postmodern crisis of manhood is an epidemic of our own creation.

INDUSTRIAL AGE VERSUS DIGITAL AGE: BLACK MASCULINITY, HEROISM, AND EMASCULATION

Myra Jehlen, in her essay "Gender," states that gender is perceived as a cultural concept rather than a biological determination. Similar arguments have been proposed in terms of other identities such as those of "class, of race, [and] of national or religious association."[25] When discussing manhood, values and behaviors of men are regarded as universal attitudes and experiences for all humans. Dispelling "the social and cultural assumptions of literary language" can complicate the reading of classic works. Jehlen expresses how the tragic downfall of Shakespeare's Hamlet is projected to society as an example of the human condition. In reality, treating the characteristics and attitudes of Hamlet as the "portrait of universal manhood" presumes "that young men of the dominant class are universally representative."[26] Ultimately, Jehlen argues that this method works to "submerge the complexities of human difference: while in order to explicate the particular, a critic needs to focus precisely on distinctions and qualifications, on the complexities of human difference."[27] In essence, if we are to analyze how black masculinity functions in *John Henry Days*, as readers we should not assume that the mainstream or popular views on masculinity automatically apply to John Henry or J. Sutter. Nor should we singularly interpret Henry through a postmodern digital lens and Sutter via industrialized views of manhood.

Industrial Era ballads and legends mythologize the harsh reality of the tunnel-building men who worked with Henry. As previously mentioned, there are those people who believe that Henry was a member of the "convict labor force that helped to build the South's infrastructure in the late nineteenth century."[28] In Nelson's *Steel Drivin' Man*, he subverts "the Bunyanesque, individualistic, macho Henry" with a historian's account "of a short abused laborer whose song originated in a tale of power and death in a tunnel."[29] Nelson believes that Henry was actually from New Jersey. Yet, after he was "wrongfully convicted of a burglary of a store," at the age of nineteen in 1866, he ended up in a Virginia prison.[30] Unfortunately, "Despite the Freedmen's Bureau, a fair trial was not available under the state's new black codes." Henry was a symbol of "the human sacrifice that built the South's railroad system." Assisted by the military, instead of the Transatlantic Slave Trade, there was a tripartite system of American capitalism—prisons, corporations, and legislators—used to ensure a prisoner workforce for Industrial Age infrastructure. The Richmond Virginia penitentiary provided "cheap labor just as a privatized railroad system bought legislators to create railroads." The physical prowess of black male bodies was utilized as a commodity for Southern infrastructure that oftentimes barred them from access and social equality. Henry's life is "emblematic of the racial injustice of the postwar South." Historically in America, black manhood is often tied to the abuse and exploitation of their physical worth for capitalistic endeavors. In the postwar Reconstruction era, if a man was "sentenced to ten years at the Richmond Virginia penitentiary," his punishment was equivalent to a death sentence.[31] Nelson suggests that the Henry ballads represent the gothic costs of "magnificent transformations of political economy and landscape, the haunting costs of industrialization that lie beyond the contest of a man with a machine."[32]

Since Whitehead writes *John Henry Days* in the postmodern tradition of Southern discourse, the discourse does not dwell in the context of black manhood in a racially oppressive south. William Ramsey, author of "An End of Southern History: The Down-Home Quests of Toni Morrison and Colson Whitehead," writes, "Once a contested monolith, the singular South has morphed into multiple narratives of a South that function with increased freedom from the past."[33] In other words, Whitehead focuses his vignettes on Henry's heroic strength, as opposed to focusing his narrative on the crippling hardships of Appalachian Southern living. Whitehead resists exchanging a "white grand narrative with an Afrocentric history claiming its own core truth."[34] Instead, Whitehead makes the reader question all versions of historical truth. Whitehead "dramatizes instead the slipperiness of all historical representation." How should the audience interpret Henry? Ramsey wonders, "Was John Henry a sacrificial martyr? Or was he a non-ethnic symbol of common man against the machine? Was he indeed a victim of anything at all?"[35] However, by choosing J. Sutter as the narrative's main character, there is subtle coverage centering on the politics of blackness and black male bodies in the South.

Occasionally, the consequence of black male presence is treated with irony in Whitehead's text. Ramsey questions, "By parallel, is J. Sutter an updated version of the ritual racial martyr?"[36] Does the initial *J* tie him to the folk hero John Henry? For Whitehead, history represents slices of truth. Objective truth is exchanged for a subjective simulation enhanced by the social constructions of journalistic spin. Whitehead "invite[s] readers to construct rather than receive historical truth" with the parallel narratives of Sutter and Henry. In the prologue, Whitehead's list "juxtaposes accounts that invalidate each other." Various personal accounts differ on the skin color and/or skin tone of Henry: "One states he was a white man, another that he was a coal black, another that he was a chocolate, and another that he was a yellow Jamaican." Why do race and/or culture matter in an aspiring postracial society? America has a history of implementing laws and social policies that adversely impact one race in favor of another. Henry's race determined some of the obstacles he faced as a black man living in the late 1800s. But Whitehead allows readers to examine race and manhood through their own personal interpretations. Why? Because everything that we read has been compromised by historical accounts, historians' biases, tainted and/or faded memories, and journalistic spin. At the inception of the Henry documenting process, a 1929 folklore study by Guy B. Johnson finds "huge discrepancies in folk sources."[37] Johnson even appears in *John Henry Days* as a black academian.[38] But one Appalachian historian insists Johnson was actually a white male. The racial identity of Johnson may or may not matter to the reader. For the purposes of heightening the intensity of the story, Whitehead may have consciously chosen to reconstruct the folklore surrounding Henry. One person even states that Johnson has been mistaken for black in previous historical accounts. Within the folklore tradition, characters and history fall prey to subjective truth. In American folklore, there are always varying versions of the perceived truth to further the storytellers' objective.

Nevertheless, in "The Career of 'John Henry,'" Richard M. Dorson writes that Johnson initially believed Henry was a "myth." Eventually, he accepts "Big Bend Tunnel as the factual basis for the ballad."[39] Even the governor of West Virginia, W. A. McCorkle (1893–1897), published an article "mixing John Henry with John Hardy, a Negro desperado hung in West Virginia in 1894."[40] If American history has multiple narratives that conflict with one another, we as readers must interpret Henry the man and/or the myth with a protective gaze. We should not assume anything about Henry based on his race or gender and the region and era in which he lived. Readers must investigate for themselves and reconstruct the memory of Henry and investigate scholars such as Guy Johnson for themselves. Within the multiple narratives of John Henry, Whitehead acknowledges these discrepancies. The celebration of the postage stamp brings everyone together.

J. Sutter is a postmodern man. Consciously, he does not interpret his manhood or individuality with respect to his blackness. Yet, when he lands in West Virginia, he arrives in the South with a set of presuppositions. Subconsciously, he bears the weight of a slave history that plagues all Americans. As a Northern black man, he is consumed with the fear that he will be killed in the South. Ramsey writes that "in the trope that governs his perceptions, he sees himself as a colonialist explorer venturing into a jungle of savage whites, all of this a reversal of the Eurocentric perception of a 'civilization' being a binary antithesis to a 'savagery.'"[41] Sutter is "unnerved" by the confederate flag decal of his taxicab. For him, this is a symbol of a backward region that is submerged in the glory days of confederate power. When he is riding in the car with a black female named Pamela Street and other freelancing junketeers, his trepidation reveals that he's watched too many cowboy western movies or Jim Crow–era movies set in the South. Since Sutter is black and there are white occupants in the car, he conjures a Southern male voice: "We don't abide no consortin' with nigruhs in Summers County. Get out of the car. Maybe one of his comrades puts up a little resistance against the taking of J. and the young lady. Then the ropes, the guns, the fire. The South will kill you."[42] Metaphorically and literally speaking, Sutter fears the consumption of the South. There is racial anxiety that his identity, masculinity, and individuality will be eaten up by the history and contemporary prejudices of the South.

Whitehead brilliantly extends this black male consumption motif with a "mock-heroic" episode. Ramsey writes, "This ecstasy of consumption [is] framed by a local entertainer's singing to the diners of the legendary John Henry. Sutter's own heroic exploit is to swallow a huge chunk of roast beef."[43] Due to Sutter's obsession with food, he ends up on the floor, choking, with helpless diners, who are mostly white. Now, he thinks his fears are

justified all along. Ramsey believes that Sutter is "thinking in absurd para-
noia." Ramsey wonders if "the inside joke . . . like John Henry and Captain
Ahab, [is that] he bit off more than he could chew."[44] Sutter rebukes himself
for traveling to this Southern junket. He says to himself, "A black man has no
business here, there's too much rough shit, too much history gone down here.
The Northern flight, right: we wanted to get the fuck out. That's what they
want, they want us dead. It's like the song says."[45] But, within the frenzied
irony of the situation, Sutter erroneously thinks the diners are refusing to
save him because he's black. He believes his "eyes must be popping out . . .
like some coon cartoon."[46] But remember Sutter refers to himself as "a
sophisticated black man from New York City."[47] Thus, he should not have to
die in the South. There was a black migration to the North for a reason.
Whitehead ends the choking scene with these words: "All these crackers
looking up at me, looking up at the tree. Nobody doing nothing, just staring.
They know how to watch a nigger die."[48] Whitehead leaves the reader in
limbo. Does Sutter die because of the consumptive history and nature of the
South? Or is Sutter dead because of his own hedonistic desire to consume as
much prime rib as his stomach would allow? Perhaps, Sutter is not dead at
all. Maybe one of the white diners saved him. After all, the diners express no
racial hostilities that would lead Sutter to believe they want to see him die.

Sutter is an unreliable narrator of sorts. He is disconnected from his black
heritage. He belittles everything and everyone in the South, black and white,
because he believes he is too good to die in the region. Nevertheless, Sutter is
likeable because he is ridiculously humorous. He appropriates black history
for the purpose of supplying substance to his empty existence and potential
death by prime rib. Whitehead intends for the reader to question Sutter's
reporting of the John Henry Days festival. We should not trust Sutter any
more or any less than the white journalists. Why? Because "J. Sutter's last
name implies falseness."[49] He almost dies at the Millhouse Inn, which is a
"fake waterwheel attached for the commercial manipulation of an agrarian
myth."[50] By placing Sutter's possible demise at the Millhouse, there is an
allusion to "Sutter's Mill, site of the California gold rush, suggesting that the
gold Sutter makes as media hack is false currency."[51] Sutter is not a man of
character. He makes money as an Internet journalist. He's an empty poser of
the American Dream. Sutter's name implies the "abandoned content of character for contemporary seductions of style."[52] For those reasons, Sutter's
interpretations of blackness, black manhood, or even the John Henry Days
festival is questionable. But these failings are not due to a presumed inferiority of the black male. Sutter's personal failings are attributed to his questionable values as an American. Sutter collects other people's receipts to receive
a higher travel reimbursement. Ramsey declares that "a sham paper slip now
constitutes an ironic reality, just as the publicity articles that J. writes offer
readers imitations of real experiences."[53] Like other journalists, Sutter is

constructing an American experience with a mixture of fact and fiction based on his personal biases and fears. Sutter's slanted interpretations of real events should make the reader question any one-sided view of history. We should question traditional texts and Internet sources that may be colored by gender, racial, cultural, regional, and/or national perspectives. In the Digital Age, when the average American reports on the news via social media or blogging, a semblance of objective truth is achieved when varied accounts are taken into consideration.

Ramsey states that "Sutter's story is not about the power of a region but about a contemporary, postmodern man's being enmeshed in the virtual cyber-realities of a technological world."[54] Therefore, what does the Sutter's soulless image reveal about the postmodern black man who lives in the Digital Age? The postmodern interpretation of black manhood acknowledges the personal experiences of the Southern narratives of Douglass, Wright, and Ellison. However, postmodern narratives negate the interpretation that black manhood is monolithic. Whitehead achieves the multiplicity of the black male experience by juxtaposing the character of J. Sutter with John Henry. Furthermore, the postmodern narrative suggests that a black male's experiences are not predominately determined by his blackness. *John Henry Days* is not a postracial narrative because Whitehead does not ignore racial differences or imply that racism is over. Nevertheless, Whitehead's narrative transcends traditional notions of black male identity by negating stereotypical labels or limiting definitions of African American male identity. In other words, Sutter makes an equal living to his fellow white male junketeers. He is privy to the same benefits and freebies as his junketeer freelancing friends. Instead, postmodern narratives declare that a character's internal and external conflicts may encompass other issues such as class, religion, region, sexuality, education, job status, and/or career choices. Therefore, Sutter's experiences as a sophisticated black man in New York or journalist visiting West Virginia are not universal. Sutter offers one of the multifarious accounts of black manhood. Thus, the state of black manhood should not be based on historical views of masculinity. But we cannot impute a mainstream definition of masculinity to Sutter, to the average black man, or even to the average American man. Sutter is a man in crisis; he is soulless, and he feels displaced in the Southern environment. But he is not a man in crisis in the traditional sense. He does not feel entitled to dominate based on his gender, and he does not have a cowboy sense of justice.

MASCULINITY IN THE DIGITAL AGE OF GUN VIOLENCE

John Henry Days is full of unexplained mysteries that are further frustrated by the multisided narratives of others. Joan Acorn's first journalism assignment is the final event of John Henry Day.[55] However, the extent of her experience is an introductory course in journalism and an internship devoted to reporting on fashion.[56] Joan, flustered by the shooting, gets details wrong at the inception of the story. Joan reports that a postal worker is killed after "critically wounding three people."[57] Later in the novel, two postal workers discuss the shooting while having drinks "at a bar on M Street in Washington D.C."[58] One guy says that the mayor was at the podium when a guy starts firing his gun in the air. But initially the shooter is misidentified by Joan as a postal worker; the shooter, Alphonse Miggs, is a collector of railroad stamps. Therefore, as a journalist "even if Joan is an eyewitness, she does not transcribe reality so much as arrange stylish semblances of it."[59]

Whitehead crafts a minor character with major importance in the characterization of Alphonse. Alphonse is a white male with a good job, but he is not in a management position.[60] His marriage to his wife Eleanor is devoid of sex. He sleeps on the couch downstairs, and he's fine with it because they've "grown bored with each other's bodies."[61] Also, he is the man who saves Sutter's life when he was choking. Two years later he saved a choking woman's life when she gobbled down some shrimp too fast. Alphonse saves his life not because he is hero. Instead, Alphonse saves "the black man" because he was unsympathetic to whether the man lived or died.[62] But Alphonse is not a hero or even a good guy. When a plane goes down, we read that he claimed responsibility for the plane crash as the "founding member and main theorist of the Alphonse Miggs Liberation Front [AMLF]."[63] Whether this scenario occurs in real life as a prank or only in Alphonse's dysfunctional head, Alphonse is a questionable character. His past and motives for shooting are an enigma.

In a *Huff Post Media* article, Jackson Katz contributes to the theme of questioning textual authority. He warns his fellow reporters to acknowledge masculine violence as the central issue of mass shootings. At the center of many violent American catastrophes are oftentimes white males. Jackson Katz questions whether "'rugged individualism' in American culture masks" the feelings of alienation that transform suddenly "to pain, despair, and anger."[64] In what appears to be an ancillary comment, the narrator says that "Alphonse believed, you go five minutes in any direction from your house and become a stranger in your own neighborhood."[65] The reader sees a glimpse of the American shooter's sense of alienation and dislocation in his own environment.

Furthermore, in American society, boys and men are indoctrinated to believe that violence solves problems, relieves anxiety, and ends pain by "exacting revenge" against their violator.[66] Instead of directing his article to readers, Katz has suggestions on how journalists should research and report these events. Perhaps the journalistic slant and misreporting is exacerbating the occurrences and interpretations of these events in American society. He would probably disagree with Paglia's focus on biological instead of soci-ological differences between women and men. The focus of gender roles is sociological because "individual men are products of social systems." Katz implores journalists to contemplate how "the culture defines manhood, how boys are socialized, and how pressure to stay in the 'man box' not only constrains boys' and men's emotional and relational development, but also their range of choices when faced with life crises." In other words, determine if males feel like failures because of the societal pressures to fulfill precon-ceived notions of masculinity. Although some Americans don't want to pon-der it, "guns play an important emotional role in many men's lives, both as a vehicle for their relationships with their fathers and in the way they bolster some men's sense of security and power."[67] Considering America's frontier history, shootout movies of Hollywood, video games, hunting culture, and the perceived need for protection, the popularity of guns should not surprise us.

Katz insists that analysis from a wider range of individuals such as coun-selors, therapists, and educators can bring insight to situations involving mass shootings. More than one expert's perspective is necessary to prevent the dangerous nexus between masculinity and violence. But in real life, just as Joan operates in *John Henry Days*, there are unqualified journalists writ-ing with authority. Mere opinions, rash judgments, and superficial analysis are heightening an epidemic problem. Joan, the inexperienced journalist, is crying as she reports the events.[68] Although Joan's emotions heighten the suspense, she misidentifies the shooter and misreports information, which makes her journalistic account unreliable.

In a seemingly random vignette, Whitehead speaks on the popularity of guns in West Virginia and America's response to everyday shootings versus mass killings. Unless, the event is a "spectacular crime," people yawn at the "routine gas station robbery."[69] Oftentimes the default answer of mental illness is used to explain away spectacular crimes. But Katz says not to rely on the standard explanation of "mental illness" without further examination. Lastly, it is not "'anti-male' to focus on questions about manhood in the wake of these ongoing tragedies."[70] In no way am I implying that the shoot-ing in *John Henry Days* is comparable to the Newtown shooting. However, since the publication of *John Henry Days*, there are 1.3 mass shootings a week. Whitehead is making a commentary on the intersection of past vio-lence in the Industrial Era and the contemporary violence in the Digital Era.

Despite Alphonse's fantasies of leading a terrorist organization, he acts alone at the post office. When his wife is on the news she reports that "he didn't leave a note or a clue . . . nothing seemed out of the ordinary."[71] Were Alphonse's actions symptomatic of a warning sign or cry for help? Although the police kill Alphonse before he hurts anyone, is the officer guilty of reckless shooting because he kills at least one bystander and injures another?

Should we consider Sutter a hero if he died at the John Henry Days final event? These are questions that Whitehead decides not to answer. Ramsey believes that "Whitehead's irony does have a vitally progressive potential—namely its radical tendency toward openness, not fixity."[72] For a while, the public will retain interest in spectacular crime stories until it dissolves into statistics. Whitehead says that "statistics will swallow the aberration, if the aberration can endure the seven-day waiting period."[73] From the inception of the shooting, "each eyewitness will begin to construct a different version of events."[74] Whitehead refuses to blame the crisis of manhood on Alphonse's personal background, the negligence of the officer, or the overzealous gun culture of America. Even in the resolution of the novel, the reader is unsure if Sutter is one of the journalists who are shot randomly by the police. If Sutter is among the three people dead, his fears that the South would consume and kill him do not seem so ridiculous after all. If Sutter is injured or dead, he is a victim of a gung-ho gun culture and an apathetic society that has not accepted the link between men in crisis and violence. The irony of a shallow guy, dying in a meaningless manner, still makes the reader cringe. Therefore, if Sutter is not dead, the reader hopes that he is now a changed man.

As the years progress, John Henry's legend will continue to endure as long as festivals, oral and written storytellers, folk songs, and digital mediums in popular culture continue to celebrate him. Since the mid-1990s, "nearly one hundred new versions have been recorded" of his ballad. The ballad is "one of the first songs to be called 'the blues' and one of the first recorded 'country' songs."[75] Various artists such as Lead Belly, Paul Robeson, Woody Guthrie, Pete Seeger, Johnny Cash, Van Morrison, and Bruce Springsteen have recorded their own versions. By the year "1962 the most widely recorded folk song sold to the public was John Henry."[76] But Ramsey states that "although the ballad may assert, *'Lord, Lord, John Henry was a man,'* what is a John Henry stamp but a copy of a man? Literally only a receipt for money paid to the postal service, it is a paper-thin simulacrum."[77] Perhaps, America idolizes their heroes more when they are legends and/or dead. Pamela wonders at the end of the novel if human sacrifice is "The price of progress. The way John Henry had to give himself up to bring something new into the world."[78] Although J. Sutter is the protagonist, his contribution to the narrative is incomparable to Henry. Sutter has no political center. He is emotionally hollow inside. He is a freelancing junketeer with no revolutionary ideas to offer his readers.[79] Nevertheless, he is an intriguing protagonist because we're unsure whether he lives or dies. Sutter's mysterious life and possible death is the making of folk stories.

Very few authors write satire on the level of Colson Whitehead. However, he must avoid the hollow pitfalls of postmodernism. Robert L. McLaughlin writes in "After the Revolution: US Postmodernism in the Twenty-First Century" that in the "end of the century . . . irony leaves us caught inside a self-referring trap, unable to assert any belief, unable to connect with others, unable to make a new world."[80] In other words, postmodernism may leave the reader with open wounds of problems with no antidote for a healing solution. Ramsey states that "Whitehead gives us bemused skepticism rather than tragedy, and irony not political engagement[;] he may fail to satisfy readers long accustomed to seeking a solid stance for progressive social action."[81] Whether Whitehead is subconsciously or consciously holding back his political viewpoints on heroism, manhood, race, or guns, his audience trusts that he will tell us the truth, even if the healing antidote is unbearable in the midst of our pain.

NOTES

1. Colson Whitehead, *John Henry Days* (New York: Random House, 2001), 3.
2. Ibid., 4.
3. Jonathan Franzen, "Freeloading Man," *New York Times*, May 13, 2001, accessed January 3, 2014, http://www.nytimes.com/.
4. Ibid.
5. Scott Reynolds Nelson, *Steel Drivin' Man: John Henry, the Untold Story of an American Legend* (New York: Oxford University Press, 2008), 163.
6. Ibid.
7. Ibid., 164.
8. Ibid., 166.
9. Ibid., 167.
10. "Appalachian Music Fellowship Program—2006," Berea College, 2006, accessed December 3, 2014, http://community.berea.edu/.
11. Nelson, *Steel Drivin' Man*, 167.
12. John C. Inscoe, "Race and Remembrance in West Virginia: John Henry for a Post-Modern Age," *Journal of Appalachian Studies* 10, nos. 1 and 2, *Whiteness and Racialization in Appalachia* (spring/fall 2004): 85.
13. Ibid.
14. Ibid., 90.
15. James Wolcott, "Men Evolving Badly," *Vanity Fair*, April 21, 2008, accessed June 22, 2014, http://www.vanityfair.com/.
16. Ibid.
17. Ibid.
18. Bari Weiss, "Camille Paglia: A Feminist Defense of Masculine Virtues," *Wall Street Journal*, December 28, 2013, accessed June 6, 2014, http://online.wsj.com/.
19. Ibid.
20. Wolcott, "Men Evolving Badly."
21. Ibid.
22. Ibid.
23. Claire Cain Miller, "Technology's Man Problem," *New York Times*, April 5, 2014, accessed June 6, 2014, http://www.nytimes.com/.
24. Ibid.
25. Myra Jehlen, "Gender," in *Critical Terms for Literary Study*, ed. Frank Lentricchia and Thomas McLaughlin, 263–73 (Chicago: University of Chicago Press, 1995), 264.
26. Ibid.
27. Ibid., 265.
28. Rosemary Feurer, "The Elusive Search for the Real John Henry," *Reviews in American History* 35, no. 3 (September 2007): 399.
29. Ibid., 400.

30. Ibid., 401.
31. Ibid.
32. Ibid., 402.
33. William Ramsey, "An End of Southern History: The Down-Home Quests of Toni Morrison and Colson Whitehead," *African American Review* 41, no. 4, *Post-Soul Aesthetic* (winter 2007): 770.
34. Ibid., 780.
35. Ibid.
36. Ibid.
37. Ibid.
38. Whitehead, *John Henry Days*, 157.
39. Richard M. Dorson, "The Career of 'John Henry,'" *Western Folklore* 24, no. 3 (July 1965): 156.
40. Ibid., 155.
41. Ramsey, "End of Southern History," 781.
42. Whitehead, *John Henry Days*, 50.
43. Ramsey, "End of Southern History," 781.
44. Ibid.
45. Whitehead, *John Henry Days*, 78–79.
46. Ibid., 79.
47. Ibid., 77.
48. Ibid., 79.
49. Ramsey, "End of Southern History," 782.
50. Ibid., 781.
51. Ibid., 782.
52. Ibid.
53. Ibid.
54. Ibid., 783.
55. Whitehead, *John Henry Days*, 24.
56. Ramsey, "End of Southern History," 782.
57. Whitehead, *John Henry Days*, 26.
58. Ibid., 366.
59. Ramsey, "End of Southern History," 782.
60. Whitehead, *John Henry Days*, 130.
61. Ibid., 133.
62. Ibid., 133–34.
63. Ibid., 360–61.
64. Jackson Katz, "Memo to Media: Manhood, Not Guns or Mental Illness, Should Be Central in Newtown Shooting," *Huff Post Media*, December 18, 2012, accessed June 25, 2014, http://m.huffpost.com/.
65. Whitehead, *John Henry Days*, 62.
66. Katz, "Memo to Media."
67. Ibid.
68. Whitehead, *John Henry Days*, 26.
69. Ibid., 181.
70. Katz, "Memo to Media."
71. Whitehead, *John Henry Days*, 367.
72. Ramsey, "End of Southern History," 783.
73. Whitehead, *John Henry Days*, 182.
74. Ramsey, "End of Southern History," 782.
75. Jeanette Bicknel, "'John Henry': Ethical Issues in Singing Performance," *Journal of Aesthetics and Art Criticism* 67, no. 2 (spring 2009): 175.
76. Dorson, "The Career of 'John Henry,'" 161.
77. Ramsey, "End of Southern History," 782.
78. Whitehead, *John Henry Days*, 378.

79. Jesse S. Cohn, "Old Afflictions: Colson Whitehead's *Apex Hides the Hurt* and the 'Post-Soul Condition,'" *Journal of the Midwest Modern Language Association* 42, no. 1 (spring 2009): 19.

80. Robert L. McLaughlin, "After the Revolution: US Postmodernism in the Twenty-First Century," *Narrative* 21, no. 3 (October 2013): 285.

81. Ramsey, "End of Southern History," 783.

Chapter Six

Commercial Enslavement and Liberation in the Industrial Age versus the Digital Age

Colson Whitehead is considered a "hulking talent" by *Salon* critic Jonathan Miles.[1] According to Miles, America is the epic subject matter of *John Henry Days*. Based on Whitehead's debut, *The Intuitionist*, the author is determined to expose binary duplicity of commercialization as both enslaver and liberator. In both the Industrial Era and the Digital Era, John Henry is a commodity worth profiting from. During the late 1800s, he is a common laborer, a "freed slave who left the plantations for hard, often lethal, labour on the railroads" that helped surge America into world power status.[2] Although Henry is a man oppressed by the late 1800s capitalistic system, his physical strength and American spirit is triumphant "against a steam-powered drill [that] cost him his life." Thus, his death epitomizes human beings' "futile struggle" against the "soullessness of machinery." Henry's feat is transformed "into American folklore's lushest metaphor."[3] Although Henry is an African American laborer, his victory is every Americans' aspirational triumph over racism, classism, capitalism, and technology. The John Henry stamp memorializes his contribution to history; he helped build America. Synchronously, the stamp traps his romanticized image within the bounds of society's own American myth-making machine. Consequently, society is less willing to empathize with authentic hardships faced by low-wage workers because the physical sacrifice has been glamorized for profit. In today's consumer culture, American mythmaking is both a source of inspiration for Henry fans and profit for junketeers. Monetary interests cause the John Henry Days festival to embark on "the selling of a whole town, with attendant merchandising including a souvenir foam hammer."[4] Miles says J. Sutter is the "junketeering journalist [who] pursues an American legend in an epic tale of man, machine and free drinks."[5] Ironically, Sutter's ability to amass junketeering freebies exemplifies his downward spiral of soullessness that is uniquely twenty-first century. From the inception of *John Henry Days*, Sutter and his fellow writing comrades are copiously aware of the "PR Mechanism" of the "List" that controls who gets junket assignments. Whitehead juxtaposes the Industrial Age that sacrifices Henry with the Digital Age that uses information "not to enlighten but to sell" an image, brand, or a dream.[6] The John Henry motif upholds America's mythmaking as an invincible nation due to Industrial Era sacrifices; meanwhile, J. Sutter is an antihero who is enslaved to the media mythmakers of his era.

THE JOHN HENRY MUSEUM

The John Henry legend symbolizes America's transition from an agrarian slave society into a liberated industrialized era. However, the multiple narratives that construct the epic novel demonstrate various individual's enslavement to the past and the present. Even though the media inspires those who clamor for more Henry, their obsession expels other people or ideas that conflict with their mission. Pamela Street, whom J. Sutter falls for, is a modern-day sacrifice to the memory of Henry. Mr. Street, Pamela's father, collects Henry memorabilia for his home that he transitions into a museum.[7] Once her father dies, she returns to bury his ashes at the Big Bend Tunnel. In essence, Mr. Street's legacy to his daughter is Henry's legend and the items that mythologize him.

The tone of the narrative becomes prideful yet solemn when reflecting on Mr. Street's personal sacrifice to Henry's memory. Thousands of people passed by over the years, but nobody entered the free John Henry Museum. The guest book remained free of any signatures.[8] All day, Mr. Street would play John Henry ballads from the 33 rpm turntable, an eight-track tape player, cassette tapes, and CDs. The music plays "through the rooms of the museum work songs, folk songs and the blues resounded, dead voices pinioned across an array of instruments."[9]

As a child, Pamela made sure her friends never ventured beyond the first floor of their home. She didn't want to explain "a dozen identical John Henry statues" consuming the house. For there was no space where "John Henry did not heave and toil and die in paint and ink and charcoal, no tables where smaller memorabilia, diecast and ceramic figurines, did not pose in martyrdom."[10] Even Pamela's childhood toys are discarded when Mr. Street discovers them in a closet. On another occasion, expressing her frustration, as a teenager, Pamela breaks the ceramic John Henry figurine into pieces. Pamela resents "her father's planets and their interminable trajectories through her space."[11] His daughter's childhood memories are worth less than the Henry legend he voraciously buys for his American Dream. Her father's orbit rejects any entity that fails to promote the folk hero's legacy. Mr. Street nourishes his existence by emotionally feeding on more and more memorabilia. Parenting the legacy of John Henry is consuming. There is no emotional room for anything or anyone that does not feed the dream. The post–civil rights era provided more freedoms and opportunity for contemporary African Americans. However, Mr. Street's Henry obsession causes a self-imposed alienation from society; he lives in the figurines' shadow of one man's triumph. Thus, he is enslaved to the past because he is unable to liberate himself from his obsessive dream in the present. Because he is always chasing Henry, like many other Americans, Mr. Street idolizes an image that he can never measure up to. For his entire life, Mr. Street "stood like that, with his arms crossed, as he listened to John Henry, and he waited for crowds" that would never come.[12] The tragedy of Mr. Street is the universal sadness of the Digital Age. Society constantly consumes the images and products associated with commercialized images. There is an innate hope that by living through those images people will transform into the figures they idolize. But worshiping iconic folk heroes of the past breeds an endless sense of vacuousness. As Mr. Street buys more Henry statues and trinkets to occupy his home, he loses connection with the real world and the people who inhabit his existence. Ironically, he never achieves his American Dream of a successful John Henry museum. Since he has severed everyday interactions with people, he is inept at promoting his Henry souvenirs to those who might have been interested in the great American folk hero.

J. SUTTER "SOULLESS" JUNKETEER AND JOHN "THE MAN AGAINST THE MACHINE" HENRY

Although the novel is named after John Henry, who is the "epitome of black strength and heartbreak," the central character J. Sutter is representative of any culture in America.[13] Updike argues that "the disgusted junketeer . . . need not be black at all." Sutter's disgruntlement could "be that of a young white or Asian-American of literary bent." His privileged educational background and "his relatively race-blind milieu of pop culture" deprive him of the heroic struggle of slave narratives and black characters from the Jim Crow and civil rights eras. Writers in the world of Sutter lack the prophetic and honorable stances of Frederick Douglass, W. E. B. Du Bois, Richard Wright, and James Baldwin. Now, protest writing has "dwindled to the mumbling ambivalences of freedom in a money-driven, publicity-mad consumer society."[14] In a sense, Sutter lacks the depth of characters from a Douglass, Du Bois, Wright, Ellison, or Baldwin era because his New York–privileged upbringing has shielded him from sociopolitical obstacles and deprivations of the past.

In "The Second Elevation of the Novel: Race, Form, and the Postrace Aesthetic in Contemporary Narrative," Ramón Saldívar explains the postmodern distance from race in contemporary narratives. For many writers of this age, "the heroic era of the struggle for Civil Rights is not a personal memory but a matter of social history."[15] Since these postmodern writers were born in the 1960s and 1970s, "writers of color have to invent a new 'imaginary' for thinking about the nature of a just society and the role of race in its construction."[16] Therefore, the decision to hoist up John Henry, who worked for white contractors like a slave, ten years after Lincoln's Emancipation Proclamation, is a substantive choice.[17] Saldívar writes that novelists, like Whitehead, construct narratives not from a "position of memory" but instead from the standpoint "that struggle is an element of history, a distant history whose heroic days seem, sadly, to have passed."[18] Saldívar's interpretation of Whitehead's authorial intent is consistent with Updike's literary analysis. Due to "assimilation and integration," African Americans share in the universal American experience of disillusionment and the irony of the American Dream: "What remains worth fighting for? How does a black man save his soul? Fortunate black citizens are now privileged to share the moral inconsequence of the entire society; this is progress of a sort, but not necessarily aesthetic progress."[19] In other words, when privileged African Americans such as Sutter share the universal moral questions of the Digital Age, this is only an element of social progress. Probing questions of enslavement versus liberation, in terms of a commercialized era, lack a level of social depth and moral character. By contrast to his African American predecessors, Sutter is an inferior protagonist because he lacks the substance and social quests of Wright's Bigger Thomas and Ellison's Invisible Man.

Perhaps Sutter creates an emotional bond with Pamela, because of not only their shared skin color but also the shared dissatisfaction by both Sutter and Mr. Street. Although they have never met, Sutter is chasing the demagoguery and stories that journalists create and uphold for society to embrace. Sutter is not guilty of worshiping past African American icons of the Reconstruction era, Industrial Era, or civil rights era. Nevertheless, Sutter is disconnected from the past just as Mr. Street is bound to the past. Sutter has no sense of racial struggle because the civil rights era is a distant memory in the Digital Age. In 2001, when *John Henry Days* is published, Trayvon Martin has not been killed, and the fiftieth-year anniversary of the 1963 March on Washington and Freedom Summer has not occurred. Lastly, the racial triumphs and struggles of the first African American president Barack Obama will not begin until 2008. As a result, Sutter is disassociated by both experience and memory from the struggles of the average, everyday African

American. Sutter experiences enslavement and freedom from a pop culture sense of justice.

Even in Sutter's memory of a former professor, Nkumreh, black militancy eventually sells out to pop culture and commercialization. After the civil rights struggle appears to have subsided, some of the professor's comrades forsake the movement for more mainstream political and commercial endeavors. One friend became a conservative Republican. The congressman became the "voice of black reason" and denounced his black militancy as the passion of youth, spoke of quotas, and resented "the popularity of male-bashing black female writers." Another comrade marketed a barbecue sauce with a label featuring "the infamous curling panther."[20] Sutter remembers that the condiment was a successful hit at soul food restaurants across the Midwest. For those comrades who had not chosen pop, they "were dead by bullets or drugs." However, it's unclear whether they died before or after they had an opportunity to sell their souls for the commercial aspect of the American Dream.

In this inextricable parallel between the commercial forces that both enslaved and liberated John Henry and J. Sutter, there is a sense of sad irony surrounding Henry's accomplishment. Henry and other men toiled "where transcontinental railroads once joined a nation (although their black labourers were barred from towns and lived in shanties near the work camps)." But the folk hero's historical contribution is largely replaced by "today's lines of communication . . . fibre optics."[21] Ironically, the steel Henry drove "to blast tunnels for the railroads, a system of transport now doubly obsolete, having been replaced once by interstate highway system and now by the virtual superhighway of information," provides a generational connection between the past, symbolized by Henry, and the present, represented by Sutter.[22] Henry is "an exemplar of the supremacy of the human body over the machine." But he is a mortal that is "defeated ultimately by the very thing he has supposedly defeated."[23] Sutter has achieved assimilation into the pop culture world that highlights folk heroes like Henry. In Sutter's world, the discrimination of the past only exists now in the South. In West Virginia, first Sutter is almost defeated by his race to gobble up as much prime rib as possible, which would make him a hedonistic victim of America's excess. But then, Sutter is possibly defeated by an injury or death at the hand of Alphonse Miggs. Alphonse is the catalyst, but the officer who shot Alphonse is the final shooter. The stamp collector starts shooting, implying "his culture and way of life are coming to an end; there is something almost quaint about this postal culture that knows it is doomed, and yet continues to do everything possible to avoid admitting so."[24] Sutter is a postmodern sacrifice in the gimmicky world of pop culture that brands everything from products to people for profit.

In the Digital Age, "the emergence of the Internet as a site of publication, distribution, and discussion" has assisted in equal access to information.[25] Thus, the social progress of Sutter is not surprising in a society where the Internet has enabled more access to the American Dream. In the last two decades of the twentieth century, the separation between nonwhites and images emblematic of the American Dream has been destroyed by media, marketing, and technology.[26] Sutter's industry is part of this revolutionary access to a universal American experience. Robert L. McLaughlin, author of "After the Revolution: US Postmodernism in the Twenty-First Century," believes that millennial writers such as Whitehead have a "conflicted attitude . . . toward their postmodern forbears" and that this is both a sign of inspiration and "a sign of cultural collapse and psychological malaise."[27] These millennial writers suffer from a wave of disillusionment that also occurred during the modernist era circa World War I and World War II. The catastrophic event of 9/11 signifies a lost era. Therefore, this post-9/11 narrative trap that ensnares Whitehead is typical of this millennial era. Somehow millennial writers such as Whitehead have disassociation caused by the disillusionment in a post-9/11 world, preventing the ability to imagine a new world.[28] *The Intuitionist* provides a futuristic solution to the fractured world of the pre–civil rights era New York. But Whitehead's *John Henry Days* ending is "strikingly problematic."[29] He intentionally leaves the readers with more questions than answers. In the reader's state of disillusionment, writers such as Whitehead attempt to "connect the reader in her loneliness to a larger social world but to do so with an awareness that the reader's loneliness is to a great extent the result of her immersion in the digital-media entertainment culture that both isolates her and mediates between her and the world at large."[30] Thus, unlike the industrialized era that exploits John Henry's strength, J. Sutter is complicit in his amoral decline. Sutter is the average, everyday American who is entrapped in their alienated milieu. Due to an obsession with pop culture ideology, the technology that offers equal access collectively binds us to a lonely world of personal disassociation.

J. SUTTER IS A POSTMODERN HERO LIBERATED BY THE DIGITAL AGE

Although many critics are dumfounded and perplexed by the ending of *John Henry Days*, they should not feel completely deprived. The postmodernist writers' quest involves questioning the very texts that purport to retell that history and the institutions and systems that these past tellings rely on. In a way, the Internet has increased the disruption to established principles, values, and culture by freeing us from the restrictions of the past. In the industrialized age, the labor men's deaths on the railroads is the human price of progress. In a search for meaning, Americans attach historical significance to people so their deaths would not seem to be in vain.

Now, ordinary people become heroes when they die or survive mass shootings. Everyday journalists may die working junkets. Subsequently, I offer a less cynical interpretation of Whitehead's *John Henry Days* ending. Whitehead withholds Sutter's fate because unanswered questions will potentially transform Sutter into an urban legend. Journalists and ordinary people will retell the stories of people who were injured or died at the first John Henry Day Festival. The Internet will bear multiple narratives on social media that speak of the martyrs for years to come. Like John Henry's multifaceted fate, J. Sutter's parallel narrative must end in ambiguity and render a mythological yearning for solving mysteries: How did he die? When did he die? Where did he die? Why did he die? Did he really survive the shooting? Enigmas are the substance of legends. Folk history is now narrated on the personal posts of everyday Americans at digital speed. Pictures from the unveiling of the John Henry stamp will surface and appear over and over on the Internet. Of course, some photos will be photoshopped to reflect the images society seeks to believe. Ordinary stories about Sutter become e-mails and blogs about the man's best qualities. Memorabilia survived from the John Henry Day Festival will end up auctioned on eBay. Sutter is a problematic antihero because he inhabits society's worse consumer traits: hedonism and gluttony. Inevitably, Pamela and Sutter's fellow junketeers will elevate his importance and moral character for the purposes of finding meaning in their own lives. But society will remember Sutter for his tenderness with Pamela and digitally manufactured last acts of heroism. Various interpretations of Sutter's fate will transform him into a postmodern folk hero; a generational bridge between the past and present renders meaning. In metaphorical or literal death, Sutter achieves a level of dignity and heroism he never achieved in life. Meanwhile, the John Henry legend will continue to reinvent itself with new narratives linking the historical figure and those who died at the first John Henry Day Festival. For in the Digital Age, history is binding; freedom is the ability to reinvent ordinary day occurrences into mythic significance and transform everyday existence into heroic occurrences.

NOTES

1. Jonathan Miles, "John Henry Days," *Salon*, May 11, 2001, accessed June 30, 2014, http://www.salon.com/.

2. Maya Jaggi, "Railroad Blues," *Guardian*, June 22, 2001, accessed June 30, 2014, http://www.theguardian.com/.

3. Miles, "John Henry Days."

4. Jaggi, "Railroad Blues."

5. Miles, "John Henry Days."

6. Jaggi, "Railroad Blues."

7. Colson Whitehead, *John Henry Days* (New York: Random House, 2001), 380.

8. Ibid.

9. Ibid., 381.

10. Ibid., 346.

11. Ibid., 348.

12. Ibid., 383.

13. John Updike, "Tote That Ephemera: An Ambitious New Novel from a Gifted Writer," *New Yorker*, May 7, 2001, accessed January 1, 2014. http://www.newyorker.com/.

14. Ibid.

15. Ramón Saldívar, "The Second Elevation of the Novel: Race, Form, and the Postrace Aesthetic in Contemporary Narrative," *Narrative* 21, no. 1 (January 2013): 5.

16. Ibid.

17. Updike, "Tote That Ephemera."

18. Saldívar, "Second Elevation," 6.

19. Updike, "Tote That Ephemera."

20. Whitehead, *John Henry Days*, 333.

21. Jaggi, "Railroad Blues."

22. Daniel Grausam, "After the Post(al)," *American Literary History* 23, no. 3 (fall 2011): 635–36.

23. Ibid., 635.

24. Ibid., 636.

25. Farah Jasmine Griffin, "Thirty Years of Black American Literature and Literary Studies: A Review," *Journal of Black Studies* 35, no. 2, *Special Issue: Back to the Future of Civilization: Celebrating 30 Years of African American Studies* (November 2004): 166.

26. Lawrence R. Samuel, *The American Dream: A Cultural History* (New York: Syracuse University Press, 2012), 176.

27. Robert L. McLaughlin, "After the Revolution: US Postmodernism in the Twenty-First Century," *Narrative* 21, no. 3 (October 2013): 285.

28. Ibid.

29. Grausam, "After the Post(al)," 637.

30. McLaughlin, "After the Revolution," 287.

Chapter Seven

Apex

The Metaphorical Bandage That Masks but Never Heals

In terms of addressing race, Colson Whitehead's books are consumed with literary angst. Yet, in Whitehead's *Apex Hides the Hurt*, the subtleties of race are made evident by the multifaceted history of a town in transition. At the center of this mass media, consumer culture, and racial allegory is the literal and metaphorical meaning of names, both personal and geographical. According to *Kirkus Reviews*, "Within the supersizing, homogenizing and mass-merchandising of American culture, names are crucial, the protagonist insists, as signals for cognitive response." Thematically, the concept of this novel is "ambitious and provocative."[1] When Linda Selzer interviews Whitehead, she refers to "the effects of a media culture that runs the risk of reducing community to mere 'demographics.'"[2] Admittedly, Whitehead is "leery of systems," such as organizations or technologies. When interpreting social advancements, he is always measuring the cost to the individual, society, and/or institutions. Both *John Henry Days* and *The Intuitionist* speak to the perils of branding and labeling things "that effectively reduces them to a formula."[3] With *Apex*, Whitehead features a nomenclature consultant as his protagonist. Whitehead's central character "makes a living condensing sensations into syllables, ensuring the success of a company's product by giving it a name that enhances its appeal."[4] Basically, he is a branding guy who creates names for various products. For instance, when naming a "brand of multi-cultural adhesive bandages that are produced in a variety of skin colors," the appeal is enhanced but the bandages are still of low quality.[5]

Intentionally, Whitehead is launching a literary assault on multicultural pluralism. In other words, efforts at diversity are sometimes a "quick patch for racial tensions."[6] Ineffectually, they mask institutional and structural problems, but they fail to heal the wounds from a legacy of inequality. According to Whitehead, "Certain forms of multicultural cheerleading are as susceptible to corruption as capitalist boosterism and frontier idealism, two other systems I talk about in *Apex*. Every-ism has its weakness. Ideology, philosophy can transform and transport us."[7] Basically, exchanging one system for another does not ensure systematic change. For Whitehead, he is examining the dysfunctional elements of the system as opposed to the functional aspects. Therefore, *Apex* is just one type of Band-Aid depicted in the novel. Nevertheless, opportunity arises again when the protagonist's "old boss calls him back for a special assignment: the fathers of the small town of Winthrop want a new name and need some help getting it."[8] In the summation of the narrative, the unnamed protagonist successfully creates a new name for the town. However, in usual Whitehead fashion, the philosophies, ideologies, and resolutions are left open ended. For Selzer, this is an appealing aspect of Whitehead's fiction. Yet, for some critics this lack of clear resolution leaves room for misinterpretation of characters and creates holes in the plot: "Whitehead disappoints in this intriguingly conceived but static tale of a small town with an identity crisis."[9] Nevertheless, the identity crisis of the emotionally, psychologically, and physically injured protagonist is representative of the town's fragmented identity. Typical of Whitehead, the nomenclature consultant's wounded toe is symbolic of the burden of blackness that is frustrated by the complexity of black identity, vestiges of slavery, and the mythology of racial progress.

THE ELLISONIAN COMPLEX: THE ANONYMOUS BLACK PROTAGONIST

A prominent characteristic of Whitehead's novels is the unnamed black protagonist who is struggling with his individual and collective identity as an American. Consequently, some critics may misinterpret the signifiers of double consciousness. Thus, they may misjudge the central character's anonymity as an indication of self-importance or a stylistic flaw. A reviewer for the *New Republic* writes, "I am not sure what the purpose of his anonymity is, but it leaves a wounding cloud of portentousness over his head."[10] Previous readings of Whitehead's entire body of work make evident the intentions behind Whitehead's literary technique. Jesse S. Cohn writes in "Old Afflictions: Colson Whitehead's *Apex Hides the Hurt* and the 'Post-Soul Condition'" that the final words of the protagonist in *John Henry Days* invites the reader to speculate on the main character's name and his destiny. Whitehead follows a similar identity motif in *Apex Hides the Hurt*. The main character in *Apex* is "a highly paid specialist in branding, who has been tasked with breaking the Winthrop town council's deadlock over a decision about whether (and what) to rename itself."[11] Consequently, it is evident that Whitehead has a preoccupation with questions of identity. Since before the era of Ralph Ellison's *Invisible Man*, authors of African American descent express a fixation on the tripartite nexus between names, double consciousness, and identity. Whitehead brilliantly interweaves these threads in the profession of an unnamed nomenclature consultant.

For the duration of the novel, the audience wonders which name will best represent this town's attempt at collective reinvention. Will the town keep the current name that is representative of the Winthrop (barbed-wire factory) family? Will the town accept Lucky Aberdeen's name New Prospera?[12] After all, "Lucky" is a white hometown "boy turned software magnate."[13] Or will the town "revert to the name originally given the town by the freed slaves who founded it, 'Freedom,' as proposed by mayor Regina Goode (herself a direct descendant of the founder known simply as Goode)?"[14] In order to delay the suspense, Whitehead takes the present narrative to uncover the past of the protagonist. *Publishers Weekly* claims that "the Apex backstory spins out in a slow, retrospective treatment that competes with the town's travails."[15] As the unnamed nomenclature consultant is contemplating a new name for the town, he is recovering from his own fall from grace. After rising to the top of his profession, he has a breakdown as a result of an infected toe that eventually has to be amputated.[16] Naming this town is "the first assignment he'd taken since his misfortune and he didn't know how things would play out once he started working again."[17] But within this individual and collective quest toward identity, the nomenclature's only identification is with his "misfortune."

Cohn alludes to the Greek tragedy *Oedipus* for further interpretation of wounded heroes. Is the nomenclature consultant representative of "an incarnation of one of the most notorious archetypes?" For indeed, "he is literally 'limping,' his limp a kind of self-inflicted curse or an incarnate personality disorder, a continual reminder of who he is in the absence of a name or a place."[18] What unites Sophocles's tragedy with Whitehead's narrative is the guilt that inhabits both characters. Cohn states that like the nomenclature consultant, "the self-cursed Oedipus, another king banished from his own kingdom, marked by his wounded feet," suffers from regret.[19] Troubled by the fact that "he never got to the heart of the thing, he just slapped a bandage on to keep the pus in."[20] But what exactly does the wounded toe represent in *Apex*? How does the symbol signify an archetype for the black or human condition in America? Cohn concludes that "in social terms, the 'hurt' that is hidden is the historical harm of slavery, which will be covered up no matter which of the three proffered options is chosen for naming the town."[21] Thus, changing the name will not transform the identity, the character, or the history of an entity.

Eventually, the nomenclature consultant views himself as an agent of repression and begins to detest himself for this newfound belief.[22] Is racial guilt the human cost of progress? At the expense of succeeding professionally in a white-dominated field, does this achievement transform the oppressed into the oppressor? Throughout the narrative, the protagonist "encounters plenty of white people (and white values) within the social and professional circles in which he operates."[23] Fearing himself an agent of societal repression, he believes that his fraudulent nature is subject to discovery. The nomenclature consultant considers that "if everyone could see everyone else's true name, we could cut out all this subterfuge and camouflage."[24] In other words, what if your name truly represented your identity? What would happen "if everyone everywhere wore their true names for everyone to see." He surmises that the mask of deception begins "at birth—by giving their children names, parents did their offspring the favor of teaching them how to lie with their very first breath."[25] Is Whitehead alluding to the fragmented identity of African Americans who bear surnames that most likely fail to represent their ancestral homes? Or perhaps Whitehead is referencing the idealism and the hope that factors into first names that fail to indicate people's true character, lifestyle, or even their destiny. Instead, Whitehead says, "Because what we go by is rarely what makes us go. GRIFTER. SINNER. DOOMED."[26] Ultimately, the culmination of the tragic history of naming, identity, and the vestiges of slavery overwhelm the protagonist. There is an element of "deception that their stock in trade" facilitates in the branding and marketing profession. Once the protagonist hears them call his name at a ceremony he flees the room: FUGITIVE. The unnamed protagonist is now "sweat-soaked and near collapse. His name is called, presumably as an award-winner for Apex, but he hears only 'FUGITIVE' . . . suggesting that, like a runaway slave, he is seeking his freedom from an unjust and harmful environment."[27] Is the audience able to connect the protagonist's identity crisis and alienation with the slave history that plagues all Americans?

THE OEDIPAL COMPLEX OF LITERARY ANGST: POSTSOUL, POSTBLACK, OR POSTRACIAL

As America's premiere African American novelist, his treatment of race continues to frustrate critics of all cultures. Of course, Whitehead is not expected to solve a legacy of institutionalized racism or heal the wounds of white supremacy in America. However, his cynical view of systems renders his narrative inconsolable on the issue of racial angst. Thus, his literary racial redress leaves the reader in a quandary to acknowledge America's troubling racial history, twenty-first-century symbols of racial progress, and the commodification of black identity. In essence, the unnamed protagonist represents Whitehead's social angst, which reveals the depth of black America's fragmented identity. In terms of America's legacy of racism, Whitehead's literary angst leaves the narrative in a vacuous state of hopelessness. Perhaps, when Chloë Schama deems the characters and by extension the plot as unsatisfactory, her expectations are too high:

> Whitehead acknowledges that the linguistic techniques of marketing will avail us little in the realm of history and identity. But *Apex* creates the expectation that Whitehead—an admired African American writer—will demonstrate some special competence, some genuine eloquence, on the subject of race and language. Why read a novel that recognizes the linguistic complications of a social issue, if not to be enlightened about a way around these complications? But in this regard *Apex* consistently disappoints. The conflict in the novel is so starkly and simplistically drawn that it almost immediately assumes a dry allegorical tenor, reducing the people in the book to a kind of shorthand for cultural and historical forces. Whitehead's people are never quite individuals. More often they are occasions for the writer tiresomely to exercise his wit. [28]

A major source of Schama's disappointment is the atypical protagonist who "fails as a means to 'inch closer' to a right way of speaking about race."[29] Consequently, even if the characters in *Apex* remained stereotypes or static in nature, if the protagonist offered insight to the racial questions proposed in a postblack or supposedly postracial era, the narrative would occupy vacuous space on racial questions.

According to Cohn, a key to Whitehead's literary angst is rooted in the postsoul aesthetic. Due to the exclusion of cultural representations from the civil rights movement and Black Power movement, writers of the postsoul generation, such as Colson Whitehead, discovered normalcy in the mass consumer culture/mass media. The concept of soul means realness, "painful history dues paid, a sense of group belonging, and commitment to the project of cultural nationalism built on that foundation."[30] When people fail to have soul, they may exhibit the following characteristics: "unreality, fakery, crossing over and selling out, betraying the culture and the history of sacrifice (the 'hurt') that created it."[31] Based on the aforementioned definitions, Whitehead does not fall neatly into the aforementioned or the former category. Cohn agrees that "Whitehead's writings betray a sense of anxiety over the source of cultural value, of guilty indebtedness to the past."[32] As a matter of fact, the postsoul generation seeks to transcend their artistic production beyond their forefather's foundational accomplishments. Transcending beyond the prescribed signifiers of blackness is often deemed as postblack. Yet, ignoring race and its significant contribution to America's fragmented identity is postracial. Therefore, *Apex* falls into the category of a postsoul or postblack narrative based on those distinctions.

As evidenced by Schama's criticism, the "spiritless prose of the protagonist enacts the argument that emerges as the central thrust of the novel: that the authority of eloquence is specious, that no one person is more entitled (or able) to name a town, or a race, or a human, than any other person."[33] In other words, Whitehead questions the textual authority of the civil rights generation, the Black Power movement generation, and even the postsoul generation to determine authenticity of blackness and its subsequent signifiers: identity, language, and naming. But, this continuous literary angst over textual authority exposes "a hollowness at the heart of its cleverness." For those reasons, the emptiness of the protagonist is also "a casualty of the empty world that it invents."[34] Unfortunately, this narrative set in "brand-centric times" succeeds at taking halfhearted "jibes at modern consumerism . . . while the ostensibly heavy subtext of race and memory adds little, especially after *John Henry Days*, a tragicomic farce about, among other things, the commodification of history and expunging of racial guilt."[35] In other words, *John Henry Days* succeeds where *Apex Hides the Hurt* fails. Within this "blank prose and ghostly setting," Whitehead expresses the meaninglessness of "modern life, but that expression is obscured by a lot of dead ends and dramatic busywork."[36] Perhaps Whitehead's work would benefit from promoting textual authority from one source over the others. By taking a definitive position with the protagonist and the overarching themes, the reader will receive the enlightenment they seek when reading Whitehead's books. Lastly, Cohn insists that Whitehead's work indicates "questions of African-American literary and cultural ancestry, if not necessarily the same as those of a nearly all-white, all-male Western Canon." In essence, his literary production is "fraught with Oedipal anxieties, haunted by debts to shadowy cultural fathers and to the names they have bequeathed."[37] Whether Whitehead acknowledges it or not, his Oedipal anxieties manifest themselves in the identity crisis of the protagonist, the shallowness of *Apex*'s minor characters, and the continuous textual tension over African American literary and cultural ancestry.

Apex Hides the Hurt emerges from an ingenious premise. The questions of black identity in a postblack and supposedly postracial era are wonderfully complex. Nevertheless, since Whitehead admittedly questions systems and institutions, he chooses to deconstruct rather than reconstruct viable options for his characters. By the summation of the narrative, the protagonist is no more enlightened on blackness and culturally acclimated than he was at the inception of the novel. Consequently, Whitehead leaves the narrative open ended with prevailing questions. For instance, how does a society progress and maintain "a real sense of history—when a language for that history doesn't exist and progress itself seems bankrupt?"[38] Issues of racial progress that are frustrated by the vestiges of slavery and postsoul identity deserve redress. Nevertheless, Whitehead "doesn't give the problem enough room to develop, and none of his characters is rich enough to give it weight."[39] As previously stated, Whitehead refuses to take sides with any of his characters or their professed ideologies "neither Winthropian nostalgia—and forget Freedomist nostalgia, too—nor New Prosperian progressivism: and he's an anthropologist, not a controversialist."[40] Leif Sorensen explains Whitehead's disillusion with naming the town by quoting from *Apex*: "They come at him, lurching, wearing the same clothes they used to wear, normal-looking yet in complete exile from themselves and their histories. Surrounding him, after pieces of him."[41] As symbolized by the zombies in *Zone One*, the protagonist's vision in *Apex* exemplifies the pressure from the town's inhabitants. Furthermore, the zombie metaphor expresses Whitehead's leeriness with the possibility of change in a mass-media-infused and consumer-based culture. Sorensen states that "in both of these moments, zombies stand for the potential that the future will consist only of an incessant repetition of capitalist cycles of consumption, labor, and branding."[42] Indeed, there is always the likelihood that America's plagued history will repeat itself. But if Whitehead is willing to pose the overarching racial questions, he must be willing to provide palatable solutions or at least a level of enlightenment for those readers who hope for societal transformation.

NOTES

1. "Apex Hides the Hurt," *Kirkus Reviews*, January 1, 2006, accessed December 3, 2014, https://www.kirkusreviews.com/.

2. Linda Selzer, "New Eclecticism: An Interview with Colson Whitehead," *Callaloo* 31, no. 2 (spring 2008): 397.

3. Ibid.

4. Chloë Schama, "Review of *Apex Hides the Hurt: A Novel*," *New Republic*, July 24, 2006, accessed December 7, 2014, http://www.newrepublic.com/.

5. Selzer, "New Eclecticism," 399.

6. Ibid.

7. Ibid.

8. Review of *Apex Hides the Hurt*, by Colson Whitehead, *Chicago Reader* Books, April 21, 2006, accessed December 3, 2014, http://www.chicagoreader.com/.

9. Review of *Apex Hides the Hurt*, by Colson Whitehead, *Publishers Weekly*, accessed December 3, 2014, http://www.publishersweekly.com/.

10. Schama, "Review of *Apex*."

11. Jesse S. Cohn, "Old Afflictions: Colson Whitehead's *Apex Hides the Hurt* and the 'Post-Soul Condition,'" *Journal of the Midwest Modern Language Association* 42, no. 1 (spring 2009): 15.

12. Ibid.

13. Review of *Apex*, *Publishers Weekly*.

14. Cohn, "Old Afflictions," 16.

15. Review of *Apex*, *Publishers Weekly*.

16. Cohn, "Old Afflictions," 16.

17. Colson Whitehead, *Apex Hides the Hurt* (New York: Doubleday, 2006), 21.

18. Cohn, "Old Afflictions," 17.

19. Ibid., 18.

20. Whitehead, *Apex Hides the Hurt*, 183.

21. Cohn, "Old Afflictions," 18.

22. Ibid., 19.

23. "Apex Hides the Hurt," *Kirkus Reviews*.

24. Whitehead, *Apex Hides the Hurt*, 170.

25. Ibid.

26. Ibid.

27. Derek C. Maus, *Understanding Colson Whitehead* (Columbia: University of South Carolina Press, 2014), 75.

28. Schama, "Review of *Apex*."

29. Ibid.

30. Cohn, "Old Afflictions," 20.

31. Ibid., 21.

32. Ibid.

33. Schama, "Review of *Apex*."

34. Ibid.

35. Review of *Apex*, *Chicago Reader*, 30.

36. Ibid.

37. Cohn, "Old Afflictions," 21.

38. Review of *Apex*, *Publishers Weekly*.

39. Ibid.

40. David Gates, "Name That Town," review of *Apex Hides the Hurt*, by Colson Whitehead, Sunday Book Review, *New York Times*, April 2, 2006, accessed December 7, 2014, http://www.nytimes.com/.

41. Whitehead, *Apex Hides the Hurt*, 195.

42. Leif Sorensen, "Against the Post-Apocalyptic: Narrative Closure in Colson Whitehead's *Zone One*," *Contemporary Literature* 55, no. 3 (2014): 578.

Part III

The Colossus of New York

Chapter Eight

New York

A Postracial Dream Realized or an American Dream Deferred

In *The Colossus of New York: A City in Thirteen Parts*, Colson Whitehead journeys through New York as an anonymous aracial commentator on the American experience.[1] John Freeman writes in the *Pittsburgh Post-Gazette* that "against the city's back-beat, grooved by the melody of its voices, Whitehead's style is best described as Duke Ellington crossed with Run DMC, with the occasional sampling of Frank Sinatra."[2] The rhythmic tone of every sentence is delivered with a mid-tempo jazzy swing. Each essay is orchestrated by a "verbal virtuoso who can write, dance, build and sing with nothing more than the English language."[3] In his tightly construed yet melodic sentiments, he gracefully "traipses across tenses and points of view."[4] Unapologetically, within one sentence, perspectives may fluctuate between second-person singular and first-person singular: "The New York City you live in is not my New York City."[5] Then, in the same paragraph, he switches to third-person singular and first-person plural. The intended effect is to encapsulate the collective consciousness of New Yorkers as they experience work life, intercity travel, leisure, and home life. When Whitehead's words fluctuate between past, present, and future tense, he is stressing the ever presence of the personal and collective history of the city's inhabitants. By grounding his thirteen essays in the cyclical and humdrum disappointments of residents on the incessant verge of change, various essays such as "City Limits," "Broadway," "Brooklyn Bridge," and "Times Square" dispel the glamour of the New York metropolis. Consequently, Whitehead confronts New York's mythical archetype with aracial commentary and distinguished discernment; the city's fable is exposed as both an untenable promise land and a splintered symbol of the American Dream.

MANIC PERSPECTIVES: *THE COLOSSUS OF NEW YORK'S* COMPETING VOICES

Whitehead's *Colossus* and E. B. White's *Here Is New York* "are, at least on the surface, ripe for comparison, in that they are both brief, personal love letters to New York City." Nonetheless, the "authors are separated by, among other things, time and circumstance."[6] According to White, there are three types of New Yorkers: commuters, natives, and settlers. However, Whitehead broadens his tribute to New York. By consolidating the voices of eight million residents, he expands his prose beyond three primary perspectives. Each voice is like "eight million naked cities in this naked city" offering his or her own plot sequence to the American story.[7] Although Whitehead is considerate of these voices, he knows that "they dispute and disagree."[8] Whitehead acknowledges that these voices are distinct because they compete for recognition as the authentic New York story. Thus, he must consolidate the predominating New York attitude from a scattered web of voices. With the exception of Whitehead's preeminent perspective, none of the voices are significant enough to outweigh the viewpoints of others; therefore, they are interlocked anecdotes vocalized by the dominant arbiter.

In Whitehead's essay compilation, he bends the standard syntax rules to mimic the manic and uncompromising voices of a complex city. By using poetic language, "he eschews question marks, commas, and much other interior punctuation."[9] Strict grammarians will lose their minds, but most readers will find freedom in the lax application of grammatical conventions. From a linguistic perspective, there is no singular way to define New York, New Yorkers, or the New York experience. As the primary storyteller, the native New Yorker issues himself permission to disrupt prescribed grammar rules. The unpunctuated interior monologue signifies the fragmented memories, feelings, and opinions that constitute a typical New York state of mind. Thus, *Colossus*'s fragmented prose mirrors the city's identity.

New York is a promise land of dreams and broken, bitter streets of reality. According to Freeman, "The anonymity of the city and the collective weight of its dreams, the way it inspires visions of a better self only to smash such fantasies to bits," are *Colossus*'s overarching themes.[10] Whitehead knows people may differ with his native narrative of New York. Perhaps Whitehead's New York is not everyone else's New York.[11] Nevertheless, Whitehead's observations occupy tension-filled space between elitist conformity and common-man authenticity: "I started building my New York on the uptown No. 1 train. . . . It's the early seventies, so everything is filthy."[12]

Mostly, his prose is "natural (and as uncomfortable) as looking in a full-length mirror."[13] The omniscient voice of New York is as ominous as the billboard eyes of T. J. Eckelburg in *The Great Gatsby*. Whitehead says in "City Limits" that "the city saw all that. Remembers, too."[14] If structures could talk, Whitehead says there are no real secrets. What would "all your old apartments . . . say if they got together to swap stories. They could . . . gossip about who you are after midnight."[15] Therefore, it's not necessary to wonder how he knows: "It's as if Whitehead has heard all of our conversations, smelled our fears, tasted our successes, recognized our falseness, tapped our phones and our fantasies, and, yes, felt our pain."[16] Despite his disdain for the commercialized aspect of the dream, the collective voice of a city is dependent on Whitehead. With every carefully constructed sentence, a mythical city is indebted to him for exposing their grand dreams and colossal failures.

NEW YORK: THE 9/11 SURVIVING MACHINE

Despite New York's symbolic designation as the mecca of America's ingenuity, *Colossus* contemplates the infinitesimal existence of New Yorkers. In an allusion to 9/11, Whitehead says, "One day the city we built will be gone, and when it goes, we go." Since American society measures our might by the fortitude of our structures, "When the buildings fall, we topple too."[17] New York survives because she reinvents herself during endless transitions. Whitehead says that "if you didn't witness it, it is not a part of your New York."[18] Although New Yorkers exemplify the determination of the American spirit, everyone and everything is pro tempore. Dreams drive people to transplant themselves from "really drab and tiny" towns to see New York icons: Broadway, the Brooklyn Bridge, and Times Square.[19] But for a native New Yorker, their metropolis is much more than a shiny emblem representing the American Dream.

The 9/11 catastrophe exemplifies the resiliency of New Yorkers' American spirit. Whitehead suggests that "maybe we become New Yorkers the day we realize that New York will go on without us."[20] Memories of former monuments are edificial ghosts of a past existence. In Whitehead's New York, buildings are likened to people. People are likened to buildings. Whitehead reminisces about the structures that he inhabited or "were part of a skyline" that he "thought would always be there."[21] Each paragraph is a weighty block devoted to the ever-present spectral of inhabitants' existence. Maybe it's the mundane routines that keep people moving. Perhaps, it's the dream of a better life or the purchasable "postcards of the new skyline" that maintains and gains believers.[22] New York's mythologized glitz and glamour enigmatically deceives transplants and outsiders with her shiny American

Dream. Freeman writes that "the New York of Whitehead's imagination is an occult world made up of tall tales and legends."[23] To Whitehead's credit, *Colossus* spends numerous pages discrediting this romanticized view of New York. With satiric mockery, Whitehead speaks of the currency associated with selling the dream, "with all the movies, TV shows and songs—the whole If You Can Make It There business."[24] Songs like Sinatra's "New York, New York" and George Benson's "Broadway" laud New York's mythic powers to grant dreams.[25] Jay-Z and Alicia Keys contribute an urbanized view in "Empire State of Mind." Jay-Z mentions that he lives on billboards, but there are "eight million stories out there, and they're naked / Cities is a pity, half of y'all won't make it."[26] Conversely, their gritty lyrics present a darker side to the journey. Don Henley, former member of the Eagles, keeps in time with *Colossus*. Henley sings that everything can change in a quick "New York Minute."[27] In a city that never sleeps, these songs motivate pilgrimages to New York as a symbolic site of entertainment, economic success, and even emotional disappointment. Hence, the multifarious voices of *Colossus* are walkers, drivers, riders, or the architecture itself: homes, buildings, bridges, or destinations like the Brooklyn Bridge, Broadway, or Times Square. Existing buildings fulfill the illusion of the dream. People are constantly on the move, traveling in and out of structures, searching for the self-actualization of the dream. Inhabitants know this; collectively they say, "Up there in the corporate headquarters of the entertainment combine, executives decide your dream life."[28] But, those who still believe offer another anecdote. There was a former pickpocket that abandons his criminal ways. The man "pushes nosebleed seats to faded Broadway shows."[29] In Whitehead's New York, "Everybody [is] selling something."[30] Ultimately, as they fruitlessly peruse the promise land, everyone is eager to buy relics of the untenable and elusive dream.

THE POSTRACIAL AMERICAN DREAM AND WHITEHEAD'S NEW YORK

In *The American Dream: A Cultural History*, Lawrence R. Samuel examines the origins, definition, and actualization of the mythic American Dream. The dream lives because individuals and institutions devote themselves to maintain its "mythological power." The dream promotes "our special mission of democracy and experiment in pluralism."[31] When confronted by groups who sometimes feel excluded from the dream, society offers up the dream as proof that equality exists even for immigrants, racial minorities, women, or various religious groups. Samuel believes that the government utilizes the power of the dream "as a tool of propaganda, that is, a powerful ideological weapon of persuasion both here and abroad."[32] America preserves a "popular image despite there being many flaws in the product itself."[33] Movies set in New York and songs about New York celebrate the dream, while they are complicit in the preservation of America's mythology. Studies prove that Americans work the longest hours, easily change jobs, and when presented with a new opportunity will move at a moment's notice. Thus, these facts further substantiate America as a land of opportunity. Remember, the iconic Statute of Liberty, her torch thrusting forward as a beaconing light, welcoming people from abroad. But Whitehead warns us not to move too fast as we try to capitalize on the dream. Don't believe the hype! Chasing the American Dream is far more exciting than the arrival. The American Dream has become "a staple within popular and consumer culture."[34] Frank Capra and Walt Disney's theme song "When You Wish upon a Star" for *Pinocchio* participate in the cultural mythmaking of the dream. Movies, radio, and television have advocated for "the Dream, with every sitcom family from *The Goldbergs* to *The Jeffersons* to *The Simpsons* trying to climb the ladder of success while facing the trials and tribulations of modern life."[35] We're "Movin' on Up," *The Jeffersons'* theme song says, "To the East side / To a deluxe apartment in the sky. . . . We finally got a piece of the pie."[36] For every American Dream, whenever the country is facing troublesome times, there is the "American nightmare, this evil twin always lurking in the shadows."[37]

Are we now in a postracial society because the American Dream is more accessible to everyone? During a 2009 article with the *Collegian*, interviewer Maria Ribas asked Whitehead his view of the term *postracial*.[38] Obama's election as the first African American president signaled for some that America is in a postrace era. At this high point of American exceptionalism, when Whitehead is presented with this question, it admittedly caused him personal and social angst. Whitehead adamantly opposed the concept of postracialism. He stated that "it's silly to think that we're post-race. Obviously racism didn't disappear overnight."[39] Although, in his op-ed article entitled "The Year of Living Postracially," he mentions that Obama's election has some great aspects. Nevertheless, this does not mean that race relations will improve instantaneously; progress is slow.[40] In other words, the first black president does not signify that America is living up to the dream of equal access and opportunity for all. Nevertheless, Samuel says that "a myriad of illustrious characters, including" Frank Sinatra, Henry Ford, Oprah Winfrey, and "Barack Obama have been considered the very embodiments" of the American Dream.[41] Therefore, associating Obama's success with the term *postracial* is not an invalid question. Nevertheless, Whitehead was motivated to write his op-ed because he "was getting asked inappropriate questions" about his politics.[42] Whitehead refrained from explaining why he deemed these questions to be inappropriate. As the most successful male literary author of African American heritage, his opinions on sociopolitical issues have value. Whitehead claims that he does not "worry about politics, but people kept asking" him his feelings about a "post-racial society." Therefore, he wrote the satiric article to get himself "off the hook." Whitehead believed that "now no one's going to ask" him what he thinks anymore because he is "just going to make jokes."[43]

Whitehead may presume that witty quips and satiric op-eds get him off the hook, but humor does not relieve him of his literary responsibility to comment on cultural interests of critics and readers. Perhaps this is why J. Sutter is a satirical character who experiences no racism except for his own racial angst. Despite the rumors he has heard about the South, the people in the town show no visible signs of racism. As one of the most successful literary authors, he has the clout that causes his audience and critics to contemplate his potentially insightful commentary on various issues. Since Whitehead feels comfortable responding to cultural questions via writing, his nonfiction and fiction books present the opportunity for him to address contemporary social issues, such as, Are poor African Americans more likely to experience the American Nightmare than African Americans with economic mobility or educational privilege? Or is race no longer a factor in African Americans' lives once they achieve success? Many literary and cultural critics concur with Whitehead's assertion that this is not a postrace era. However, in terms of literary messages, Whitehead's texts have postracial elements, such as characters, themes, and settings that support the inverse of Whitehead's purported disbelief in postracialism. Although both *The Intuitionist* and *John Henry Days* explore the racial hindrances on mobility, despite the dream's promise, they address race in terms of a historical fact instead of a contemporary adversity.

The multifarious voices of *Colossus* are comprised of postracial or aracial voices. They bear no hints of cultural or racial distinctions, yet they speak as the universal authority of New York–style mobility. There are references to class differentiations in terms of zip codes, owners, and renters. But there are no racialized voices expressing whether they feel included or excluded from the dream. As everyone navigates their way through the metropolis, Whitehead's collective voice exposes the illusory elements of the dream. Although Whitehead disavows belief in a postracial society, class and race play no role in shattering the delusion of the dream. Everyone is "trapped at corners . . . conniving tortoises, ratified by fable."[44] During the 1940s, "John La Farge's book *The Race Question and the Negro* also exposed how blacks were excluded from sharing in the American Dream."[45] From a new millennial perspective, comparing the protagonist Jay Gatsby to the rapper Jay-Z, fragments of the dream are sprinkled throughout "the landscape of American culture."[46] The success of Jay-Z, the executive producer of *The Great Gatsby* (2013), manifests the illusion that the dream is attainable despite economic hardships and racial differences.[47] Samuel acknowledges that "popular music (especially hip-hop, with its adoration of money and the luxuries it could buy)" fuels the belief that the dream is inclusive rather than exclusive.[48] During the media-crazed decade of 2000–2010, Jay-Z and P. Diddy were "musical king[s] of the dream." However, after the New Jersey native Bruce Springsteen's album *The Rising* (2002) responded to the 9/11 tragedy, he was "considered a virtual saint because he and his music were almost synonymous with the American Dream."[49] Springsteen is "the son of a bus driver and legal secretary . . . a rich rock and roller with a strong moral conscience."[50] To some Americans, the early struggles of New York natives Jay-Z and P. Diddy represent anomalies. Theoretically, Jay-Z and P. Diddy's glamorous bling is unattainable for the average black or white American. Thus, both entertainers buffer the delusional belief in the dream.

To Whitehead's credit, he highlights the commercial forces that propagandize New York as the dream maker. However, Whitehead should probe deeper into the consumer forces that promise material relics of the dream yet provide a lack of real access to the dream. Why does Whitehead refrain from discussing the racial, economic, and political factors that inhibit the dream? For writers during the eighteenth and nineteenth century, "the economic and political realms" were indistinguishable "from the political and industrial revolutions."[51] In the twentieth century, an "author's genius was invoked to explain the irrelevance of economic and political issues to questions of strictly cultural interest."[52] Around the time of the *Colossus*'s 2003 post-9/11 publication, Whitehead resists treating New York as a political and gentrified space. Furthermore, Whitehead abstains from the social and racial commentary that he offers in *The Intuitionist* and *John Henry Days*. In the context of those aforementioned books, as previously stated, structural and institutional racism are treated as issues whose centrifugal force remains in the past.

Amongst Whitehead's multitude of voices in *Colossus*, and out of the eight million naked cities he portends to unify in his essay collection, his prose lacks any ethnic perspectives. Whitehead says that "talking about New York is a way of talking about the world."[53] Since Whitehead observes New York in terms of a universal manner of experiencing global life, he negates human differences in race, economics, or gender. If a writer unveils "the social and cultural assumptions of literary language," he or she complicates the reading.[54] Therefore, when authors separate "the cultural from the political and economic realms," they demote the social purpose of their work.[55] From a historicists' perspective, they link "the author and critic in a shared project."[56] Thus, the critic may restore the work to a "social, economic, political, and gendered" contextual meaning.[57] Whether Whitehead acquiesces or not to his literary duty as a culture maker, the author is "determined by the social and economic forces whose shapes he reflected or altered in his work." From a psychoanalytic and phenomenological standpoint, "their criticism takes place at that moment within an author's work when the author becomes critically aware of dominant social, psychological, and political forces."[58]

J. Hillis Miller writes in "Narrative" that the purpose of fiction functions to dethrone "reigning assumptions of a given culture,"[59] for instance, dispelling the myths associated with the dominant American culture, such as economic and racial equality. Nonfiction texts have the same opportunity to dethrone commonly held assumptions. However, *The Colossus of New York* operates as universal commentary on the myth's power to consume everyone without regard to race. Whitehead's *Colossus* lacks social, psychological, and political awareness of forces that capitalize from the dream ideology. At the socioeconomic expense of the average New Yorker, their everyday commute and living arrangements are influenced by forces not discussed in the *Colossus*. Instead, Whitehead frames the New York experience as problematic for those who transplant themselves in a feigned pursuit of the dream. A story "can propose modes of selfhood or ways of behaving that are then imitated in the real world."[60] Nonfiction texts have the same capacity to influence culture by transforming lives. Fictional texts have extreme magnitude "not as the accurate reflectors of a culture but as the makers of that culture and as the unostentatious, but therefore all the more effective, policeman of that culture."[61] Whitehead, with his excellent body of work, is a culture maker. Many people look to Whitehead to provide insight into the African American culture. At this time, Whitehead has fulfilled his obligation to the dominant American culture; however, he has not met his obligation to the complexities of the African American culture. In *Colossus*, Whitehead misses an opportunity to sew a thread into the tattered blanket of the American Dream. He speaks of pop culture as the only dark side of the dream's myth. In terms of the myth's power, strains on equal access, class, gender, and racial commentary are excluded from his discussion on failed dreams.

Although Whitehead espouses disbelief in postracialism, he passively upholds the theory by neglecting opportunities to offer multiracial perspectives. Direct socioeconomic, political, and racial commentary would make him a formidable voice in the literary landscape. As the most accoladed African American author of the early twenty-first century, his platform is wide. Yet, he is reluctant to step up to the podium. At this juncture, he does not occupy the shoes of Don Delillo or Ralph Ellison, who are his literary foreparents. In the age of Obama and the New Millennium, if Whitehead seeks to maintain his humongous space on the stage, he must occupy the vacuous space left by the mortal absence of his literary predecessors. He must walk up to the podium and offer an inclusive, cultural, sociopolitical, and anti-postracial view of the entire American experience.

NOTES

1. Zoe A. Y. Weinberg, "Raceless Like Me: Students at Harvard Navigate Their Way beyond the Boundaries of Race," *Harvard Crimson*, October 13, 2011, accessed July 11, 2014, http://www.thecrimson.com/. The term "aracial" is rarely used in American society. Phrases such as "transcendent identity" or "raceless" are sometimes used. Dr. Kerry Ann Rockquemore claims, "Someone who is race transcendent or raceless may choose to identify by ethnicity instead, or emphasize another part of their personal heritage, such as nationality, language, or culture." Furthermore, aracialism further reiterates the fact that race is a social construct not a biological construct. Lastly, Weinberg writes that "racelessness" functions as an avenue for people "who do not wish to identify by race at all."

2. John Freeman, "'The Colossus of New York: A City in Thirteen Parts': Poetic Prose Dance to the Many Rhythms of the City," *Pittsburgh Post-Gazette*, December 14, 2003, accessed July 11, 2014, http://old.post-gazette.com/.

3. Rick Kleffel, "*The Colossus of New York* by Colson Whitehead," Agony Column, October 28, 2003, accessed July 11, 2014, http://trashotron.com/.

4. Ibid.

5. Colson Whitehead, *The Colossus of New York: A City in Thirteen Parts* (New York: Anchor, 2003), 6.

6. Youkie Otah, "Here Is the Colossus of New York," NewYorkBoundBooks.com, June 22, 2013, accessed July 11, 2014, http://www.newyorkboundbooks.com/.

7. Whitehead, *Colossus of New York*, 6; Whitehead's reference to the "naked city" is possibly an allusion to the TV series *Naked City* (1958–1963), IMDb, accessed July 11, 2014, http://www.imdb.com/. The crime-drama television show featured guest stars such as Dustin Hoffman, Jack Klugman, and Christopher Walken. The series depicted the lives of cops and the crimes they investigated in the city of New York.

8. Whitehead, *Colossus of New York*, 6.

9. "The Colossus of New York: A City in Thirteen Parts," *Kirkus Reviews*, July 15, 2003, accessed July 11, 2014, https://www.kirkusreviews.com/.

10. Freeman, "Colossus of New York."

11. Whitehead, *Colossus of New York*, 6.

12. Ibid., 4–5.

13. "Colossus of New York," *Kirkus Reviews*.

14. Whitehead, *Colossus of New York*, 9.

15. Ibid.

16. "Colossus of New York," *Kirkus Reviews*.

17. Whitehead, *Colossus of New York*, 9.

18. Ibid., 5.

19. Ibid., 3.

20. Ibid., 9–10.

21. Ibid., 8.

22. Ibid., 10.

23. Freeman, "Colossus of New York."

24. Whitehead, *Colossus of New York*, 3. Whitehead is making an allusion to Sinatra's classic song "New York, New York." See Frank Sinatra, "New York, New York," Metro Lyrics, CBS Interactive, 2013, accessed July 12, 2014, http://www.metrolyrics.com/. Sinatra sings, "If I can make it there / I'll make it anywhere / It's up to you / New York, New York."

25. See George Benson, "On Broadway," Metro Lyrics, CBS Interactive, 2013, accessed January 12, 2014, http://www.metrolyrics.com/. Benson sings, "They say the neon lights are bright on Broadway / They say there's always magic in the air." He responds back to people who say he won't make it: "'Cause I can play this here guitar / And I won't quit till I'm a star on Broadway."

26. Jay-Z and Alicia Keys, "Empire State of Mind," Metro Lyrics, CBS Interactive, 2013, accessed July 13, 2014.http://www.metrolyrics.com/.

27. See Don Henley, "New York Minute," Metro Lyrics, CBS Interactive, 2013, accessed July 12, 2014, http://www.metrolyrics.com/. At the beginning of the song, a man who works on

Wall Street and dresses in black commits suicide at the train tracks. But Henley says if you hold onto the one you love, "In a New York minute / Everything can change / In a New York minute / You can get out of the rain." In essence, everything moves fast in New York. Life can change for the worse or the better in a quick New York minute.

28. Whitehead, *Colossus of New York*, 146.

29. Ibid.

30. Ibid.

31. Lawrence R. Samuel, *The American Dream: A Cultural History* (Syracuse, NY: Syracuse University Press, 2012), 7.

32. Ibid.

33. Ibid., 7–8.

34. Ibid., 8.

35. Ibid.

36. "Movin' on Up," *The Jeffersons* (theme song), YouTube, September 28, 2011, accessed July 12, 2014, http://www.youtube.com/.

37. Samuel, *American Dream*, 9.

38. Maria Ribas, "Q&A with Colson Whitehead," *Collegian*, December 18, 2009, accessed July 11, 2014, http://thecollegianur.com/.

39. Ibid.

40. Ibid.

41. Samuel, *American Dream*, 9.

42. Ribas, "Q&A with Colson Whitehead."

43. Ibid.

44. Whitehead, *Colossus of New York*, 76.

45. Samuel, *American Dream*, 38.

46. Ibid., 9.

47. See "Jay-Z Confirms Great Gatsby Executive Producer Role," BBC Newsbeat, March 15, 2013, accessed July 13, 2014, http://www.bbc.co.uk/. The article states that "He has been acting as executive producer, helping director Baz Luhrmann put together the jazz performances on screen and arrange the soundtrack." Baz Luhrmann and Jay-Z were introduced by Leonardo DiCaprio, who stars as Jay Gatsby "in the adaptation of F. Scott Fitzgerald's novel set in the 1920s."

48. Samuel, *American Dream*, 182.

49. Ibid., 183.

50. Ibid.

51. Donald E. Pease, "The Author," in *Critical Terms for Literary Study*, ed. Frank Lentricchia and Thomas McLaughlin, 105–18 (Chicago: The University of Chicago Press, 1995), 110.

52. Ibid.

53. Whitehead, *Colossus of New York*, 158.

54. Myra Jehlen, "Gender," 264.

55. Ibid., 265.

56. Pease, "Author," 111.

57. Ibid.

58. Ibid., 112.

59. J. Hillis Miller, "Narrative," in *Critical Terms for Literary Study*, ed. Frank Lentricchia and Thomas McLaughlin, 66–79 (Chicago: University of Chicago Press, 1995), 69.

60. Ibid.

61. Ibid.

Chapter Nine

The Colossus of New York

A Tribute to Gothic Urban Spaces

Colson Whitehead's *Colossus of New York* bears the same title as a classic sci-fi film set in the 1950s. In the 1958 movie *The Colossus of New York*, a scientist dies on the eve of receiving the Nobel Peace Prize. Due to this untimely and tragic death, the scientist's father implants his son's brain into a robot that eventually terrorizes the citizens of New York. The theme of *The Colossus of New York* derives from Mary Shelley's *Frankenstein*.[1] Shelley's classic pioneered the "theme of an uncontrollable creature wreaking vengeful destruction upon the heads of his monomaniacal scientific Creator."[2] Universally, contemporary society uses the term "Frankenstein" to mean "creativity gone wrong and monstrosity gone wild."[3] Contrary to popular public perception, Frankenstein is the name of the scientist not the monster. Yet, in contemporary culture, "the creature often takes on the name of the creator, as if there were no differences in the monstrosity of outcomes."[4] Even though Whitehead's ode to New York bears the same name as the creature in the aforementioned movie, his episodic and tightly strung together anecdotes are nonfiction. Unlike *Zone One*, instead of writing a sci-fi version of New York, Whitehead pays homage to the bedlam and beauty of his birthplace in *Colossus*. Nevertheless, the questions still remain: Is New York City the monster that consumes the moods, stories, and lives of New Yorkers? Or are New Yorkers the robotic creatures of habit that hide a semblance of monstrosity deep within their souls? In a *New York Times* article, Whitehead publishes a horrific and descriptive gothic view of gargantuan flames obscuring the skyline.[5] The poignant reflection of a tumbling Twin Towers is eloquently written in Whitehead's "Way We Live Now." He refers to his own emotional detachment and disassociation as aesthetic distance. Whitehead's use of aesthetic distance exposes the suppressed monster that looms on the exterior of New York and dwells within the inner beings of strangers abroad. Historically, the term *Frankenstein* has been used to express the fears of democratic government: politicians who advocated the abolition of slaves or a voting populous were warned against creating a "Frankenstein monster" that would eventually turn on them.[6] Then, in the post-9/11 era, there were media pundits who criticized the US government for its military response during the Gulf War. For instance, Saddam Hussein was deemed a Frankenstein of America's own creation.[7] However, in *The Colossus of New York*, there are only allusions to 9/11 amongst the populous. In a city where the impossible is possible, both the city and its inhabitants struggle for authority over one another in the 9/11 aftermath. The New York skyline has changed. But has the way people travel, live, and work altered as a result of the emotional detachment and disassociation? Although Whitehead's *Colossus* lacks the science-fiction elements of a Colossus or gigantic robot, he expands the metaphor of Frankenstein to explore the automation of humankind. In a post-9/11 era, as a result of bearing witness to the destruction of American ingenuity, Whitehead presents the subsequent mechanization of humans and their resulting dehumanization. Thus, *Colossus* explores the technology that governs New Yorkers' modes of living, working, and transporting themselves in a milieu of posttraumatic remembrance.

The locals of Whitehead's *Colossus* live, work, and travel in a routine, robotic, and humdrum manner. Meanwhile, the anthropomorphic structures sit in contrast to the residents; the buildings house their stories like spirits who live and breathe, in memory of those who once inhabited the space.[8] The personal stories and histories of New Yorkers are the heart and soul of the buildings they inhabit. The structures participate in the narrative like characters in a play directed by Whitehead. He seamlessly depicts this symbiotic, automaton-like relationship between the city and its inhabitants. Within this interdependent, master-servant relationship, do the roles reverse? Does the city serve the people? Or, do the people serve the city?

As usual, Whitehead leaves narrative conclusions to the reader. He presents the urban landscape but leaves the depth of humanity up to the audience's perception. Perhaps the zombie infestation in *Zone One* is a metaphor for post-9/11 New York City. Throughout Whitehead's *Colossus*, with the exception of New York transplants, humanity moves in a dehumanized, routine, and soulless way. Are the ancestors of the apocalyptical zombies in *Zone One* the unnamed straggler-like and skel-like residents of Whitehead's *Colossus*? For the citizens in the movie, the Colossus creature represents a predominating desire to dominate and consume the lives of New Yorkers; yet, in "The Way We Live Now," Whitehead offers a gothic depiction of disassociation in the face of horror and the subsequent and collective detachment that occurs in *Colossus*.

COLOSSUS OF NEW YORK: THE MOVIE

As previously stated, Whitehead's *Colossus of New York* bears the same title as the 1958 "overlooked classic" film *The Colossus of New York*. Although the horror movie is considered a "little silly" and definitely implausible, the movie resonates amongst science-fiction movie fans. In an "oversaturated decade of monster movies," this movie "carries the torch from past landmarks like Mary Shelley's *Frankenstein* and Fritz Lang's *Metropolis*." Jeremy Spensser (Ross Martin) is "a brilliant young scientist" who dies "on the eve of his acceptance of the Nobel Peace Prize." Jeremy's sudden death cuts short his potential "impact on human progress."[9] Jeremy's father is unable to accept his son's accidental death; therefore, "rather than having his son's body driven to the morgue, William insists that it be taken to his home, where he secretly removes Jeremy's brain from his dead body."[10] As a "renowned brain surgeon and unyielding man of reason, [Jeremy's] father William (Otto Kruger) believes the mind can be reactivated independent of the body."[11] John, Jeremy's fellow scientist and friend, disapproves of William's decision to save Jeremy's brain. Adamantly, John insists that a man "needs to feel emotions to remain human."[12] Therefore, a brain without emotions would "become dehumanized in monstrous proportions." William's creation is "an eight-foot colossus."[13] The huge and clunking "metal mass" with "forever-open white eyes and a gaping mouth" is reminiscent of an "archetypal mask of Greek tragedy."[14] Once Jeremy sees himself in the mirror, he "collapses on the floor," horrified by his own reflection.[15] Initially, Jeremy wants his father to destroy him. Yet, Jeremy acquiesces to pressure from his family in order to continue his work for humanity. When Jeremy befriends his son at his own gravesite, he realizes that the family has lied to him. The Colossus robot, Jeremy, thinks that his family died in the automobile accident with him. Learning of his family's betrayal sets Jeremy into a rage. In a fit of madness, Jeremy "destroys the remote control box that William and [his brother] Henry use to control his mechanical body when he becomes overly excited."[16] Upon discovering that Henry has unrequited love for his wife Anne, "Jeremy murders his brother with laser beams from his x-ray eyes." Once he arrives back "to his father's lab, the now deranged Jeremy announces that he is turning his back on humanity, arguing that the weak should be destroyed, not saved, and such extermination should begin with all humanitarians."[17] Inevitably, the disconnection between human intellect and human emotions causes Jeremy discord. His desire for love and death to those who have betrayed him conflict with the "suffering of his mourning family and the love and generosity that defined him."[18] Suddenly, Jeremy's urge to aid in human progress has transformed "into contempt and, ultimately, bloodthirsty hate."[19] When the police "investigate Henry's death," William disavows all knowledge "of any 'monster.'"[20]

At a United Nations conference, held by John to honor Jeremy's contributions to humankind, the Colossus barges into the meeting. Jeremy's son Billy, who attends the conference with his mother Anne, becomes the innocent voice of reason. Since the young man has developed a rapport with the monster, he gets close "to the colossus" and admonishes him for behaving badly. At this moment, Jeremy realizes "that he has truly lost his humanity, [so he] asks Billy to turn off the power switch hidden beneath his left arm." Billy obeys the monster who has asked him earlier in the movie to call him "Daddy." The tragic life of the Colossus ends when he "collapses to the floor."[21]

Finally, William realizes that he should have listened to John; therefore, William "tells John he was right, that a brain without a soul is nothing but monstrous."[22] In essence, this creation (the Colossus) turned on its master and father (William). By inventing a mechanical body for his son's brain, but without his son's heart, the Colossus lacks an essential element of humanity. William becomes the master at the mercy of his own invention. Growing resentful of a mechanized life, the creation is devoid of the necessary compassion and civility that makes a person human. Inevitably, the people of New York are now prey for the advanced technology built by one of the city's own citizens. Once an entity transforms its purpose from advancing the progress of humans into an existence that preys on the very beings it was constructed to protect, the society is now dealing with a monstrous creation of its own invention: the emotional disconnection between the rationale of the mind and the actions of the body. This is the inevitable result of a routine, automaton-like lifestyle in urban spaces.

WHITEHEAD'S POST-9/11 NEW YORK: CATASTROPHE AND TRAGIC DISASSOCIATION

From an intimate distance, when Whitehead views the grotesque beauty of the burning towers, there is a nexus between catastrophe and tragic disassociation in urban spaces. His authorial perspective emphasizes the inevitable dehumanization that occurs when an individual and/or community experiences tragedy on epic scale. Thus, the open space of the New York skyline is mirrored by the emotional vacancy of the disconnected narrator. As evidenced by the September 23, 2001, publication date of "The Way We Live Now," the posttraumatic 9/11 disassociation is real for Whitehead. Thus, the reader must examine "The Way We Live Now" as a companion piece to *The Colossus*. In a crowd of "small groups, [of] strangers," the memory of "the top halves of the twin towers" resonates because the structures "overpowered the scene like bullies."[23] But as the fire rages in the New York skyline, the Twin Towers are forced to submit to the forced cremation. Casually, he suggests to his wife that they should "frame it" because "it was a nice shot." Once the smoke travels in the distance, Whitehead realizes that the second tower was gone. The top levels of the second tower had "buckled out, spraying tiny white shards, and the building sank down into itself, crouching beneath the trees and out of frame." Upon this realization, Whitehead and his wife head home. Toward the end of the personal reflection, he says, "And certainly it had been easier to shape the horror into an aesthetic experience and deny the human reality."[24] When Whitehead frames the terrifying fall of the Twin Towers as an "aesthetic experience," he expresses the dehumanization of the city's habitants in the midst of tragedy. By sharing an aesthetic version of the grotesque, there is a disconnection between Whitehead's intellect and the reader's expectation of natural emotions. Consequently, through the anthropomorphic description ("buckled out" and "crouching") of the towers, Whitehead creates a gothic image of urban space via his own dehumanization as the author.

The manner in which an individual witnesses, perceives, and responds to a tragic experience is difficult to evaluate as a critic. But an author's response to an aesthetic image exposes their emotions or lack of emotions to the world. Yet, according to Wyatt Mason, who writes in his review for the *New Republic*, the gothic image and the dehumanization expressed by Whitehead appears disingenuous. As Whitehead stood there that "morning of September 11 in Fort Greene Park in Brooklyn" with his wife, there is an air of "self-mockery."[25] Mason writes that "the pastoral image that Whitehead thought to freeze—all blue skies and bicycles, racial harmony and distracted dogs—was grotesquely misleading: it masked the truth that the image should have been unveiling." Despite the realization of the dangers presented by aesthetic distance, Whitehead employs an understatement such as "Tower 2 sighed."[26] Whitehead's use of literary irony is problematic for Mason. He insists that "the collapse of one hundred thousand tons of steel and glass—which made a cloud visible from space and a sound audible forty miles away" is carelessly transformed "into a mild human wind."[27] Furthermore, Mason objects to Whitehead's choice of the word "sighed," since the word "sighed" distracts the reader "from the thing described" and projects attention onto the description. Moreover, Mason is distressed by Whitehead's use of the word "crouching" for an instance where "dismemberment, immolation, suffocation, impact" is synonymous with "a metaphorical bending of knees."[28]

Despite Mason's commentary, it is doubtful that Whitehead is minimizing the horrifying deaths of those who worked and lived in the city he adores. Instead, by employing the word "crouching" there is a structural image akin to a human being cowering. The unwitting submission of a grandiose structure is likened to the finite nature of humanity. Perhaps Whitehead is underscoring the aesthetic beauty present in the partnership between human beings and the structures of their own ingenuity; their common bond is mortality.

Admittedly, Mason realizes that "Whitehead was merely trying to alleviate our distress by transforming a thing of great ugliness into a thing of some beauty."[29] But what troubles Mason is the literary abandonment of the people who are dying. Subsequently, focus is transported to the writer himself. For Mason, this artistic method of placing a distance between oneself and the image is disingenuous. To Mason, Whitehead's authorial technique in this piece is inferior to his narrative command in *The Intuitionist* and *John Henry Days*. Even though Mason has a compelling argument, comparing a short personal anecdote to fictional novels such as *The Intuitionist* and *John Henry Days* is a faulty comparison. Within a span of a novel, Whitehead has an opportunity to expand, elaborate, and strengthen his connection with his audience.

Rightfully so, Mason compares Whitehead's genius to "echoes of techniques and tones drawn from predecessors both American and continental, whether elders (Joyce, Woolf, Gaddis) or nearer contemporaries (Barthelme, Pynchon, DeLillo, Foster Wallace, Moody)."[30] Mason describes Whitehead's method in *The Colossus* as "impressionistic, imagistic, for Whitehead is not presenting the city as it stands, but as it sits within him." *The Colossus* should be "read as a devotional text, written by a congregant from his pew." For Whitehead, "the loss of the twin towers has been gently absorbed into the city's history of losses. A facet of being a New Yorker." Innately, for every New Yorker, is the awareness "of those sudden voids, to be as aware of them as of the actual presences before us. That observation is something of a commonplace. It is called memory." Mason claims that "Whitehead seems to resort to the language of death only when there is something genuinely pretty to look at." Mason admits that "in the past" Whitehead's work has been marvelous; Whitehead "can produce aesthetic transformations as true and rich as those in *The Colossus of New York* are empty and false."[31]

Although Mason exemplifies Whitehead's implementation of aesthetic distance and posttraumatic disassociation, there is no doubt that Whitehead's writing is always brilliant. In fact, Mason misses the mark by not understanding that grotesque beauty is an element of Gothicism. Therefore, I disagree with Mason's conclusions rendering the episodic essays as "empty and false." The vacuous space, intentionally created by Whitehead, is an emotional distance that allows the witness of a horrific event an opportunity to cope with the scene. Consciously, Whitehead seeks to heighten Mary Shelley's warnings about the mechanization of humankind and the dehumanization that results when there is no emotional connection between the hand and the mind. With every technological invention in the Digital Age, there is another opportunity for human beings to destroy themselves and the monstrous structures they create. As evidenced by the implementation of airplanes, used as torpedoes to demolish the Twin Towers, the events of 9/11 demonstrate how human ingenuity may result in tragedy. Heeding Shelley's warnings in the scientific age, the inventions that aid in human progress will eventually result in the inevitable demise of humanity. The technological warnings of *Frankenstein*, which are considered elements of scientific progress, are reiterated in *Zone One*'s zombie apocalypse and the semblance of civilization that remains.

NOTES

1. Rob Humanick, "The Colossus of New York," *Slant*, June 25, 2012, accessed October 18, 2014, http://www.slantmagazine.com/.
2. Maurice Handle, introduction, in *Frankenstein*, by Mary Shelley (New York: Penguin, 2003), xi.
3. J. Paul Hunter, introduction, in *Frankenstein*, by Mary Shelley, ed. J. Paul Hunter (New York: Norton, 2012), ix.
4. Ibid.
5. Colson Whitehead, "The Way We Live Now: 9–23–01; Close Reading: Elements of Tragedy; The Image," *New York Times*, September 23, 2001, accessed October 12, 2014, http://www.nytimes.com/.
6. William St. Clair, "*Frankenstein*'s Impact," *Frankenstein*: A Norton Critical Edition, 2nd edition, ed. J. Paul Hunter (New York: W. W. Norton and Company, 2012), 262.
7. Elizabeth Young, "Frankenstein as Historical Metaphor," *Frankenstein*: A Norton Critical Edition, 2nd edition, ed. J. Paul Hunter (New York: W. W. Norton and Company, 2012), 271.
8. "Anthropomorphosis," Urban Dictionary, 2014, accessed October 12, 2014, http://www.urbandictionary.com/. "Anthropomorphosis" is defined here as "the attribution of human characteristics to animals or other non-human objects/inanimate objects (eg, trees, birds, buildings, etc.)."
9. Humanick, "Colossus of New York."
10. "Overview," *The Colossus of New York* (1958), Turner Classic Movies, 2014, accessed October 12, 2014, http://www.tcm.com/.
11. Humanick, "Colossus of New York."
12. "Overview," *Colossus of New York* (1958).
13. Ibid.
14. Humanick, "Colossus of New York."
15. "Overview," *Colossus of New York* (1958).
16. Ibid.
17. Ibid.
18. Humanick, "Colossus of New York."
19. Ibid.
20. "Overview," *Colossus of New York* (1958).
21. Ibid.
22. Ibid.
23. Whitehead, "Way We Live Now."
24. Ibid.
25. Wyatt Mason, Review of *The Colossus of New York: A City in 13 Parts*, by Colson Whitehead, *New Republic*, December 4, 2003, accessed October 12, 2014, http://www.powells.com/.
26. Whitehead, "Way We Live Now."
27. Mason, Review of *Colossus*.
28. Ibid.
29. Ibid.
30. Ibid.
31. Ibid.

Chapter Ten

Subways, Rush Hour, and Downtown

New Yorkers Lead Quiet Lives of Desperation

For the duration of Colson Whitehead's essays entitled "Subway," "Rush Hour," and "Downtown," he emphasizes the downward and upward mobility of the wage slave earners and dreamers of New York City. Underlying the hopes and dreams of those who transport to, reside in, and retreat to New York are the "lives of quiet desperation" led by the everyday residents or the common person. For that reason, this chapter will compare the unfulfilled promise and purpose of Whitehead's text with Henry David Thoreau's critique of the societal complacency in "Civil Disobedience." Even though Thoreau's essay focuses on his withdrawal from society into a place of nature, in resistance of an immoral government that abuses its inhabitants (in particularly slaves), Thoreau offers criticism on the apathetic mode of his Concord community. Although Thoreau has inspired political movements in the United States and abroad, he himself was not personally involved in organizations. Perhaps Thoreau could be considered an isolationist due to his elevation of the individual above the community. Based on extensive research of Whitehead's fiction and nonfiction texts, his work shares the preponderance of individualism. To be fair, Thoreau's essay was written in 1849.[1] Thoreau wrote during a time that witnessed the passage of fugitive slave laws in the 1850s and John Brown's raid on Harper's Ferry in 1859.[2] A year before his death in 1862, the onslaught of the Civil War would erupt. Nevertheless, Thoreau didn't receive popularity until the Labour Party in England used his text as an inspiration text for social change.[3] Mahatma Gandhi utilized the essay for "nonviolent resistance in Africa and India, and Martin Luther King, Jr., cited it often during the civil rights movement of the 1960s, as did the activists who protested against the war in Vietnam.[4]

In contrast with Thoreau, his fellow Harvard alum Whitehead has received celebrity status during his lifetime. Yet will his post-9/11 text have similar social and political impact on future audiences? Most likely, the episodic essays of *Colossus* will remain only a picturesque snapshot of New York. Whitehead's narrator gazes at the skyline and the architecture while in traveling mode, but he neglects opportunities to speak on the personal, social, and political impact of post-9/11 New York. Instead, Whitehead focuses on mass transit, cabs, and cars as a means to survive or thrive in New York City. Considering the fact that Whitehead personally witnessed one of the planes fly into the second Twin Tower, he offers no commentary on this moment in *The Colossus*. Thus, readers are left with a vacuous space that Whitehead's angst-filled narration refuses to occupy. How does Thoreau's statement on desperation in "Civil Disobedience" compare to Whitehead's depiction of the social angst of New Yorkers who use transport for the purpose of ingress and egress from New York? Further examination will determine how Whitehead's postmodern voice on city mobility compares to Thoreau's message of desperation of "mankind" in "Civil Disobedience."

In Brent Powell's "Henry David Thoreau, Martin Luther King Jr., and the American Tradition of Protest," he discusses the motivation behind "Civil Disobedience." Thoreau, who lived from 1817 to 1862, expressed frustration with the citizens of his hometown in Concord, Massachusetts. He chastised them for satisfying their material yearnings with their drive for profit and their lack of concern for social issues such as the abolition of slavery. Unlike many individuals who espoused their noble beliefs, "Thoreau lived what he preached. In opposition to slavery, he stopped paying taxes in 1842. He defended his actions, claiming he would not support an institution that tolerated injustice."[5] By today's standards, Thoreau may be considered anti-American and lacking in patriotism. But in those days, Thoreau was not seeking best-selling author or best literary author status. Instead, he sought to change individual minds for the purposes of radically altering society. After all, he railed against "the Constitution and national government. Thoreau opposed both of these institutions because he believed they protected slavery and hindered individual freedom."[6] By objecting to the Constitution and the national government, he believed that society would enhance their individual rights and economic freedoms. As previously stated, King was influenced by Thoreau's message in "Civil Disobedience." However, both men realized that "violence might result from civil disobedience . . . but this should not keep one from protesting."[7] Now here is where the two Harvard alums, Thoreau and Whitehead, differ in their message of individualism. Thoreau advocates a social response or protest to an unjust system. But Whitehead neglects in-depth criticism of the systematic, structural, and institutional consequences for individuals living in a post-9/11 New York.

Yet Whitehead not only resists criticism of America's infrastructure in *Colossus* but also lacks an urge for transformation of the individual living in a desperate age of terrorism. Whitehead offers his disapproval of the mechanization of the individual and the subsequent loss of freedom in a maze of subways, but he neglects the opportunity to chastise the system that compels a person to operate in a repetitive and mentally frantic-like manner. In the essay entitled "Subway," Whitehead writes, "This is the fabled journey underground, folks, and it's going to get a whole lot worse before it gets better. On the opposite track it's a field of greener grass, you gotta beat trains off with a stick."[8] The term *fabled* implies that the daily journey has been mythologized or even glamorized for generations. Derek C. Maus states in *Understanding Colson Whitehead* that in the opening paragraph Whitehead clearly discusses New York in terms of a geographical location and as a "somewhat abstract and artificial concept that is constructed to entice outsiders."[9] There is a sense that the New York experience is a ragged road and the passage is not likely to become any smoother with time. Then, Whitehead makes an allusion to the idiom "the grass is always greener on the other side." American Dream mythology dictates that an individual must persevere because there is a more viable alternative on the opposite track. Whitehead's commentary of the subway traveler segues further into Maus's analysis of *The Colossus*.

Maus writes that the well-received Whitehead reveals "a dynamic tension that includes both love and loathing" of his beloved birth city. However, Whitehead's love for the city overshadows the "New York-identified forms of transportation" that play a role "in managing potential anxiety" that may occur from living there.[10] With all the constant modes of transportation, individuals may easily lose their way. Maus argues that "'getting lost' in the city is primarily a form of physical disorientation; it also speaks to a metaphysical sense of loss that pervades Colson Whitehead's New York." For the transitory population of New York, abandoning the past "and coming to New York for a fresh start" is a positive notion. But Maus also insists that this constant state of traveling and the sense of loss express "a regretful sadness that ranges from melancholy to outright trauma."[11] New York, the city that never sleeps, is always mobile and in survivor mode. Even in the wake of the 9/11 tragedy, politicians made it clear that New York was open for business ventures and tourism.[12] In Whitehead's *New York Times* article entitled "The Way We Live Now: 11-11-01; Lost and Found," he offers a hint of criticism for the commercialism and monetary motives that pervade everyday living in New York City. He writes, "The cement trucks will roll up and spin their bellies, the jackhammers will rattle, and after a while the postcards of the new skyline will be available for purchase."[13] Buried within this statement Maus detects "an undertone of cynicism."[14] This is the cynicism that elevates a text from a series of anecdotal moments about New York mobility to a politically and socially transformative text. As a matter of fact, *The Colossus* edits out Whitehead's direct reference to the Twin Towers. In the *New York Times* article Whitehead says, "I never got a chance to say goodbye to the twin towers. And they never got a chance to say goodbye to me. I think they would have liked to; I refuse to believe in their indifference."[15] But in the book, it reads, "I never got a chance to say good-bye to some of my old buildings. Some I lived in, others were part of a skyline I thought would always be there."[16] In both contexts, Whitehead reveals a sense of loss and anxiety for the emotional and structural loss of the Twin Towers. However, the indirect reference to the towers avoids rather than expounds on life in post-9/11 New York.

For the duration of *The Colossus*, Maus states that the chapters are "loosely held together by a 'fly-on-the-wall' narrator whose words frame momentary glimpses into the perspectives of other people, both native New Yorkers and visitors from out of town."[17] The result is an incomplete or fragmented narrative that is a hodgepodge of voices acting as a singular and collective narrator. Perhaps Whitehead's text is a foreword-thinking collection of essays that is beyond the understanding of modern-day critics. Conversely, Whitehead's text is vacuous in terms of physical descriptions and historical details.[18] Despite the various "sections titled with place-names like Broadway, Coney Island, Times Square," the narration lacks the research that may actually inhibit "the baritone sonorities of improvised lament." These details prevent the reader from fully grasping the social and political implications of traveling on the subway during rush hour, leaving or headed downtown, for the everyday New Yorker. Maus refers to another reviewer, Nicholas Howe, when he reiterates various sentiments of cultural critics: "Whitehead's politics are never explicitly ideological and they rarely register the daily facts of elections and governments. But they are powerfully democratic in suggesting that the city is above all else the place that can erase social and economic distinctions."[19] Perhaps this is where the cracks in the text expand due to textual tension. The lack of geographical context and the sense of loss that is both directly and indirectly attributable to the posttraumatic stress of 9/11 is experienced on the subways, during rush hour, and downtown. But this anxiety of loss is never directly addressed by Whitehead. Furthermore, if Howe is right about Whitehead's persistent intention to eradicate social and economic distinctions with his collective voice, there is an element of postracialism. As previously stated in earlier chapters, Whitehead disavows the existence of such a notion. Regardless of this, the Americanized voice of *The Colossus* denies the multifarious identities that inhabit New York. Consequently, the essay collection is disjointed in a way that reiterates Thoreau's assessment of humanity: "The mass of men lead lives of quiet desperation."

Cristina Beltran, an expert on multicultural politics and political theory, has spoken extensively on the "univocal racialized experience" that is constantly pushed in American society. [20] Although people are aware that "identity is influenced by education, class, region," there are many more ways to interpret identity. She believes that art can occupy "the gaps and pauses that politics does not always address: subtleties, contradictions, and paradoxes." But by not directly addressing posttraumatic angst after 9/11, *The Colossus* thwarts an opportunity to express a nexus between the constant state of ingress into New York and egress out of New York for the purposes of escape from social angst. If New Yorkers were not leading quiet lives of desperation before the fall of the Twin Towers, Thoreau's indictment on Concord, Massachusetts, is extremely appropriate in this context:

> The mass of men lead lives of quiet desperation. What is called resignation is confirmed desperation. From the desperate city you go into the desperate country, and have to console yourself with the bravery of minks and muskrats. A stereotyped but unconscious despair is concealed even under what are called the games and amusements of mankind. There is no play in them, for this comes after work. But it is a characteristic of wisdom not to do desperate things. [21]

In reality, New Yorkers who can afford to retreat to places like Sag Harbor and the Hamptons no doubt are not frolicking with "minks and muskrats" in their place of refuge. Furthermore, Thoreau writes "Civil Disobedience" for the purposes of criticizing the social apathy of a community. On the last line of Whitehead's essay entitled "Rush Hour," Whitehead offers insight into the desperation that is derived from fear of discovery: "You have paid to sit, so pray. As if these daily humiliations and sacrifices mean something, are tallied by the ones who keep the books. Tomorrow we pick up where we left off. Sleep tight. Sleep deep. Sleep the sleep of the successful because somehow you made it through the day without anyone finding out that you are a complete fraud." [22] With this blunt conclusion to the essay, Whitehead expresses the daily thoughts that consume upwardly mobile and so-called successful people of New York. Most people fear they will lose everything: money and the material things that accompany this prosperity. With this in mind, there is a quiet state of desperation that consumes New Yorkers when they travel to and fro from their homes. Consequently, there is not time to occupy one's head with the political implications of 9/11. Instead, upon the discovery that your lifestyle or worse your identity is constructed on a fraudulent basis, the mind delves into an inward state of helplessness. Thoreau makes reference to this egress from work when he says that the "unconscious despair is concealed" under the distractions and amusements of humankind.

In the essay entitled "Rush Hour," Whitehead makes reference to the desperate state of post 9/11 New York: "Escape from midtown. Make a break for the wall or tunnel under." [23] In this section, New Yorkers are seeking refuge from work into their homes. Yet these sentiments may have been the same prior to 9/11. But as stated later, in the essay, Whitehead makes reference to the history of the New York skyline instead of directly speaking to the Twin Tower loss. Whitehead writes, "The skyline graphs the hubris of generations, visible for miles, and inevitably all who see it extract the wrong morals from the stories."[24] When Whitehead makes the statement that "the skyline graphs the hubris of generations," he is speaking of how the skyline has transformed over the years. Perhaps this is also an allusion to the vacuous space that followed the tumbling of the towers. Whitehead refers to human's manmade creations as prideful in nature. After all, the word "hubris" is often associated with the great tragedies of Greek mythology. When Whitehead refers to how individuals see the skyline and "extract the wrong morals from the stories" or they conceive the mythologized perspective of New York's emergence, he is making a slight indictment on those who are swayed by the legendary tales of New York City. But by that critique of those who revered the Twin Towers as evidence of New York's godlike preeminence, he appears to judge the transplants more than the natives. Despite the pride that accompanies the grandiose nature of the city and those who build and maintain it, many New Yorkers lead quiet lives of desperation; inside they fear the discovery of their own inner natures and truth. Perhaps the constant mobilization is a shield for the fear of detection. If individuals move fast, talk fast, live fast, and work fast, the post-9/11 angst that remains or desperation that consumes an individual's soul will escape the discovery of the masses.

Both Thoreau and Whitehead demonstrate a commitment to the individual. They both understand the necessity of removing oneself from the community for the purposes of introspection. But from Thoreau's perspective, "the true America was yet to be discovered, and its revolution was still only a promise rather than an achievement."[25] Throughout the narrator's anxiety of loss, even in the midst of escape, Whitehead appears to be discovering America as well. Although the narrative focuses on New York, the famous city of lights is a mythologized and recognized symbol of the American spirit of individualism, freedom, and dreams. Thoreau would have probably retreated quickly from the commerce, technology, industrialism, and material progress that pervade Whitehead's New York. After all, Thoreau believed that "reform was interior, private, and wholly individual."[26] However, Whitehead's collective and desperate voice of New York seeks refuge, but this is not an individual seeking transformation or social reform of one's existence. *The Colossus of New York* demonstrates no desire to frame the New York experience within a sociopolitical context that renders a narrative classic for generations to come. Thoreau believed that a life well lived sought connection with one's soul and the transformative power of the individual to impact society. For Thoreau, living "deliberately" is a viable alternative to living a life of quiet desperation.[27]

Within the fragmented narrative of Whitehead's New York, individuals live moment by moment without extensive contemplation of their existence. As the writer, Whitehead must take responsibility for the gaps and the pauses that pervade *The Colossus*. Meanwhile, Thoreau believed that authentic freedom is derived from living "without the trappings of a more complicated life."[28] After all, party girls in "Downtown" symbolize a life led without contemplation: "A delegation of corpses staggers by on structurally unsound heels."[29] Yet, these ladies are only a few of the endless symbols of New Yorkers who constantly move while in a catatonic state. This constant mobility is disallowing of the deliberation needed to forge a meaningful life—perhaps one that results from the disengagement from the material world and the questioning of commercial and institutional factors that compel humanity's state of quiet desperation. Considering the aforementioned argument, *The Colossus of New York* lacks the social and political resonance of Whitehead's literary forebears, such as Thoreau, amongst others. Still, Whitehead's writing is equivalent to those who impacted generations before him. But even so, the literary angst of Whitehead's *Colossus*, his resistance to directly address 9/11, in essence mirrors the anxiety or quiet desperation of New Yorkers. This desperation surfaces as the persistent and ailing fear that society will discover their authentic self or the pain that still resonates in a post-9/11 New York. Sadly, *The Colossus of New York* creates a vacuous space due to the author's frayed connection between not only himself and his subject matter but also himself and his audience. For Whitehead's *Colossus* to meet the expectations of both critics and audiences, the essays must relay geographical, political, and social relevance into the literary landscape and beyond.

NOTES

1. Henry David Thoreau, *Walden and Civil Disobedience* (New York: Penguin, 1986).

2. Michael Meyer, introduction, in *Walden and Civil Disobedience*, by Henry David Thoreau (New York: Penguin, 1986), 33.

3. Ibid., 30–31.

4. Ibid., 31.

5. Brent Powell, "Henry David Thoreau, Martin Luther King Jr., and the American Tradition of Protest," *OAH Magazine of History* 9, no. 2, *Taking a Stand in History* (winter 1995): 26.

6. Ibid.

7. Ibid., 28.

8. Colson Whitehead, *The Colossus of New York: A City in Thirteen Parts* (New York: Anchor, 2003), 49.

9. Derek C. Maus, *Understanding Colson Whitehead* (Columbia: University of South Carolina Press, 2014), 93.

10. Ibid.

11. Ibid.

12. Ibid., 94.

13. Colson Whitehead, "The Way We Live Now: 11-11-01; Lost and Found," *New York Times*, November 11, 2001, accessed November 9, 2014, http://www.nytimes.com/.

14. Maus, *Understanding Colson Whitehead*, 95.

15. Whitehead, "Way We Live Now: 11-11-01."

16. Whitehead, *Colossus of New York*, 8.

17. Maus, *Understanding Colson Whitehead*, 96.

18. Phillip Lopate, "New York State of Mind," review of *The Colossus of New York*, by Colson Whitehead, *Nation*, December 1, 2003, accessed November 9, 2014, http://www.thenation.com/.

19. Nicholas Howe, "Bi-coastal Myths," review of *The Colossus of New York*, by Colson Whitehead, *Dissent* 51, no. 2 (2004): 86–90 (quoted in Maus, *Understanding Colson Whitehead*, 99).

20. Cristina Beltran, *Melissa Harris-Perry Show*, MSNBC, November 1, 2014.

21. Thoreau, *Walden*, 51.

22. Whitehead, *Colossus of New York*, 121.

23. Ibid., 113.

24. Ibid., 114.

25. Meyer, introduction, 7.

26. Ibid., 13.

27. Ibid., 15.

28. Ibid., 17.

29. Whitehead, *Colossus of New York*, 129.

Part IV

Sag Harbor **and** *Zone One*

Chapter Eleven

Social and Philosophical Divide

The Intersection of Class and Race for an Adolescent and Adult Colson Whitehead

With Colson Whitehead's autobiographical novel *Sag Harbor*, he explores black upper-middle-class lives. With determined desire, the nerdy teenage protagonist, Benji, seeks independence from his younger brother and long-time shadow, Reggie.[1] In a summer that stretches from Memorial Day to Labor Day, as Benji hangs with his clique of friends, he is discovering his identity in the prosperous area of Sag Harbor. Upon speaking to Deborah Treisman for the *New Yorker*, Whitehead insists that *Sag Harbor* is a work of fiction.[2] Nevertheless, Whitehead shares some similarities with the novel's adolescent hero. During the school year, Whitehead lived in Manhattan until the advent of the summer when he and his friends lived in their respective homes in Sag Harbor. Meanwhile, their parents would work in the city and retreat to their summer homes for the weekends. During the 1930s and 1940s, blacks developed this plot of land. Since many people have heard of the resort town of Oak Bluffs, outside of Martha's Vineyard, Whitehead wanted to bring attention to Sag Harbor and its connection to the Hamptons in New York. Now, Whitehead says, the homes in Sag Harbor are bigger and there are white families who summer there as well.

As the story follows the escapades of Benji and his friends, Whitehead delves into "idiom, the styles, the mind-set of the boys."[3] In other words, Whitehead creates a coming-of-age story that depicts the typical summer of upper-middle-class black boys. Treisman refers to Whitehead's style as an "anthropological, sociological study of the mid-eighties adolescent."[4] In this case, Benji is a child of hip-hop and alternative rock that is caught between two worlds, one black and one white, in a post–civil rights era. As usual,

Whitehead presents his narrative without projecting his moral judgments onto his readers. In addition to Benji, *Sag Harbor* features his entertaining gang of buddies: Marcus, NP, Kevin, Bobby, and Clive. During their casual summer, they "make the most of it, hitting the beach, practicing elaborate handshakes, shooting one another with BB guns, trying to talk their way into a rap concert and exchanging hilariously profane takedowns."[5] But despite Whitehead's lackadaisical presentation and laborious anecdotes of a nonpro-ductive summer, there are contemplative themes such as black male identity that make *Sag Harbor* worthy of study. But in terms of black male identity, *Sag Harbor* reconsiders black militancy and black upper-middle-class guilt from a postmillennial and postracial standpoint.

THE LABORIOUS STYLE OF *SAG HARBOR*: THE MEANDERING DAYS OF SUMMER

Despite receiving the MacArthur Genius Grant, Whitehead still receives crit-icism for his meandering writing style. Yet, the richness of his subject matter implores most readers' forgiveness. With Whitehead's *Sag Harbor*, Natalie Bakopoulos writes in *Fiction Writers Review* that the narrative "is driven not by plot but by time, by the fleetingness of summer and its constant reminder of that fleetingness."[6] Basically, the narrative mirrors the momentary pace of summer. Bakopoulos refers to the inception of the narrative as "slow, with the sense of months ahead, time to digress and ponder and imagine and internalize, with the thickest, most dense prose socked in the middle of July, the more desperate, urgent bursts as we careen toward Labor Day." Notwith-standing Whitehead's laborious manner, the story is "wonderfully languor-ous throughout, like summer itself, and a perfect match for adolescence: unrestrained and indulgent but wonderfully self-conscious as well."[7] Bako-poulos insists that from a less skilled writer "such long digressions and detailed explanations may begin to feel like a literary tic, but here it emerges as Whitehead's rich, well-appointed style. In a sense, these diversions are the story. The absence of structured narrative is a reflection of summer itself."[8] In essence, Whitehead is always in control of the narrative despite its languid pace that meshes with the leisurely attitude of the story's characters.

Touré refers to the pacing of the narrative with more patience than Bako-poulos. He refers to Whitehead's language as delicious and his "sarcastic, clever voice fit this teenager who's slowly constructing himself."[9] Contro-versially speaking, Benji and his friends access privilege in the same manner as do their white schoolmates. For that reason, uncovering "Benji's destiny beyond his sharp-eyed way of looking at things, his writerly voice and his desire to provide a historical and sociological context for blacks in the Hamptons" is engaging for the audience.[10]

Meanwhile, Taylor Antrim claims that the book's vernacular, humor, and anecdotes attempt to disguise the absent story line. Although Antrim refuses to deny Whitehead his due as a masterful writer, he considers the author's method as "idling and indolent."[11] Antrim laments that *Sag Harbor* reminded him of *The Colossus of New York* because it was "stylistically virtuosic but stubbornly hard to finish." Due the "amusements and felicities of language," the novel fails to delve below the superficial narrative. For Antrim, *Sag Harbor* is emotionally unsatisfying, and "it's a low-stakes affair, which is another way of saying it's a little too much like summer for its own good."[12] In other words, Antrim found no real significance in learning about the privileged and leisurely lives of Benji and his friends.

With these lackluster criticisms in mind, Nikesh Shukla credits Whitehead's *Sag Harbor* for motivating her to write her first novel. The episodic structure and humorous "dialogue and brilliantly observed characters" effectively bring the narrative to a satisfying conclusion.[13] According to Shukla, each chapter "contains its own discrete story, is its own episode." As usual, Whitehead's authorial effect never leaves his grasp. He concurs with Shukla to a certain extent when he says that the chapters "work best in concert." Nevertheless, Whitehead wanted each chapter to inhabit its own subject matter "as if they were mini essays on summer, or being a kid, or finding your voice."[14] Whitehead intentionally matched the intermittent action with the rhythms of summer. As a matter of fact, Benji does not grow much as an individual. But he is a little "smarter on Labor Day than he was at the beginning of the summer, and that's the most that the majority of us can hope for as we go through life." From Whitehead's prospective, gaining more wisdom is the most people can expect in their lifetime. For purposes of realism, Whitehead tempered the pace of the action and contemplated "what happens in each day" of a lethargic summer of adolescent males.[15]

SAG HARBOR: POSTBLACK REALISM OR POSTRACIAL MYTHOLOGY

Not only do critics differ on the pacing of *Sag Harbor*, but they also differ on the depth of meaning in this coming-of-age tale. Since *Sag Harbor* was a PEN/Faulkner award finalist, the novel deserves a more introspective analysis than mere criticism of Whitehead's narrative style. By delving into Touré's determination of Whitehead's postblack status in the Obama era, there is a necessity to examine his narrative style in terms of postblackness or postracialism. Although some interviewers attempted to probe Whitehead on his perspective of postracialism, Whitehead's literary angst resists confining labels and rigid designations of an authorial African American identity. Moreover, Whitehead resists critics' attempts to place him in a rigid box. Thus,

Sag Harbor's tendency to avoid sensational racial encounters with whites and vicious intraracial incidents between black youth prohibit affirmative and stereotypical depictions of blacks. Based on some critics' presumptions, they deem the plotline as devoid of action and meaning. For those reasons, one must ponder if preconceived notions of black male adolescence cause critics to expect more in-depth subject matter? Or does the universality of the American coming-of-age tale make a novel about race seem somehow beyond race, postblack, or postracial in the authorial hands of Whitehead?

From the inception of Touré's review of *Sag Harbor*, he addresses black identity and the concept of postblackness. In the past, black identity was dominated by perceptions of "the '60s street-fighting militancy of the Jesses and the irreverent one-foot-out-the-ghetto angry brilliance of the Pryors and the nihilistic, unrepentantly ghetto, new-age thuggishness of the 50 Cents."[16] But now, Touré insists that it is time to "reshape the iconography of blackness." Basically, Touré objects to the images that society conjures when defining black male identity. Generally, in terms of their achievements, individuals who were not considered "ghetto" or referenced white influencers as inspiration for their success were labeled as "Oreos." Touré credits the art world with redefining black identity in a postblack era. Various African American artists refused the labels defining them as "black artists" because "their work redefined notions of blackness." For decades, blacks whose work resonated beyond their own race were deemed as "inauthentic and bullied into an inferiority complex by the harder brothers and sisters," but now Touré claims it is time for postblacks "to take center stage." Touré names Colson Whitehead, hip-hop artist Kanye West, and the award-winning novelist Zadie Smith as artists who can "do blackness their way without fear of being branded pseudo or incognegro." With this reconfigured definition of blackness, black artists are liberated from the burden of asserting black pride or having to justify their blackness. For instance, in *Sag Harbor*, Benji is "a Smiths-loving, Brooks Brothers–wearing son of moneyed blacks who summer in Long Island and recognize the characters on 'The Cosby Show' as kindred spirits."[17] In many ways, the character of Benji fits Touré's notions of a postblack character. Due to Benji's upper-middle-class status, his family summers in a well-off beach town. Furthermore, Benji's family is more reminiscent of characters from *The Cosby Show* than the characters of the 1970s hit *Good Times*. Since Benji does not fit within the preconceived determinations of blackness, does that make him any less black? According to Touré, postblacks thrive outside the preconscribed notions of black identity. Thus, postblack writers such as Colson operate inside and outside the established and traditional realms of black identity.

Nevertheless, the question remains, Does *Sag Harbor* redefine or deconstruct notions of blackness and black masculinity? Within Benjamin Alsup's *Esquire* review, he considers *Sag Harbor* and its author to be postracial rather than signifiers of a postblack consciousness. Alsup's primary argument is based on Whitehead's comfort as part of the literary establishment or elite class of writers who are revered by the literary power structure. According to Alsup, if Whitehead disrupted the status quo or risked being "despised" by critics, readers would find more fulfillment in Whitehead's narratives. By the same token, Alsup realizes that Whitehead is widely revered, smooth, and "a master of writing important books (and his newest, *Sag Harbor*, doesn't disappoint)."[18] Furthermore, Alsup credits Whitehead with his ability to garner praise of English majors, editors, and reviewers. Yet, Alsup wishes that Whitehead "would try pissing people off." Benji and his friends make their own rules by enjoying the bar-mitzvah circuit and roller skating in their summer home in the Hamptons, on Long Island. Admittedly, Sag Harbor "contributes to the upending of our (white) notions of what it means to be African-American." According to Alsup, this subversion of traditional notions of blackness is deemed as postracial: "Like Whitehead, these kids are cool and post-racial. They harbor a certain sense of detachment, a wariness of conflict, and a rational embrace of ambiguity."[19] Alsup refers to the characters as detached from the rest of the world. Although Benji and his friends are aware of black-white conflicts, they are comfortable in a state of ambiguity, limbo, or wavering between worlds, as they inhabit both black and white milieus. Various other critics take note of the lack of real conflict, which is why some of them referred to the narrative as plotless. But according to Alsup, he interprets the lack of conflict, racial ambiguity, and unbiased attitude of Benji and his friends as postracial.

Whitehead's leisurely narrative that occupies space between detachment and ambiguity fails to engage Alsup, and he believes these detractors affect the audience in a similar manner. As a result of the lack of conflict, there is an element of dispassion and vagueness to the characters. Alsup widens this determination of postconflict and postracialism to include the narrative. Consequently, the narrator's commentary and delivery of the postracial narrative is thereby imputed to the postconflicted Whitehead:

> This is precisely the tendency that makes Whitehead's work less engaging than it could be. He seems post-conflicted, awfully comfy in whatever skin he's in. Racial prejudice? It's out there. But it's out there like bad weather: It comes and goes and does little damage to the soul. The same goes for consumerism. And the decline of industry. Everything is cool. Which is to say that nothing is. I suppose that kind of worldview is an essential part of being cool in the first place, but I'm not sure that it's the essence of gripping literature. Doesn't the novel demand conflict? Man versus Man. Man versus Nature. Man versus Himself. The post-conflicted male, I dig him. The post-conflicted novelist? Eh. He leaves me a little cold.[20]

That is to say, Alsup is seeking definitive evaluations on racial subject matters, consumerism, and the decline of industry in the novels of Colson Whitehead. Perhaps Whitehead is content with his secure position within the mainstream and popular culture imagination. Or maybe he seeks to uphold a balance between history, sociocultural knowledge, and the privilege status he now enjoys as an esteemed member of the literary literati. For that matter, what Touré deems as a postblack state of mind is deemed as postconflict and postracial ambivalence by Alsup. From the Alsup's standpoint, lack of racial engagement in *Sag Harbor* is due to the postconflicted delivery of Whitehead. Ultimately, if there is no Man versus Man conflict or Man versus Nature conflict, there is no possibility to explore Man versus Society in the narrative.

Alsup insists that the world of literature needs books that disrupt societal comfort: "books that confront us with frightening visions, evangelical zeal, wild beauty, an alarming lack of cool self-possession."[21] Influential writers such as Whitehead should write for a larger purpose than self-satisfaction of their authorial desires. Alsup elevates Roberto Bolaño as a writer who "reminds us that writers might be motivated by something larger than themselves, some vision of the world in which our aesthetics are inexorably tied to our politics, and our politics are inexorably tied to everything else." Moreover, Whitehead neatly fits into the writing establishment because he does not challenge preconceived notions of blackness from a political or a sociopolitical standpoint. By interweaving the politics of blackness into his forthcoming narratives, he may risk "being despised. Or even loved."[22] Based on Alsup's analysis, if Whitehead followed the model of Bolaño, amongst others, he would not be a postblack writer who writes from a postconflicted or postracial perspective.

Although some critics may disagree, Whitehead plays it safe in *Sag Harbor*. The notion of well-off black people living in a formerly segregated portion of the Hamptons is treated like a radical concept. In actuality, many people never knew this segment of society existed until Whitehead broached this subject. Thus, in an effort not to offend preconceived notions of mainstream audiences, Whitehead tiptoes his literary footprints around black themes and dares not interweave the historical and cultural complexities of the region and its inhabitants into *Sag Harbor*. After all, the adult narrator states that "we knew where our neighborhood began because that's where the map ended. The black part of town was off in the margins."[23] Due to segregation in the 1930s and 1940s, the circumstances that led to the marginalization of upper-middle-class black people who vacation on a separate plot of land is rich with cultural and intellectual enlightenment. This multilayered cultural history, despite American mythmaking, would add needed weight and substance to his narrative. Undoubtedly, Sag Harbor's complex history or more-thorough references to the past struggles of residents would have enhanced the significance of Benji and his friends' carefree lives. If the reader concurs with Touré's definition of postblackness, Benji and his friends enjoy the fruits of past generations' labor without the thorough knowledge and burden of social struggle.

Admittedly, Benji is fifteen, and he does not recognize the contribution of Du Bois to the black community and his American contribution to the discipline of sociology. But based on his mother's pronunciation of the surname Du Bois, Benji knows that Du Bois had "uplifted the race."[24] Of course, there are some references to "the great narrative of black pathology" when the narrator mocks newspapers for their declarations of "CRISIS IN THE INNER CITY!, WHITHER ALL THE BABY DADDIES, THE TRUTH ABOUT THE WELFARE STATE: THEY JUST DON'T WANT TO WORK, NOT LIKE THE GOOD OLD DAYS."[25] Satirically speaking, the narrator jokes that society should just "bring back slavery already, just look at these dishpan hands."[26] But Whitehead abandons the opportunity to extensively subvert the stereotypical notions of black identity and work ethic with profound commentary. Instead, he makes intermittent quips about his friends' access to the postracial American Dream as "black boys with beach houses." In essence, this supposed paradox is the rationale for a crisis in black identity. Actually, the juxtaposition of the black struggle, the narrative of black pathology, and black privilege is definitively postblack in nature. However, the absence of profound statements on the root cause of postblack privilege guilt and their accompanying upper-middle-class struggles with double consciousness decreases the significance of the characters and the narrative. Consequently, with Whitehead's postracial sensibility he succeeds at offending neither blacks nor whites. Yet, he misses the opportunity to offer significant commentary on the postblack experience in America.

When Whitehead speaks of race, he references the past with a satirical tone that hints at not only self-mockery but also cultural mockery. Upon speaking of Bobby's black militancy, the adult Benji points toward the hypocrisy. The light-skinned and radicalized Bobby "directed most of his hostile talk at his mother, who worked on Wall Street."[27] When Bobby asked for twenty dollars, he launched racial epithets behind her back because she was subservient to white establishment. Although Bobby's father worked at Goldman Sachs, his mother received most of Bobby's black rage. The adult narrator quips, "It's not like" the father "was dashiki-clad and running a community center somewhere."[28] The anecdotes of postblack hypocrisy are hilarious and authentic in many circumstances. Nevertheless, there is no profound statement of racial struggle in a black-dominated society located within a white-dominated milieu. *Sag Harbor* could be considered postracial because racial conflicts occur but not because of social encounters with whites. Instead, postblack guilt occurs within the minds of the characters.

But for privileged blacks living in the post–civil rights era, their identities seem disaffected by white presumptions of blackness. For example, in one instance an "old white man stopped" Benji and his brother "on a corner and asked" if they "were sons of a diplomat. Little princes of an African country. The U.N. being half a mile away. Because—why else would black people dress like that?"[29] These encounters induce no real introspection or reflection of disappointment or outrage toward white society from the adult narrator. Instead, the narrative quickly moves on to the next anecdote, as if Benji and his brother are disaffected and detached from the commonplace misconceptions of the society around them. When a character is considered postblack, does that alleviate him or her from a natural or human character's response to racial prejudice or discrimination? In order to avoid designation as a black militant, do postblack writers have to subdue their characters' reactions to interracial encounters? If so, the writers risk transcending into the perception of postracialism even if they disavow the existence of postracialism. For the postblack status to resonate more than a postracial label, Whitehead should subvert structural notions of blackness and challenge institutional inequalities of black spaces and black people despite upper-middle-class status. Due to the publication of *The Intuitionist* and *John Henry Days*, Whitehead should maintain his revolutionary postblack status, instead of his recent post-conflicted, postracial, and apolitical stances that are problematic for some critics.

WHITEHEAD: POSTBLACK AUTHOR OR POSTRACIAL AMERICAN AUTHOR

During an interview, Nikesh Shukla probes Whitehead on the significance of Obama's election, black identity, and the elements of postracialism in his novels. Although Whitehead proudly identifies himself as an African American, twenty years ago he didn't consciously define himself "as an African-American writer."[30] Whitehead's labels, such as "African-American writer," are used "by the critical establishment." Specifically, Whitehead seeks to shed labels that leave him "pigeon-holed, ghettoized, held in a different category" than other contemporary authors. As a writer, Whitehead's black identity is really only one of the characteristics that inform his writing or character. Admittedly, Whitehead does not allow his blackness to define his narratives. He says that he didn't plan to write an "African-American zombie story or an African-American story about elevators." Instead, when he wrote *The Intuitionist*, he was consciously "writing a story about elevators which happens to talk about race in different ways." Or when he was composing his zombie novel, *Zone One*, he was writing a novel that "is really about survival." Even though Whitehead is describing a process that is postracial in nature, he continues to find discussions about postracialism as "very superficial." As proof of the lack of postracialism in American society, Whitehead offers racial overtones while Obama was running for president: "There was race-baiting, and racially-coded language used by some Republican candidates. There are underlying narratives which are still pretty potent. I think you're only post-racial when you stop asking if you're post-racial."[31] Perhaps this is the duality of the American paradox and African American double consciousness: evidence of racial progress intermeshed with evidence of continuous racial stigmatization. Nevertheless, Whitehead's solution to the postracialism is to stop pondering the issue. Thus, by not addressing the topic and ignoring its social relevance, Whitehead suggests this method will eventually lead to postracialism in society. Shukla refers to Whitehead's commentary as "meta-post-racial, because they're still talking about the thing that they no longer are anymore." As further proof of Whitehead's move toward postracial narratives, the interviewer comments on how the reader does not discover that the main character is black until much later in *Zone One*. Casually, the postconflicted Whitehead states that Spitz's race is really "not that important. The apocalypse is what I was thinking of." But in the same conversation, Whitehead adds that the idea that Obama's election cast a "magic spell" and signaled the end of racism is obviously not true. Perhaps Whitehead's treatment of race signifies his belief that race is really not that significant. If so, did his East Coast upper-middle class upbringing contribute to his belief? Perhaps his private schooling and Harvard education led him to these beliefs. Regardless of the cause, the next chapter will examine his postracial treatment of race with Richard Wright's autobiography *Black Boy*.

Sag Harbor is a wonderful addition to the coming-of-age story in American literature. However, critics will continue to debate its significance amongst other nonfiction and fictional autobiographical narratives. Instead of focusing on black identity in terms of postblackness and postracialism, most critics focused on Whitehead's writing style in *Sag Harbor*. Unfortunately, that is a myopic way of analyzing this text about Benji and his friends. Nevertheless, there were critics like Touré and Alsup and interviewers like Shukla who probed into postblackness or postracialism in the Obama era. Yet, Alsup is one of the few who discussed the purpose of literature and the authorial intent. Thomas L. Morgan offers a discussion on the burden of black novelists. When Morgan writes on Paul Laurence Dunbar, he mentions how the country has "existing expectations regarding African Americans."[32] These societal expectations influenced the way critics and readers interpret Dunbar's work then and now. Whitehead shares a similar concern with Dunbar: "As a black male author in a predominantly white literary world, Dunbar had to navigate the racial presumptions of editors and readers alike in order to succeed." To be financially successful, neither Dunbar nor Whitehead "explicitly confront white readers' internalized beliefs regarding blacks." Dunbar practiced this method by "maintaining his political and aesthetic

stance; Dunbar had to create literary strategies capable of critiquing the social, political, economic, and cultural problems facing African Americans."[33]
Although Whitehead does not divulge his political stance, he critiques social
and economic issues in *Sag Harbor*. Yet, he avoids addressing in depth the
cultural issues, such as intersection of racism and class in the novel. Furthermore, Whitehead utilizes sarcasm as a method of satire to address the hypocrisy of young, black, upper-middle-class males. Although Dunbar and Whitehead lived and wrote in divergent eras, the responsibility of the novelist and
the novelist who is black is still significant. Especially in an era of postblackness and supposed postracialism, Whitehead's political and cultural stances
should resonate even more in his latter narratives.

NOTES

1. Touré, "Visible Young Man," *New York Times*, May 1, 2009, accessed November 22, 2014, http://www.nytimes.com/.
2. Deborah Treisman, "Fiction: Q&A; Colson Whitehead," *New Yorker*, December 11, 2008, accessed November 22, 2014, http://www.newyorker.com/.
3. Ibid.
4. Ibid.
5. Taylor Antrim, "'Sag Harbor: A Novel' by Colson Whitehead," *Los Angeles Times*, April 26, 2009, accessed November 22, 2014, http://www.latimes.com/.
6. Natalie Bakopoulos, "*Sag Harbor*, by Colson Whitehead," *Fiction Writers Review*, May 15, 2009, accessed November 22, 2014, http://fictionwritersreview.com/.
7. Ibid.
8. Ibid.
9. Touré, "Visible Young Man."
10. Ibid.
11. Antrim, "Sag Harbor."
12. Ibid.
13. Nikesh Shukla, "Colson Whitehead: Each Book an Antidote," *Guernica*, April 24, 2013, accessed November 22, 2014, https://www.guernicamag.com/.
14. Ibid.
15. Ibid.
16. Touré, "Visible Young Man."
17. Ibid.
18. Benjamin Alsup, "Colson Whitehead: The Coolest Writer in America," *Esquire*, March 25, 2009, accessed November 23, 2014, http://www.esquire.com/.
19. Ibid.
20. Ibid.
21. Ibid.
22. Ibid.
23. Colson Whitehead, *Sag Harbor* (New York: Anchor, 2009), 24.
24. Ibid., 18.
25. Ibid., 71–72.
26. Ibid., 72.
27. Ibid., 73.
28. Ibid., 74.
29. Ibid., 7.
30. Shukla, "Colson Whitehead."
31. Ibid.

32. Thomas L. Morgan, "Black Naturalism, White Determinism: Paul Laurence Dunbar's Naturalist Strategies," *Studies in American Naturalism* 7, no. 1 (summer 2012): 7.

33. Ibid.

Chapter Twelve

Wright and Whitehead

Black Hunger in the South and Black Faces in the Hamptons

Colson Whitehead is the only postmillennial writer to yield as many accolades as Richard Wright. Thus, a comparison between *Black Boy* and *Sag Harbor* is inevitable. With that being said, Whitehead is the first to admit that his autobiographical novel is uneventful, which is a complete contrast to Wright's tragic narrative. Zach Barron refers to *Sag Harbor* as a "valedictory ode to a 15-year-old black kid named Benji with braces and buddies and a job at an ice cream shop."[1] The inception of the novel occurs "in June 1985 on the east end of Long Island . . . and ends on Labor Day, with Benji fantasizing about the shows he'll see at CBGB once he finally turns 16." Due to the lighthearted context of Whitehead's autobiographical novel, Barron considers *Sag Harbor* funnier than all three of his former novels combined. But Barron presumes that the novel is "devoid of plot" because it presents "existential literary questions."[2] However, Whitehead's venture into the autobiographical novel lends itself to comparisons of historical classics.

Since before Frederick Douglass, the autobiography has been an essential segment of African American literature. For instance, Touré sites "Richard Wright's 'Black Boy,' Claude Brown's 'Manchild in the Promised Land,' Maya Angelou's 'I Know Why the Caged Bird Sings,' Kody Scott's 'Monster'—could have been subtitled 'My Journey Out of Hell.'"[3] However, those books distinguish themselves from the postblack narrative of *Sag Harbor*. All of them detail "the horror of being black and enslaved or segregated or impoverished or imprisoned." Meanwhile, Whitehead's black protagonist lives in a post–civil rights era, and he has "tremendous class advantages and summers in a vacation paradise."[4] Furthermore, Benji is not assaulted by life.

Instead, his postblack privileged life offers the opportunity to figure out his identity and who he wants to be in life. Therefore, this chapter will compare and contrast Richard Wright's Jim Crow–era autobiography *American Hunger*, also known as *Black Boy*, to Colson Whitehead's postblack fictional autobiography *Sag Harbor*. Do differences in education, region, economic status, and era influence the delivery of the narrative? Similarly, how do *Black Boy* and *Sag Harbor* convey a sense of black identity that is emblematic of their respective era? Although both novels share emphasis on the individual over community, each novel addresses how father-son relationships play a role in black manhood and how the use of foul language signifies a rite of passage revealing black male identity.

BLACK BOY AND *SAG HARBOR*: AUTOBIOGRAPHICAL, SEMIAUTOBIOGRAPHICAL, OR FICTIONAL

Essential to the process of interpreting *Black Boy* and *Sag Harbor* is the determination of the author's authenticity and by extension the authenticity of the narrative itself. For years, critics have analyzed the veracity of *Black Boy*'s purported truth and the untold truth in *Sag Harbor*. Since both books are written by influential authors, they bear comparison in terms of their authentic depiction of the African American experience. Whitehead was born a year before Dr. Martin Luther King Jr.'s assassination in 1968. Furthermore, his 1967 birth occurred during the peak of the Black Power movement. But for Wright, who was born in 1908, his early years were wrought with unrest and harmony. The early 1900s were a time of "race riots, lynchings, and the revival of the Ku Klux Kan."[5] Since the South had a large black population, this region became fertile for racial discord. Understandably, Wright's vision of American culture was influenced by his environment. The themes of "brutality, fear, and deprivation" are prevalent in most of his fiction.[6] Consequently, he wanted "to give voice to those, who, like himself, had suffered under the extreme pressures of injustice and racism."[7] In actuality, the authorial burden of speaking for the voiceless is emblematic of Jim Crow–era and civil rights–era autobiographies. For those reasons, Whitehead's birth at the peak of the civil rights movement and in an era of black militancy makes him the paradox of the postblack era writer. *Sag Harbor* represents the progress that African American forefathers fought for, yet Whitehead's characters represent an inability to appreciate the hardships and relate to the hostile white-black relations due to their black educational and economic privilege and their unfettered access to white spaces.

Nevertheless, *Black Boy* is considered "not only as the finest autobiography written by a black author but [also] as one the greatest autobiographies ever written in America."[8] But many critics debate what genre best describes

Black Boy. W. E. B. Du Bois referred to *Black Boy* as "fiction or fictionalized biography. At any rate the reader must regard it as creative writing rather than simply a record of life."[9] Moreover, Du Bois writes that Wright portrays his father "as gross and bestial, with little of human sensibility."[10] In the words of Du Bois, he did not find Wright's words "unbelievable or impossible; it is the total picture that is not convincing."[11] Moreover, Mary McCarthy writes that no white person should consider Wright's depiction of his childhood as representative of every black individual.[12] With that being said, this book must offer that same criticism of Whitehead's postblack Benji. In no way can a critic say with certainty that Benji's carefree resort lifestyle is representative of all upper-middle-class black males or, for that matter, black people of any class level. McCarthy deems *Black Boy* as evidence of "self-aggrandizement and self-dramatization that casts a shadow of melodrama on the whole story."[13] Thus, readers and reviewers may cast off the book as twisted or embellished. As a Southern critic, there is a tendency to believe that Wright's childhood accounts of white-black relations have more truthful elements than falsifications. Therefore, there is reason to believe that as a Harvard-educated African American, Whitehead has read *Black Boy* or, at the very least, he is aware of the negative criticisms received by Wright. Perhaps, in an awareness of the melodramatic elements of black autobiographies, Whitehead intentionally downplays instances of racially tense white-black encounters and superficially addresses unintentional and intentional violence in *Sag Harbor*.

Although Whitehead shares a similar background with his protagonist Benji, he insists that this narrative is purely fictional. However, it is important to discuss some of Whitehead's promotional statements concerning his autobiographical work. Ultimately, interpretation of *Sag Harbor* is enhanced by examining Whitehead's promotion of this text. In a review of *Sag Harbor* for the *Los Angeles Times*, Taylor Antrim refers to a promotional video of the vibrantly slim Whitehead as he strolls through the Long Island area of Sag Harbor. As previously stated, Whitehead states that nothing eventful occurs in his novel, such as a dead body like in *Stand by Me*, a lynching, or a KKK chase through the Hamptons.[14] Of Course, this is more of Whitehead's acerbic wit as he alludes to a tragic aspect of American history. Yet, when Whitehead makes that sarcastic joke, one is reminded of how the Ku Klux Klan is responsible for killing Wright's uncle in *Black Boy*. Then comes the thought of the adult Benji reflecting comically on how he and his friends would respond to an unexpected encounter with the KKK. Of course, making fun of the KKK is a luxury of black privilege not afforded to their parents and grandparents. For instance, when referencing his light-skinned friend Bobby Grant, his friends joke that he is so light that the KKK would pass him over if they were hunting for blacks.[15]

Instead of attributing Whitehead's lighthearted tone toward style, Antrim draws the conclusion that "Whitehead seems uneasy with the confessional demands of autobiography."[16] In other words, he believes that *Sag Harbor* is a "memoir masquerading as a novel." According to Antrim, Whitehead admits this fact in his "Message from the Author," included with his advance copy; Whitehead confesses, "I've always been a bit of a plodder, which is why I now present my Autobiographical Fourth Novel, as opposed to the standard Autobiographical First Novel."[17] If Antrim's conclusion is to be believed, "Benji, a brainy black kid marooned at a very white Upper East Side private school, is a Whitehead stand-in, and . . . Benji's family bears some resemblance to the author's own."[18] Perhaps this explains the "skittish way he describes their rather alarming dysfunctions." In Antrim's words, he describes Benji's father as "a brutish drunk; he hits Benji in the face, calls Reggie a demoralizing (and unprintable) nickname, [and] verbally abuses their mother." Yet, Benji's response to this domestic violence is understated at best and bears a stark contrast to the wounded Richard. Basically, Benji's reaction to those family dysfunctions is unaffected. Benji treats these violent encounters with a "dissociated narration" as if this is "just one more feature of the summer landscape, no more worthy of the reader's attention than the season's Lisa Lisa and Cult Jam track."[19] Nevertheless, without documentation, it is presumptive to believe that the postconflicted Whitehead is displaying literary angst with regard to his authorial truth. After all, unless Whitehead or those close to him admit it, the readers will never know with certainty whether he wrote *Sag Harbor* under the guise of an autobiographical novel; therefore, he is willfully burying his authenticity in a fictional text.

Nonetheless, in the *New Yorker*, Whitehead makes genuine statements that are reminiscent of family traditions in his book. Now, when Whitehead visits Sag Harbor, he likes to stay "around the house, go to the beach, barbecue."[20] Whitehead continues by saying that all he "did was cook meat all day—smoke some ribs and other big chunks of pork."[21] Meanwhile, his daughter spent time on the same beaches that he played on and his mother played on years before him. Whitehead speaks of barbecuing and playing on the beach as a tradition of continuity that is quite special. Although these sentiments are quite touching, one may remember that Benji's father's specialty was his barbecue. Anecdotes about the father's barbecue are humorous, but they bear significance on the tension between Benji and his father. Derek Maus refers to Benji's constant grilling as a form of control rather than a symbol of his concern for his family.[22] Yet when Whitehead refers to his real-life devotion to barbecuing at his Sag Harbor home, there is a tone of sentimentality and love of his family and their traditions. Thus, Whitehead's reference to barbecuing may be the closest he comes to implying that *Sag Harbor* is closer to his adolescent reality than he cares to admit in print.

BLACK IDENTITY: JIM CROW–ERA RICHARD VERSUS
POSTBLACK BENJI

Due to the differences in Wright's and Whitehead's educational, regional, and economic backgrounds, there is no surprise that their protagonists' personal experiences differ in America. With that being said, black identity in America is similar regardless of the personal characteristics. Even though Benji lives a privileged life, he still faces a fractured relationship with his father like Richard faces in *Black Boy*. Yet, before probing into the problematic elements of Wright's autobiography, this chapter will briefly discuss the carefree life of Benji and his friends. In an article for the *Washington Post*, Ron Charles writes that no author "writes with more acrobatic imagination and good humor about the complexities of race in America than Colson Whitehead."[23] Charles compares Whitehead to Stephen Carter because they both write about a segment of upper-middle-class blacks who summer on Long Island. Sag Harbor straggles between East Hampton and Southampton. By America's standards, this is an ancient town because the whaling community existed before the American Revolution and it is mentioned in the classic novel *Moby Dick*. In the process of sarcastically describing the dilemma of wealthy black teenagers, Whitehead's tone oscillates "between resigned sympathy and impatient mockery."[24] For instance, Whitehead refers to the rite of passage as young educated blacks read up on classic black literature and then in a moment of impassioned activism organize marches for black professors. Even as Whitehead deconstructs the myth of the Cosby family, he wittily implores the reader to "share enough common understanding to laugh at each other without bitterness or hatred or hard feelings." Although the Cosby family is emblematic of a popular urban mythology, there are black families who live inside and outside of Sag Harbor who also experience similar upper-middle-class black privilege in America. Exposure to black professional parents and racially integrated experiences results in the sheltered upbringings of Benji and his friends. Perhaps their lives appear uneventful because they don't have the racial baggage of young Richard in *Black Boy*.

Bernard Bell writes about Wright's childhood in *The Afro-American Novel and Its Tradition*. His autobiography "reads like one of his short stories or novels."[25] Before Richard's seventeenth birthday, he encountered an onslaught of tragedy. Wright was abandoned by his father as a youth; his poverty-stricken mother placed him in an orphanage; he must flee Arkansas once his uncle is lynched; he suffered "under the religious tyranny of his grandmother and aunts; he was "bullied and beaten by white bigots"; and he engaged in petty thievery with his friends.[26] For Wright, it was not the American Dream that liberated him from a troubled childhood. Instead,

Wright became a successful writer in spite of the ideal of the American Dream.

As a matter of fact, Benji's life bears such a contrast to Richard's that he lives a postblack privileged existence that is devoid of real choices and complexity. Benji lives a life that is inundated with pop culture experiences that are perhaps as authentic to him as Richard's Southern childhood. Whitehead offers "heartfelt odes to Stouffer's frozen food, rhapsodic descriptions of the toppings at the Jonni Waffle candy bar, exegeses on old Coke versus New Coke, and dense, filigreed forays into the sociology of the ice cream store patron."[27] Benji's everyday work life is consumed with sundaes and the quotidian thoughts of a skinny-framed "15-year-old everyman virgin and his marginally less distinct friends, give or take a repressive father and a particularly evocative shoreline landscape."[28] As previously stated, Benji no more represents every black youth in the postblack North than Richard represented every black youth in the Jim Crow–era South. But both Benji and Richard symbolize the formation of black identity in America. Undoubtedly, the educational, regional, and economic experiences of a black youth will determine his perception of his identity, masculinity, and humanity in relation to the world around him.

BLACK MANHOOD FORMATION: *NIGGER* AND OTHER "BAD LANGUAGE"

Particularly, black manhood has been a fascination in America since early black narratives. Although Whitehead's postblack narrative venture into a postracial depiction of the African American experience, in terms of black manhood, *Sag Harbor* addresses the word *nigger* and its various uses to express anger, disappointment, and camaraderie amongst black males. Meanwhile, the word *nigger* in *Black Boy* signifies criticism, violence, and white supremacy over blacks. Interestingly, foul language is a rite of passage to these bildungsroman narratives. Thus, the use of bad language denotes growing up and the recipient's ability to filter the real purpose behind the foul language.

Jennifer H. Poulos writes in "'Shouting Curses': The Politics of 'Bad' Language in Richard Wright's *Black Boy*" that Wright "literally curses his way through the early part of his life."[29] Poulos vehemently argues that "Wright's deployment of bad language plays a crucial role in shaping him as an African-American artist."[30] Due to America's history of barring or curtailing African American expression, for a black artist, gaining agency over language is an even more profound act. Since slavery, "bad" language serves a dual function of expressing oneself and liberating "African Americans from the stereotypes imposed on them by an oppressive white culture."[31] However, such self-expression may result in a destabilization of "the racist status quo."[32] For some blacks, the white establishment's perception of "bad language" is absorbed as subversive verbal norms in the black community. Moreover, proper English in some segments of the African American community may result in alienation. Thus, bad language or foul language from the mouths of black people becomes a decidedly political act. Therefore, as Richard acquires the language skills to express himself, he risks criticism from both whites and blacks in America. Based on Whitehead's tendency to temper his words and speak of his novels through universal terms such as "survival," he bears the same concerns as Wright.

Young Richard's use of foul language expresses his coming-of-age process and negotiation of language as a male. Richard uses his terms purposefully. Although he upsets his family with his cursing vernacular, his use of language is "appropriate and justified" when used. When swearing is "indiscriminate, inappropriate," he places it "in the mouths of whites."[33] When Wright extensively depicts his work experience at the optician's, "he reprints in detail and at length the bad language of his employers." For the whites in the book, swearing is gratuitous and is used to degrade others.

In another instance, literacy, self-expression, and foul language intersect for white-black relations in *Black Boy*. On one occasion Richard is on his paper route selling the newspaper. When a man confronts him on the racist propaganda, he has not even contemplated the content of the paper. There is a cartoon with a "picture of a huge black man with a greasy, sweaty face, thick lips, flat nose, golden teeth, sitting at a polished, wide-topped desk in a swivel chair. The man had on a pair of gleaming yellow shoes and his feet were propped upon the desk."[34] Above the disparaging caricature of black masculinity is a bold sign that reads, "The White House." There is a distorted picture of Abraham Lincoln with the words, "The only dream of a nigger is to be president and to sleep with white women! Americans, do we want this in our fair land? Organize and save white womanhood!"[35] Ironically, Richard has no idea that the papers that he is selling are promoting the Ku Klux Klan agenda. When the man confronts his efforts at monetary gain, Richard acknowledges that the KKK seeks to stop black people from voting and working good jobs. Almost instantly, Richard realizes the importance of literacy. Also, Richard realizes how the word *nigger* signifies Southern literacy and Southern self-expression in white culture. Upon his newfound knowledge, he makes a decision without consulting any grown-up that he will no longer unwittingly act as "an agent for pro–Ku Klux Klan literature."[36] After he throws the papers in the trash, he tells his grandma that he is no longer needed at the company. Due to the power of language, racist literature conveys a philosophy and an organization's ignorance and fears of blackness. Furthermore, the realization of the power of words and how they signify meaning sheds light on the derogatory term *nigger*." Consequently, Richard's exposure to foul language and its powers helps him grow as a male and as an individual.

When Benji is confronted with the word *nigger*, he is not traumatized by the white child who insinuates this term. Instead, the power of the word is only heightened by how a black person chooses to respond to racial confrontations. Nevertheless, Mr. Cooper, Benji's father, is enraged when he learns that his son did not respond to the other child with violence.[37] Then, the father chastises his son for fearing retaliation. When a boy runs a finger down his face and says, "It doesn't come off," Mr. Cooper says the kid was calling Benji a nigger.[38] Then, he strikes his son twice across the face for not defending himself. Young Benji's response to racism is, "The lesson was, Don't be afraid of being hit, but over the years I took it as, No one can hurt you more than I can."[39] Mr. Cooper believes that he is teaching his son that there is no safety in the public sphere. But by beating Benji in the face, he is also teaching his son that there is no safety in the private sphere.[40] Thus, the message of fighting against white racism is delivered in a manner that teaches "Benji through the lens of paternal authority and violence."[41] Benji's sister suggests that he get an education and leave that house. Like Richard Wright, Benji knows the power of education will provide a semblance of safety in the public sphere. Ironically, it is the economically advantaged and privileged home that Benji derives from that enables "Benji and his siblings to escape the constraints of their domestic sphere and to presume their own entitlement to mobility within the public sphere."[42] Based on Mr. Cooper's interpretation of a school incident, Benji hears the pejorative use of the word *nigger* from his own father. For those reasons, the violence associated with word *nigger* is produced by his own father. This hostile intraracial encounter "is the principal source for Benji's conflicted sense of identity" and contemplation on his black manhood.[43] But in an earlier chapter of the book, Benji hears and uses the word for altogether different meanings.

One of Benji's comrades is nicknamed NP (Nigger Please). The narrator explains that his buddy had a tendency to exaggerate stories. Thus, the best way to characterize him is with the pejorative word *nigger*. However, this nickname is not used for the purposes of malice. Instead, it is a term of endearment and is a source of comic relief in the text. After all, according to Benji, "He was our best liar, a raconteur of baroque teenage shenanigans."[44] But there is a double consciousness with respect to the word. On the one hand, NP's nickname has become a source of unifying his friends around a narrative of black male storytelling or folklore and by extension the formation of black male identity around tall-telling or folklore. Thus, due to the "thorny history of its initial word," the group abbreviates the nickname.[45] Since the adults gave them trouble, when they heard young people use the word, the young black males censor themselves. Yet, in terms of the word *nigger*, there is generational and societal hypocrisy with regard to the degrading term. Benji notices that authority figures use the word in a familiar context yet "also to distinguish themselves from those of our race who possessed a certain temperament and circumstance."[46] Also, there is an elitist tone to black members of the resort town: "There were no street niggers in Sag Harbor. No, no, no."[47] Nevertheless, despite tones of 1960s militant philosophy there is still a desire to attain status and rise above so-called black low life.

For a member of the postsoul aesthetic or postblack era, Whitehead offers a peek at privileged upper-class black life. At the same time that he questions uplift rhetoric, he mocks the linguistic hypocrisy of the older generation. The evolutionary uses of the racial epithet *nigger* exemplify the changing times. During Richard Wright's Jim Crow era, the term was used by whites mainly to degrade, mock, and threaten African Americans. By the time Benji is growing up in the post–civil rights era of the 1980s, the term *nigger* is used by Sag Harbor residents to form camaraderie, mock the voices of the KKK, and distinguish oneself from the lower-class representatives of one's own culture. Maus asserts that "Whitehead's depiction of the Coopers shows that the postsoul condition is an extremely tenuous one, despite—or possibly because of—the relative freedom provided by greater access to material comforts."[48] In other words, access to white spaces and close proximity to white privilege does not alleviate the coming-of-age struggles of Benji and his friends. Even in the Northeast, the young Richard Wright would have never imagined that black boys with beach houses was possible. Despite the differences between Richard and Benji, language and education is the generational link that provides a semblance of hope, enlightenment, and eventual freedom.

NOTES

1. Zach Barron, "Soul Sonic Summer: Colson Whitehead's *Sag Harbor*," *Village Voice*, April 29, 2009, accessed November 29, 2014, http://www.villagevoice.com/.

2. Ibid.

3. Touré, "Visible Young Man," *New York Times*, May 1, 2009, accessed November 22, 2014, http://www.nytimes.com/.

4. Ibid.

5. John O. Hodges, "An Apprenticeship to Life and Art: Narrative Design in Wright's *Black Boy*," in *Richard Wright's Black Boy (American Hunger)*, ed. William L. Andrews and Douglas Taylor, 113–30 (New York: Oxford University Press, 2003), 113.

6. Ibid., 114.

7. Ibid.

8. Yoshinobu Hakutani, "Creation of the Self in Richard Wright's *Black Boy*," in Andrews and Taylor, *Richard Wright's Black Boy*, 131.

9. W. E. B. Du Bois, "Richard Wright Looks Back: Harsh, Forbidding Memories of Negro Childhood and Youth," in Andrews and Taylor, *Richard Wright's Black Boy*, 33.

10. Ibid.

11. Ibid., 36.

12. Mary McCarthy, "Portrait of a Typical Negro?" in Andrews and Taylor, *Richard Wright's Black Boy*, 41.

13. Ibid., 43.

14. Taylor Antrim, "'Sag Harbor: A Novel' by Colson Whitehead," *Los Angeles Times*, April 26, 2009, accessed November 22, 2014, http://www.latimes.com/.

15. Colson Whitehead, *Sag Harbor* (New York: Anchor, 2009), 73.

16. Antrim, "Sag Harbor."

17. Ibid.

18. Ibid.

19. Ibid.

20. Deborah Treisman, "Fiction: Q&A; Colson Whitehead," *New Yorker*, December 11, 2008, accessed November 29, 2014, http://www.newyorker.com/.

21. Ibid.

22. Derek C. Maus, *Understanding Colson Whitehead* (Columbia: University of South Carolina Press, 2014), 110–11.

23. Ron Charles, "Book Review: Ron Charles on Colson Whitehead's 'Sag Harbor,'" *Washington Post*, April 29, 2009, accessed November 30, 2014, http://www.washingtonpost.com/.

24. Ibid.

25. Bernard W. Bell, *The Afro-American Novel and Its Tradition* (Amherst: University of Massachusetts Press, 1989), 155.

26. Ibid.

27. Barron, "Soul Sonic Summer."

28. Ibid.

29. Jennifer H. Poulos, "'Shouting Curses': The Politics of 'Bad' Language in Richard Wright's *Black Boy*," in Andrews and Taylor, *Richard Wright's Black Boy*, 149.

30. Ibid.

31. Ibid., 150.

32. Ibid.

33. Ibid., 151.

34. Richard Wright, *Black Boy* (1945; New York: Harper Collins, 2006), 130.

35. Ibid., 131.

36. Ibid., 132.

37. Andrea Levine, "'In His Own Home': Gendering the African American Domestic Sphere in Contemporary Literature," *Women's Studies Quarterly* 39, nos. 1 and 2 (spring/summer 2011): 179.

38. Whitehead, *Sag Harbor*, 163.

39. Ibid., 164.

40. Levine, "In His Own Home," 180.

41. Ibid., 182.

42. Ibid., 180.

43. Maus, *Understanding Colson Whitehead*, 107.

44. Whitehead, *Sag Harbor*, 39.

45. Maus, *Understanding Colson Whitehead*, 106.

46. Whitehead, *Sag Harbor*, 39.

47. Ibid.

48. Maus, *Understanding Colson Whitehead*, 112.

Chapter Thirteen

Zone One

Postapocalyptic Zombies Take Over Manhattan in the Age of Nostalgia, Despair, and Consumption

Colson Whitehead's *Zone One* capitalizes on his childhood memories of a ruined city.[1] By reflecting on the economic downturn and reversal of fortunes of his 1970s birthplace, imagining a postapocalyptic, dreamless New York was a minute leap. Writing a horror novel allowed him the space to recover from the hostile landscape of his birth. *Zone One* is a tribute to how a culture reconstructs hope and rebuilds itself in the wake of an accident or trauma, such as the unfathomable tragedy on 9/11. Whitehead eloquently transforms the Manhattan landscape, centering the horrific action around the well-known and symbolic streets of Broadway and Canal, and separating the survivors from the monsters.[2] George A. Romero's *Escape from New York* and *Omega Man* served as inspirations for Whitehead's science fiction/horror–driven tale.[3] Human nature causes most people to blindly follow the crowd, submissively consuming pop culture without introspection and without purging its capitalistic effects. This docility shields the terror within American culture, American cities, and American people. For Whitehead, "Your friend, your family, you[r] neighbor, your teacher, the guy at the bodega down the street, can be revealed as the monster they've always been.[4] By using the zombie metaphor for the frustrated consumer culture that seeks nourishment from materialism, the zombie represents the consumptive nature and violent transformation within everyone when their hunger for fulfillment is ignored and denied. Whitehead is not the first African American, literary author to examine the urban monsters that live figuratively or literally in every city. Richard Wright's *Native Son* and Ann Petry's *Street* shine a light on the raw, demented monstrosity of violence lurking behind every corner, within every house, and in every building. However, while Wright and Petry emphasize the marginalization of blacks in the urban landscape, Whitehead takes a decidedly postracial view. Postplague Manhattan is a place where class is evident but race and culture are vaguely mentioned and hardly noticed by the city's inhabitants. When literary authors such as Colson Whitehead expand the genre of street lit with urban gothic novels such as *Zone One*, transformative depictions of dehumanization, corporate greed, and political capitalization of urban culture are unveiled. *Zone One* depicts socially relevant themes such as nostalgia, despair, and consumption through a zombie metaphor that is layered within the subtext of allusions, flashbacks, irony, and symbolism. This gives way to uncensored honesty in an African American authorial perspective, set within a city landscape.

LEGITIMIZATION OF STREET LIT: DEFINITION, CRITICISM, AND AUTHORS' PURPOSE

The surge in street lit may be traced to the popularity of Donald Goines and Iceberg Slim in the 1960s and 1970s. Both writers create a realistic depiction of inner-city life featuring drug dealers, pimps, and prostitutes, and expressing their stories in their uncensored, graphic, African American vernacular.[5] Yet, despite the popularity of Donald Goines and Iceberg Slim and various contemporary street lit authors, the genre remains marred with reluctance from major publishers. With the exception of Triple Crown Publications, Urban Books, and a few other independent publishers, street lit has not been a welcome presence in the industry.

Nevertheless, modern-day authors such as Teri Woods, Vikki Stringer, and K'wan Foye continue the tradition of hip-hop literature with their fast-paced novels, illustrating ghetto realism and themes exemplifying the pitfalls and glory of gangsta life.[6] Street lit authors such as Woods may argue that their creative expression seeks to connect and relate to a black audience, who lack characters in other genres reflecting their physicality and inner turmoil. Street lit provides insight into a demonized urban culture, whose humanity is realized by the passion of authors who write literature embodying the emotional, mental, and literal truth of the African American experience. In Vanessa Irvin Morris's award-winning book *The Readers' Advisory Guide to Street Literature*, Woods insists that street lit represents the marginalized voices of a people whose story was meant "to be forgotten, swept under a rug, put in a box—better yet a cell—never to have a voice, never to cry out, and never able to speak out against the injustice we" experience in urban America.[7] Ultimately, street lit "depicts tales about the daily lives of people living in lower income city neighborhoods. This characteristic spans historical timelines, varying cultural identifications, linguistic associations, and various format designations."[8] Street lit is not bound by the confines of an era, racial stereotypes, language, or narrative style. Boxing street lit into a narrow narrative style is to deny oneself the creative escape into the urban American experience.

However, critics of street lit unleash many of the same criticisms faced by rap artists. Perturbed black consumers cite an absence in originality and the exploitation of young African American minds. Charles D. Ellison argues that those criticisms are "swirls in an ugly soup of moral relativism and pop-cultural melee."[9] Ellison balks at the negative response to hip-hop literature because white novelists write gritty, real-life dramas too. Chuck Palahnuk, author of *Fight Club*, and Stephen King both "venture down that path of poor-White-trashiness that's just as ghetto as" street lit narratives. Furthermore, the words *urban experience* are not always synonymous with the word *black*. *Urban* is the expression of a city life. *The Wire* is no more urban than the depiction of hip, gentrifying white yuppies on hit television shows such as *Sex in the City* or *Friends*. Ellison is confounded by these societal distinctions and identifies such divisions in pop culture as classist and elitist. Black people's acceptance of these polarizing limitations is a manifestation of self-hatred, reminding the audience that "there are just as many ghettos in Europe, the Middle East, and Southeast Asia as there are in Philly, New York, or Oakland." For instance, English steel ghettos feature prominently in Charles Dickens's *Hard Times*. Ellison acknowledges that there are stereotypes and racism present in some street lit. However, there is a duty to share the American experience in its entirety. Readers may not agree with everything they see on the shelves, such as porn-teasing covers, giving the impression that salaciousness and street cred is more important than the literature itself. But Ellison celebrates the fact that literature has evolved and black folks are reading and writing in the twenty-first century. Generation Xers should simply open their minds and stop lamenting over the misty-eyed days of the literary remnants from the twentieth century.

RICHARD WRIGHT AND ANN PETRY: THE FOREFATHER AND FOREMOTHER OF STREET LIT

Many contemporary critics fail to acknowledge that Richard Wright was criticized for his realistic depiction of sexual and violent characters, groping for emotional and physical survival. "*Native Son*, Wright's 1940 best-selling novel about a young black man who kills a white woman by accident and then a black woman on purpose, made him immediately famous and remains a classic."[10] After *Native Son* was published, audiences began to accept not only the lonely rural narratives of African American characters but also the urban experience. Literary critic Leonard Cassuto asserts that "Bigger is a memorable inarticulate creature of the segregated Chicago ghetto, boiling with unchanneled rage against the white people who restrict his movements, and with hopeless ambition to fly airplanes he can't even approach, let alone enter."[11] With both *Native Son* and his memoir *Black Boy*, Wright highlighted the unjust and terrifying social, living, and working conditions on both sides of the Mason-Dixon Line.[12] Thus, Wright stands as the forefather of early twentieth-century urban fiction.

Despite the elements of realism and naturalism in *Native Son*, there is a vein of urban Gothicism that is relevant to the interpretation of *Zone One*. *Native Son* is intertextual, interweaving the Great Depression, capitalism, and the advent of mass culture, overlapping with allusions to Hawthorne, Dreiser, and Poe.[13] During the 1930s, when Wright was working on *Native Son*, the popularity of horror flicks emerged. These stories were often inspired by Bram Stoker's *Dracula*, Mary Shelley's *Frankenstein*, and Edgar Allan Poe's "Black Cat" and "Murders in the Rue Morgue."[14] James Smethurst asserts that the first two portions of *Native Son* mimic a typical horror flick of the 1930s. After Bigger's murderous rampage, he is pursued through an urban gothic landscape, anxiously fleeing from thousands of police officers with flashlights. This section parallels "the villagers with torches who chase Frankenstein's monster through an expressionist landscape." The demarcation between the monster and the man who bore him is blurred in both *Frankenstein* and *Native Son*. Similarly, Bigger is the monster produced by the murderous mainstream culture who views his black skin as a deformity or stain in the American landscape.

Both Richard Wright and Ann Petry depict characters that are pursuing the mythic, utopian American Dream.[15] In that process, dynamic characters are developed around the psychological and material gratification that is sought but denied when chasing the American Dream. Both of these novels are generally discussed as protest novels, which may be an archaic term for modern readers of urban literature. Nevertheless, they expose the topical and fantastical delusion, insisting that American racism has made achieving the dream a nightmare for black folks. In *The Street*, Petry's beautiful protagonist, Lutie Johnson, a single mother, is forced to work as a domestic in Harlem, because of her broken marriage.[16] Despite Lutie's optimistic outlook, she is forced to live in a decrepit Harlem apartment building, which symbolizes the filth and wretchedness of black degradation on 116th Street. The smell of the rooms is "a mixture that contained the faint persistent odor of gas, of old walls, dusty plaster, and over it all the heavy, sour smell of garbage—a smell that seeped through the dumb-waiter shaft."[17] Lutie's only issue, with regard to her race, is the institutionalized racism that prevents her from enjoying the cleanliness and financial liberty of the white family she works for. Diana Trilling, book critic for *Nation* magazine, wrote that for "Mrs. Petry, equality of opportunity means a free capitalist economy in which the Negro individual, no less than the white, can gain as much as he desires and is capable of gaining."[18] This issue of capitalism, equal access, and consumption of material goods is a pervasive theme in Wright's, Petry's, and Whitehead's texts.

Ironically, protest writers in early urban fiction did not attack the existence of the American Dream. Instead, early urban writers such as Wright and Petry sought to "protest whites' insistence on treating blacks as outsiders and interlopers." Undoubtedly, it is this constitutional amendment, stipulating the equality of all human beings, that incurs the protest, Where is my piece of the American pie? Although literary urban foreparent narratives, such as *Native Son* and *The Street*, contain the monstrous yet realistic violence, the brutality is written for a deeper purpose.[19] Smethurst argues that W. E. B. Du Bois, author of *The Philadelphia Negro*, could be deemed gothic based on his use of the term *veil*. As writers such as Wright and Petry have alluded to before, the veil "hides the black world from the white world and vice versa—or perhaps more accurately that by which the white ruling class of America conceals the black subject as human, much like a concealed skeleton in a classic novel."[20] Readers are asked to acknowledge the racism, the sexism, the capitalism, and their symbiotic relationship to the veiled masquerade of the American Dream. Subsequently, the emotionally invested audience is barraged with a violent narrative, compelling them to resist the status quo and overturn the wrongs perpetrated by the powers that be. In so doing, equal access will be a cure to the plague of broken American Dreams and the endemic virus within modern-day Biggers and Luties, birthing inner-city lawlessness and criminals, who are a monster manifestation of society's own making.

ZONE ONE: LITERARY INTERSECTION OF HIP-HOP, POP CULTURE, AND POSTAPOCALYPTIC ZOMBIES

Whitehead's *Zone One* should be defined as urban gothic literature, street lit "couture," or high-art literature in an urban setting. Expansion of the term *street lit* should include a literary author who creates an intersection between hip-hop, pop culture, and postapocalyptic zombies invading Manhattan. In the process of penning *Zone One*, Whitehead was obsessed with horror flicks such as *Night of the Living Dead*, *Dawn of the Dead*, and *Day of the Dead*, which was the first George Romero trilogy.[21] Ghastly aesthetics consume the pages of the narrative. Delightful nauseam of cinematic proportions fills one's stomach as if watching a horror flick. Suspension builds as the protagonist reflects on his childhood prior to the zombie plague.

With the sidewalks hidden from view, the boy conjured an uninhabited city, where no one lived behind those miles and miles of glass, no one caught up

with loved ones in living rooms . . . and all the elevators hung like broken
puppets at the end of long cables.

The city as ghost ship on the last ocean at the rim of the world. It was a
gorgeous and intricate delusion, Manhattan, and from crooked angles on over-
cast days you saw it disintegrate, were forced to consider this tenuous creature
in its true nature. [22]

Whitehead's complex language describes the city as a grandiose entity,
weaving mystery and beguiling language into such gothic subject matter as
the apocalypse. The term "ghost ship" alludes to the deaths from the plague
rendering the City of Lights barren of life. Meanwhile, the words "last
ocean" imply that Manhattan is the world's final destination and possibly the
last hope for recapturing America's grandeur. Yet, phrases like "intricate
delusion," "crooked angles," and "tenuous creature" have gothic implications
that veil the true nature of New York City and its inhabitants. "Millions of
people tended to this magnificent contraption; they lived and sweated and
toiled in it, serving the mechanism of metropolis and making it bigger, better,
story by glorious story and idea by unlikely idea."[23] Again, there is a sense
that Manhattan is a larger-than-life character, even before the zombie apocalypse, more important than its survivors, corporate sponsors, or bureaucracy.
However, beneath this grotesque beauty of the city is the darkness that lives
inside each brooding structure—the skels and the stragglers—the urban gothic nightmare.

Urban Gothicism is a literary genre that is dominated by African
American authors yet is not exclusive to one ethnicity. Urban decay and
moral dilapidation is the essence of the inner city. These characters are struggling with issues of poverty, broken families, drug abuse, and crime, yet their
plight is aggravated or enlightened by the issues of the supernatural. Characters confront the nature of man's cruelty while fighting nightmares, visions,
omens, ghosts, and spiritual conversions. Inner-city genocide, homicide, and
suicide are realistic yet detrimental evolutions of their pain. Their eventual
rise may be wrought with regret, violence, or immorality, but the character
will feel that he or she is justified. Sometimes they flee the metropolis or
abandon the values of their heritage or class in hope of salvation in the
mainstream culture, only to find a tainted American Dream that bleeds tragedy in both the city and the suburbs. Ultimately, the protagonists must return
to the city, mostly ruined by the time of their discovery, oftentimes to the
place of their birth. Emotional, mental, or physical transformation may only
derive from reuniting with one's personal and cultural identity. Redemption
may be discovered in the streets, with their family, the community, or in
becoming one with their inner spirituality. If catharsis occurs, an element of
peace may be attained for the protagonist.

Street lit couture is Whitehead's unique blend of hip-hop, pop culture, and classic literature. Whitehead's eloquent sentence structure stretches the common perception of street lit as lowbrow and common. Critic Glen Duncan states that "in the action sequences we get essayistic asides and languid distentions, stray insights, surprising correspondences, ambivalence, paradox."[24] *Zone One*'s sentence structure is varied and complex, utilizing various techniques such as historical allusions and collective disillusionment to describe the Manhattan descent into the zombie takeover. "Their mouths could no longer manage speech, yet they spoke nonetheless, saying what the city had always told its citizens, from the first settlers hundreds of years ago, to the shattered survivors of the garrison. What the plague had always told its hosts. . . . I am going to eat you up."[25] Whitehead's literary interpretation of urban decay, moral dilapidation, and the grotesque nature of the American Dream turned sour is a transformative signifier, deserving a designation within street lit as urban gothic literature.

Pop culture references, classic literature, and horror movie tropes are fused into a city landscape swarming with zombies, who are a metaphor for the corruptive influences consuming the streets, uptown and downtown, and condemning residents to a mindless cycle of misfortune. Undoubtedly, Whitehead's experience growing up in Manhattan influenced his awareness of the types of characters who make street lit such a phenomenon. *Zone One* is a dark ode to the Big Apple, the living dead version of Whitehead's exquisite essay collection *The Colossus of New York*.[26] Later in the narrative, he describes the starving monsters as angry and ruthless chaos made into flesh. Affirming the gothic beauty of New York and its troubled citizens is facilitated by the lyrical allusions familiar to most audiences.[27] Whitehead's selection of epigraphs—quotations from Walter Benjamin's "Dream Kitsch," Ezra Pound's "Hugh Selwyn Mauberly," and Public Enemy's "Welcome to the Terrordome"—"suggests that [he was] tackling head-on the challenge of marrying intellectual and literary substance with pop culture."[28] Whitehead refers to this harmonious marriage, metaphorically, as a worldly junkyard, garnishing the parts that function and maneuvering the machine to work as the operator pleases. However, Whitehead does not regard his style with such serious intentions. Pound's epigraph is a lyric that can be sung in transit, while Public Enemy's epigraph to move as a community is a sensible recommendation. Both lyrics operate as a literary work that breathes beyond its conception by speaking to divergent generations and cultures, or functioning within various contexts. Thus, references to Public Enemy's lyrics and Ezra Pound's poetry in *Zone One* are transcendent in nature and linguistically revolutionary in its merging of hip-hop and pop culture into an urban gothic narrative.

POSTAPOCALYPTIC CORPORATE INFRASTRUCTURE AND RECONSTRUCTION

Mark Spitz is a member of the Omega Unit, which is an allusion to one of Whitehead's favorite movies—*Omega Man*. Their job is to reclaim the island for the chosen, the privileged amongst the survivors—the intellectuals who will reside in Buffalo. This three-person squad must clean up the meandering monsters in Zone One, after a massive military unit has eliminated most of the skels.[29] The Omega Unit people live life five minutes a time, which is a reactionary mindset that takes the readers through three days: Friday, Saturday, and Sunday.[30] Throughout the thrill, Spitz is revealed to the reader in bite-size pieces, and as a direct result of his job, he is fighting legions of teeth and fingers. There is the modernistic element of stream of consciousness as Spitz's mind travels from one flashback to the next, all the while annihilating zombies, as a sweeper.[31] Thankfully, Spitz and his team are not the only barricades preventing a potential blood fest. The barrier is guarded by snipers, patrols, and "woven-plastic miracle fabric that is the final separation between undead teeth and fresh flesh."[32] Despite the trauma faced by survivors, they have succumbed to a recovery plan called the "American Phoenix Campaign" that has a slogan, anthems, buttons, and hats from the merchandising department.[33] Sadly, this marketing distraction fails to heal the survivors of postapocalyptic stress disorder (PASD), which is caused by the trauma of witnessing loved ones becoming carnivorous, flesh-eating monsters. There are two types of zombies: skels and stragglers. The skels are bloodthirsty and representative of the classic zombies of the average American's youth or from AMC's *Walking Dead*. Whitehead reinvents the zombie genre with the stragglers, who are frozen in time. Instead of walking slowly in the streets, they are stuck wallowing in their "'subconscious' choosing, be it flying a kite, photocopying their buttocks, or reading a palm."[34] They are doomed to one act for eternity. They are like ghosts who fail to pass into the afterlife, operating in a permanent state of purgatory. Sadly, they represent 99 percent of the zombies. Meanwhile, the drooling skels, half-decomposed shells of a monster, represent the violent 1 percent of the zombies. Whitehead turns the zombie survivalist narrative on its head; he creates a story where the survivors are more horrific than the empathetic zombies. Spitz and his team don't hesitate to play "solve the straggler," as they meditate on what brought the zombie there, sometimes drawing Hitler mustaches across their faces.

Drawing Hitler mustaches is a historical reference to race discrimination, genocidal behavior, and the monstrous attempts at human destruction. However, Whitehead does not explicitly make ethnicity or racial heritage an element of his zombie narrative. After all, Spitz and his team are the good guys, the zombie exterminators. On the surface, zombies and the survivors epitomize respectively the malevolence and benevolence of the human race.[35] Within that broader metaphor, there is a more specific interpretation. Zombies are effective allegories, but what demographic are they symbolizing? African Americans? Minorities? White-collar workers? Or delusional suburban families? Arijit Sen, a writer for the *Missouri Review*, suggests that zombies are an allegory for the race relations in America. Postplague, there are segregated living areas, and there is the constant concern over gentrification once Manhattan has been obliterated of skels and stragglers. Mark Spitz and his team must eradicate all the structures of nondangerous stragglers. After all, Whitehead's narrative creates the impression that the zombie epidemic must be wiped out as the country reconstructs itself. But the black protagonist sweeps and cleanses the buildings for whom? The underclass? Or the privileged class? Who is the enigma controlling the tentacles of recovery? The audience never lays eyes on the individuals that operate in the shadows of the Buffalo headquarters. These dark figures delegate orders in this postapocalyptic milieu to the laborers, who clear the spaces without question, feeling thankful to have survived the plague. Spitz and his team's supplies are sponsored by the surviving corporations; therefore, the sweepers have rigid directives to create minimal structural damage. Jess d'Arbonne, an expert zombiephile, writes in the *Examiner*, "The new government, based in Buffalo, is obsessed with PR and image, often forgetting what the men and women working toward rebuilding are facing on a daily basis."[36] Gentrification is a necessary part of this postplague reconstruction motif, that the streets are ruled by a distinct, distant few. Manhattan is barren with the exception of the legions of the damned and the soldiers who dispose of them.[37] Even Spitz and his team realize that. In this way, low-income urbanites' fate is synonymous with the skels. Anyone can and will be eradicated if they are deemed uncivilized, dangerous, or subhuman, like the monstrous zombies in Zone One. The rebuilding motif is personal, physical, and structural. Personal reinvention is the domain of the intellectuals, athletes, corporate sponsors, and shadowy figures in Buffalo bureaucracy. After the zombie virus erupts, the American Dream is now being resuscitated but only for the benefit of a privileged few.

POSTRACIAL MARK SPITZ AND THE RELEVANT THEMES OF NOSTALGIA, DESPAIR, AND CONSUMPTION

Spitz, who is now a civilian soldier in the recolonization of Manhattan, meanders through the streets, where the plague ridden are sometimes indistinguishable from the survivors who are suffering from PASD.[38] Spitz's story alternates between nostalgic flashbacks of his childhood and the postapocalyptic Manhattan. Frequently, Spitz's mind flashes back to his suburban childhood, which is a time of normalcy and warm memories of the city. But the monster transformation of all things rational and normal is essential to the zombie metaphor. In one scene, Whitehead treats his readers like sexual exhibitionists, peeping into the bedroom of Spitz's parents. When he was six, waking up from a nightmare, he regretfully seeks solace in the arms of his parents.[39] Spitz creeps into the master bedroom and discovers his mother "gobbling up his father" as his father snarled for him to leave. On the Last Night, before the zombies take over Manhattan, Spitz returned as an adult from Atlantic City and "witnessed his mother's grisly ministrations to his father. She was hunched over him, gnawing away with ecstatic fervor on a flap of his intestine, which, in the crepuscular flicker of the television, adopted a phallic aspect."[40]

Whitehead webs a connection between the stragglers and the sweepers who kill them. He is concerning himself with the demons of people by describing the transformation that is both metaphorical and literal. Whitehead's personal evolution, as the writer of the nostalgic *Colossus of New York*, is "from beloved New York semi-flaneur to the blacksmith of a myth that outlasts a movie season."[41] Whitehead depicts a nation fluttering their eyes, trying to determine who in the ruined city is there to destroy us. This distinction is difficult because, like the stragglers, those survivors suffering from PASD move in a catatonic state, reveling in the past and reminiscing on the good times, when everything seemed normal. Ironically, there is not only an emotional price for nostalgia but also a mortal price for those who succumb to the temptation of pondering the past.[42] One of the more striking moments in the narrative is when the marines lose their way in the monstrous spectacle. Drifting off into "over idealized chapters of their former lives," they are overcome by memories, making them vulnerable to the zombie feast.

Overlapping the theme of nostalgia is the interweaving sense of hopelessness that is supposedly caused by PASD. Replaying the past and living in the present consumed by yesteryear demonstrates a lack of faith in the future. Grand buildings will remain grotesquely beautiful despite their plague-ridden history. But who will live in these spectral-like altered spaces? After the sweeper's mission is completed, Whitehead analogizes the hopefulness of postplague occupancy by everyday survivors to the optimism of immigrants freshly arriving to the harbor.[43] Yet, Whitehead swiftly gnaws at this American myth of dreams realized in the zombie city. Despite the tireless work of the military and the sweepers, Buffalo headquarters remained secretive about Manhattan's postplague residents. Mark, Gary, and Kaitlyn discuss the dismal opportunities in their future living arrangements. Gary says to the group that rich people, politicians, pro athletes, and chefs from cooking shows are the most likely occupants, while Kaitlyn remains hopeful that there will be a less plutocratic process, such as a lottery. Gary insists that the government has other plans like Staten Island. "But we wouldn't live on Staten Island if they were giving out vaccines and hand[ing] jobs right off the ferry."[44] Hope rises and falls, instilling a state of despair amongst the characters and audience, because nothing in society has changed.

Spitz is like an overseer, wage slave, working for the establishment, but he will never enjoy the spaces he sweeps. As a zombie sweeper, clearing the spaces for the rich, he works in a subservient role, for a minimal reward called everyday survival. In the words of Henry David Thoreau quoted earlier,

> The mass of men lead lives of quiet desperation. What is called resignation is confirmed desperation. From the desperate city you go into the desperate country, and have to console yourself with the bravery of minks and muskrats. A stereotyped but unconscious despair is concealed even under what are called the games and amusements of mankind. There is no play in them, for this comes after work. But it is a characteristic of wisdom not to do desperate things.[45]

This state of despair causes men to seek solace outside the confines of the city. In this subconscious search for meaning, men conceal their despair in the games and choice of entertainment they seek. For Spitz, there is no form of escape except for the memories and the games he and his team play with the stragglers. Manhattan is the chosen place for reconstruction-style gentrification. Spitz's job is to kill harmless stragglers for the benefit of the capitalistic structure. Unlike the street narratives of Wright and Petry, Spitz feels incorporated into this laborious process of rebuilding America. In a sense, he is at the bottom ladder of the American Dream. Although Whitehead hints to the fact that Spitz and his comrades may touch the ladder of opportunity, the powers that be will never let them climb into the buildings he sweeps for them. Thoreau advises against resorting to desperate acts while in a state of despair. Unlike his modern counterparts, the murderous Bigger and Lutie, Spitz is complacent in his exclusion from the trappings of success. After all, Spitz is a mediocre man with mediocre expectations of his future, even before Last Night. Spitz's "averageness makes him the perfect Everyman Survivor," but Whitehead quickly reminds us that "hope is a gateway drug; don't do it" lest you be consumed by nostalgia.[46] Then, the despair comes with the eradication of normalcy or the realization that nothing ever was, or ever will be, normal in the city. Whitehead remarks, "Everybody's fucked up in a different way, just like before."[47] Memories of the horrors drag people down. Society has not changed; thus, they behave desperately and erratically.

Sag Harbor, John Henry Days, and *The Intuitionist* all demonstrate a concentration on the issue of race.[48] Yet, in *Zone One* he neglects to make casual reference to Spitz's racial heritage until the forty-six-page finale. Does

Spitz's race add to his social angst? On the contrary, Spitz seems to realize both sides of this issue. "There was a single Us now, reviling a single Them."[49] If the world was attacked by a common enemy, do all Americans treat each other as one race—the human race? At first Whitehead wants his readers to believe that *e pluribus unum*, out of many one. But even Spitz comes to the conclusion, "If they could bring back paperwork . . . they could certainly reanimate prejudice, parking tickets, and reruns."[50] Spitz's racial heritage is revealed because a character assumes that he can't swim due to his race. Therefore, literary critic Sen believes that Whitehead wants society to think about race. Furthermore, Whitehead is asking the audience to examine the way in which society dehumanizes, devalues, and degrades those whom we perceive as our enemy. When the clearing squad ceases shooting chaotic zombies to paint their faces and pose with them, there is a message about how Americans treat those who appear "faceless, blending into one, non-understandable, ciphers and mysteries that pose some sort of danger even though we're not sure what" inside and outside this country.[51] Dehumanization of the marginalized other facilitates the capacity to kill without a conscious.

Ron Charles views Spitz as blank and colorless. Although Whitehead sought inspiration from *Night of the Living Dead*, which featured Duane Jones, an African American at the center of a white mob trying to devour him, this racial element is absent from *Zone One*. "Mark is also a young black man, but strangely that element of his identity is bleached away in this novel, as though color blindness and zombie-ism came to America at the same moment."[52] Yet, Charles's faith is restored in the narrative when Whitehead's prose novel elevates to the status of T. S. Eliot, F. Scott Fitzgerald, and Cormac McCarthy, while maintaining the macabre elements of cinematic horror. Even without the racial implications, "no matter the hue of their skins, dark or light, no matter the names of their gods or the absences they countenanced, they had all strived, struggled, and loved in their small, human fashion. Now they were mostly mouths and fingers."[53] Consciously, Spitz suffers from PASD but experiences no despair with regard to race. He has witnessed the plague infect humans without concern for race, creed, or color. He misses those he loved. His family is now his team. Living in the city, from day to day, and surviving five minutes at time is a very urban concept. In the future, the zombie equalizer gives way to race but not to issues of class, which some may argue is the real culprit of urban blight. Whitehead further transforms the genre of street lit by making his postapocalyptic narrative in a postracial America, simultaneously speaking against contemporary discrimination in the twenty-first century.

Even in Whitehead's postracial America, every social ill that plagued society prior to the apocalypse, such as class distinctions, the government bureaucracy, and corporate interest, still consume the city landscape. Whitehead deepens the zombie metaphor to represent this exchange. Within the context of the gothic genre expectation, the readers are expected to suspend their incredulity in the living dead and the supernatural. [54] Cultural references to the supernatural indicate a society on the edge of transformation. Zombies symbolize the hugest threat to humanity, other than humanity's threat to itself. This interaction between the human and the undead is always writhing with violence, usurpation, and consumption. In *Zone One*, the zombies are a reflection of our society holding a mirror to our history, our consciousness, providing a certain sense of critical insight that may only be perceived from a pop culture experience. The zombies' act of tearing and eating flesh is an act of literal and figurative consumption. In the figurative sense, there is a message about consumption as a consumer. The consumer is in a constant state of seeking an object to create a sense of individuality. However, this object fails to satisfy because it is a model of an idealized image that is mass produced. [55] Whitehead plays on this symbiotic relationship between the capitalist and the consumer. The zombie metaphor is one of consumption fueled by consumerism. Consumers have lost their souls because they are manipulated by images and norms of society, marketing to individuals and suggesting to them what they should buy. The model is an illusion but an image people seek as proof of their own aspirations or accomplishments. This obsession with material goods in a capitalistic culture transfers into an objectification of the individual. People transform into empty vessels, nothing more than the objects they seek and keep. In this instance, pop culture predisposes people to the zombie virus that causes desperate stragglers to nostalgically return to their wage slave jobs, white-collar offices, and malls—the place of their favorite sites.

Whitehead has the vantage point of not living in a segregated America like Wright and Petry. Thus, he has the opportunity to fictionalize a world in *Zone One* where he may reject the contemporary issue of racism in postapocalyptic society. Color is ambiguous in the future. Everyday survivors are unified by a common state of disenfranchisement. Oppressed not because of the differences in their skin tone, the survivors are instead deprived by their daily need to survive the last remaining skels and stragglers. Whitehead's warnings about American materialism speak to all ethnic heritages of all class levels: people who place value on pop culture figures themselves or their social status and ability to amass goods that symbolize or embody wealth are like empty vessels. Thereby, they create a state of false self-worth and a means to judge and subjugate people who do not engage in the rat race of consumerism or fail to obtain the semblance of economic mobilization. In the end, the bureaucracy and capitalists will reign supreme in the postapocalyptic new world. Benefactors of privilege are granted the option to subjugate wage slaves and other survivors, segregating them with a patriotic marketing campaign aimed at gentrification of property as opposed to reconstruction of a populace's inner selves. Whitehead recognizes that American materialism afflicts both blacks and whites; therefore, in the future it is not hard to imagine that for a decimated society that has suffered so much, race will be the last factor on their minds. Although monsters are the marginalized other that society fears, metaphorically and literally, they are really all of us and we are them. They are the grotesque monsters that dwell, in the city and beyond, waiting for a moment of consumptive despair to burst forth within us. Nevertheless, plague-free spaces in Manhattan that facilitate a sustainable future for the entire human race matter far more than the shade of black skin adorning the mediocre yet heroic face of Mark Spitz.

NOTES

This chapter was previously published in *Street Lit: Representing the Urban Landscape* edited by Keenan Norris with foreword by Omar Tyree (Scarecrow Press, 2014).

1. Eric Sunderman, "Q&A: Colson Whitehead Talks Gritty New York, Zone One Zombies, and Frank Ocean's Sexuality," *Village Voice*, July 11, 2012, accessed December 8, 2012, http://www.villagevoice.com/.

2. Michael Rudin, "The Forbidden Thought: A Review of *Zone One*, by Colson Whitehead," *Fiction Writers Review*, February 14, 2012, accessed December 8, 2012, http://fictionwritersreview.com/.

3. Sunderman, "Q&A."

4. Joe Fassler, "Colson Whitehead on Zombies, 'Zone One,' and His Love of the VCR," *Atlantic*, October 18, 2011, accessed December 8, 2012, http://www.theatlantic.com/.

5. Wanda Brooks and Lorraine Savage, "Critiques and Controversies of Street Literature: A Formidable Literary Genre," *Alan Review* 36, no. 2 (winter 2009): 49.

6. Ibid.

7. Terry Woods, foreword, in *The Readers' Advisory Guide to Street Literature*, by Vanessa Irvin Morris (Chicago: American Library Association, 2011), xi.

8. Vanessa Irvin Morris, *The Readers' Advisory Guide to Street Literature* (Chicago: American Library Association, 2011), 2.

9. Charles D. Ellison, "Define 'Urban Lit' . . . ," *Huffington Post*, June 23, 2009, accessed December 8, 2012, http://www.huffingtonpost.com/, 1.

10. Leonard Cassuto, "Richard Wright and the Agony Over 'Integration,'" *Chronicle of Higher Education* 54, no. 6 (2008): B12, History Reference Center, accessed October 12, 2012, http://search.ebscohost.com/.

11. Ibid., B13.

12. Ibid., B12.

13. James Smethurst, "Invented by Horror: The Gothic and African American Literary Ideology in *Native Son*," *African American Review* 35, no. 1 (2001): 31.

14. Ibid., 32.

15. Keith Clark, "A Distaff Dream Deferred? Ann Petry and the Art of Subversion," *African American Review* 26, no. 3 (autumn 1992): 495, http://www.jstor.org/.

16. Diana Trilling, "Class and Color," *Nation*, 162, no. 10 (March 9, 1946): 291, accessed December 8, 2012, http://search.ebscohost.com/.

17. Ann Petry, *The Street* (New York: Houghton Mifflin, 1946), 16.

18. Trilling, "Class and Color," 291.

19. Ibid.

20. Smethurst, "Invented by Horror," 30.

21. Fassler, "Colson Whitehead on Zombies," 1.

22. Colson Whitehead, *Zone One* (New York: Anchor, 2011), 7.

23. Ibid., 5.

24. Glen Duncan, "A Plague of Urban Undead in Lower Manhattan," *New York Times*, October 28, 2011, 2, accessed December 8, 2011, http://www.nytimes.com/.

25. Whitehead, *Zone One*, 304.

26. Ron Charles, "'Zone One,' by Colson Whitehead: Zombies Abound," *Washington Post*, October 19, 2011, Accessed December 8, 2012, http://www.washingtonpost.com/.

27. Jeremy Keehn, "*Zone One*: Six Questions for Colson Whitehead," *Harper's*, October 17, 2011, 2, accessed December 8, 2012, http://harpers.org/.

28. Ibid.

29. Jess d'Arbonne, "Zombie Book Review: 'Zone One' by Colson Whitehead," *Examiner*, January 16, 2012, 2, accessed December 8, 2012, http://www.examiner.com/.

30. Rudin, "Forbidden Thought," 1.

31. d'Arbonne, "Zombie Book Review," 2.

32. Rudin, "Forbidden Thought," 1.

33. d'Arbonne, "Zombie Book Review," 2.

34. Rudin, "Forbidden Thought," 2.

35. Arijit Sen, "Zombie Nation," *Missouri Review*, April 5, 2012, 3, accessed December 3, 2014, http://www.missourireview.com/.

36. d'Arbonne, "Zombie Book Review," 2.

37. Whitehead, *Zone One*, 35.

38. Tom Chiarella, "How It Ends," *Esquire*, September 19, 2011, 2, accessed December 8, 2012, http://www.esquire.com/.

39. Whitehead, *Zone One*, 87.

40. Ibid., 88.

41. Chiarella, "How It Ends," 2.

42. Whitehead, *Zone One*, 87.

43. Ibid., 73.

44. Ibid., 89.

45. Henry David Thoreau, *Walden and Civil Disobedience* (New York: Penguin, 1986), 51.

46. Duncan, "Plague of Urban Undead," 2.

47. Charlie Jane Anders, "Colson Whitehead's *Zone One* Shatters Your Post-apocalyptic Fantasies," Io9, December 29, 2011, 2, accessed December 8, 2012, http://io9.com/colson-whitehead.

48. Charles, "Zone One," 2.

49. Whitehead, *Zone One*, 288.

50. Ibid.

51. Sen, "Zombie Nation," 6.

52. Charles, "Zone One," 2.

53. Whitehead, *Zone One*, 303.

54. Clifford D. Deaton, "Seeing the Specter: A Gothic Metaphor of Subjectivity, Popular Culture, and Consumerism," *Gnovis Journal* 8, no. 2 (spring 2008): 95, accessed December 8, 2012, http://gnovisjournal.org/.

55. Ibid., 99.

Conclusion

Few writers possess the class, social grace, and intellect of Colson White-head. For any fan, including myself who has met Whitehead in person, no doubt they will deem him as a personable and well-spoken individual. Al-though he would probably resist the following descriptors, his upper-middle-class upbringing, private school education, and collegiate Harvard back-ground informs his experience as an African American of privilege. Perhaps the aforementioned statement is paradoxical. But as a postblack writer there is no absolute or monolithic way for him to perform blackness in the Obama era. However, it is an oblivious position to pretend that cultural identity is not informed by economic status, education, family structure, and regional back-ground. Although Whitehead states on numerous occasions that Obama's election does not signify the end of racism and satirically refers to himself as a postracial czar or secretary of postracial affairs, there is an element of truth to his proclamations. In an unprecedented manner, Whitehead has reached heights and acceptance amongst mainstream critics, academia, and the liter-ary establishment. Furthermore, each of his books offers a world where his-torically race mattered, but the main character feels socially alienated from both whites and blacks due to their empty lives despite their personal suc-cess. Also, the main characters in his narratives achieve in a manner that makes racism appear obsolete. On the other hand, Touré would consider Whitehead's writing postblack, and Derek Maus refers to Whitehead as an emblem of the postsoul aesthetic.

All things considered, Whitehead's nonfiction books *The Colossus of New York* and *The Noble Hustle* and fiction books *Apex Hides the Hurt* and *Zone One* choose not to address race in a meaningful and in-depth manner. Thus, he is providing postracial treatment to his characters, themes, and by extension his narrative. Even critics who despair over the superficial or sketch-like characters in Whitehead's fictional works acknowledge the genius of Whitehead's writing skills. At times, Whitehead's novels are critiqued as a series of interrelated anecdotes and witty observations, such as in *Sag Harbor*. However, those critiques are even more applicable to his nonfictional works, such as the *Colossus of New York* and *The Noble Hustle*. Perhaps, problematic concerns of superficial characters and anecdotal writing would cease if Whitehead addressed race in a contemporary context like he addresses class. Respectfully speaking, Whitehead should cast off his literary angst with racial subject matter and his distrust of literary forebears. After all, he once said to Kevin Larimer, "I'm going to have black characters, and this being America, it's going to end up being about race anyway, it seems to me."[1] By offering commentary that revolutionizes the way Americans interpret blackness and whiteness, he will remain a trailblazer. Thus, Whitehead's ambivalent positions and stances on race must resonate deeper in future narratives. He must resist the facile position of the everyman who is liked and accepted by everyone. In order to reach his highest heights as the premier African American writer, he must risk offending critics, some readers, academics, and even some members of the literary establishment.

Like the great Richard Wright, Ralph Ellison, and James Baldwin, Whitehead's literary works are consumed with the double consciousness of his African American and American identity. The aforementioned literary predecessors not only reconstructed black identity but also redefined notions of white identity, and they inextricably linked blackness and whiteness in the configuration of American identity prior to Toni Morrison's *Playing in the Dark*. Those African American forebears represented the voiceless, and they realized that despite social obstacles, they were in a privileged position of having a literary pulpit. In actuality, Whitehead should continue to resist proselytizing to his audience or the preachy pitfalls of protest literature. Perhaps this is why he leaves so many questions unanswered. Nevertheless, with the publication of *The Intuitionist* and *John Henry Days*, Whitehead forced America to examine not only race but also the intersection of race and class. Moreover, his signature themes of independence, freedom, and equality are reinterpreted in a mass-media-infused and consumer-based culture. Nevertheless, by inserting insightful and distinct commentary as in *The Intuitionist*, *John Henry Days*, and *Zone One*, these postmodern classics should be his self-imposed standard, not merely exceptional representations of his literary works. Regardless of what Whitehead chooses to do, his footprints are deeply imbedded in the literary path he continues to forge before us!

NOTE

1. Kevin Larimer, "Industrial Strength in the Information Age: A Profile of Colson Whitehead." *Poets & Writers*, July/August 2001, 23.

Bibliography

BOOKS BY COLSON WHITEHEAD

Apex Hides the Hurt. New York: Doubleday, 2006.
The Colossus of New York: A City in Thirteen Parts. New York: Anchor, 2003.
The Intuitionist. New York: Anchor, 1999.
John Henry Days. New York: Random House, 2001.
Sag Harbor. New York: Anchor, 2009.
Zone One. New York: Anchor, 2011.

UNCOLLECTED WRITINGS BY COLSON WHITEHEAD

"Visible Man." *New York Times*, April 24, 2008. Accessed January 1, 2014. http://www.nytimes.com/.
"The Way We Live Now: 9-23-01; Close Reading: Elements of Tragedy; The Image." *New York Times*, September 23, 2001. Accessed October 12, 2014. http://www.nytimes.com/.
"The Way We Live Now: 11-11-01; Lost and Found." *New York Times*, November 11, 2001. Accessed November 9, 2014. http://www.nytimes.com/.
"When Zombies Attack Lower Manhattan." NPR, July 20, 2012. Accessed December 8, 2012. http://www.npr.org/.
"The Year of Living Postracially." *New York Times*, November 3, 2009. Accessed January 1, 2014. http://www.nytimes.com/.

SECONDARY SOURCES

Alsup, Benjamin. "Colson Whitehead: The Coolest Writer in America." *Esquire*, March 25, 2009. Accessed November 23, 2014. http://www.esquire.com/.
Anders, Charlie Jane. "Colson Whitehead's *Zone One* Shatters Your Post-apocalyptic Fantasies." Io9, December 29, 2011. Accessed December 8, 2012. http://io9.com/colson-whitehead.
"Anthropomorphosis." Urban Dictionary, 2014. Accessed October 12, 2014. http://www.urbandictionary.com/.

Antrim, Taylor. "'Sag Harbor: A Novel' by Colson Whitehead." *Los Angeles Times*, April 26, 2009. Accessed November 22, 2014. http://www.latimes.com/.

"Apex Hides the Hurt." *Kirkus Reviews*, January 1, 2006. Accessed December 3, 2014. https://www.kirkusreviews.com/.

"Appalachian Music Fellowship Program—2006." Berea College, 2006. Accessed December 3, 2014. http://community.berea.edu/.

Appiah, Kwame Anthony. "Race." In *Critical Terms for Literary Study*, edited by Frank Lentricchia and Thomas McLaughlin, 274–87. Chicago: University of Chicago Press, 1995.

Ashabranner, Brent. "Pecos Bill: An Appraisal." *Western Folklore* 11, no. 1 (January 1952): 20–24.

Bakopoulos, Natalie. "*Sag Harbor*, by Colson Whitehead." *Fiction Writers Review*, May 15, 2009. Accessed November 22, 2014. http://fictionwritersreview.com/.

"Barack Obama: 2004 Democratic Convention Keynote Address." American Rhetoric, 2012. Accessed January 3, 2014. http://www.americanrhetoric.com/.

Barron, Zach. "Soul Sonic Summer: Colson Whitehead's *Sag Harbor*." *Village Voice*, April 29, 2009. Accessed November 29, 2004. http://www.villagevoice.com/.

Baughman, Ernest W. "Folklore to the Fore." *English Journal* 32, no. 4 (April 1943): 206–9.

Bell, Bernard W. *The Afro-American Novel and Its Tradition*. Amherst: University of Massachusetts Press, 1989.

Beltran, Cristina. *Melissa Harris-Perry Show*. MSNBC, November 1, 2014.

Benson, George. "On Broadway." Metro Lyrics, CBS Interactive, 2013. Accessed January 12, 2014. http://www.metrolyrics.com/.

Berlant, Lauren. "Intuitionists: History and the Affective Event." *American Literary History* 20, no. 4 (winter 2008): 1–16. Accessed January 5, 2014, http://alh.oxfordjournals.org/.

Bernstein, Sanders I. "Colson Whitehead '91: One of Harvard's Recent Authors Keeps It Real." *Harvard Crimson*, April 16, 2009. Accessed January 1, 2014. http://www.thecrimson.com/.

Bicknel, Jeanette. "'John Henry': Ethical Issues in Singing Performance." *Journal of Aesthetics and Art Criticism* 67, no. 2 (spring 2009): 173–80.

"Biographical Index of America's Founding Fathers." *A New World Is at Hand "The Charters of Freedom."* US National Archives and Records Administration. Accessed January 2, 2014. http://www.archives.gov/.

Birkerts, Sven. "Carry That Weight." *Esquire*, May 2001, 30. http://search.ebscohost.com/.

Bonds, Laura. "The Intuitionist." *Memphis Reads* (blog), June 6, 2007. Accessed January 3, 2014. http://memphisreads.blogspot.com/.

Boyd, Valerie. "The Intuitionist." *Star Tribune*, May 1, 1999. Accessed January 3, 2014. http://www.startribune.com/.

Brooks, Wanda, and Lorraine Savage. "Critiques and Controversies of Street Literature: A Formidable Literary Genre." *Alan Review* 36, no. 2 (winter 2009): 48–55.

Cassuto, Leonard. "Richard Wright and the Agony Over 'Integration.'" *Chronicle of Higher Education* 54, no. 6 (2008): B12–B13. History Reference Center. Accessed October 12, 2012. http://search.ebscohost.com/.

Charles, Ron. "Book Review: Ron Charles on Colson Whitehead's 'Sag Harbor.'" *Washington Post*, April 29, 2009. Accessed November 30, 2014. http://www.washingtonpost.com/.

———. "'Zone One,' by Colson Whitehead: Zombies Abound." *Washington Post*, October 19, 2011. Accessed December 8, 2012. http://www.washingtonpost.com/.

Chase, Richard. *The American Novel and Its Tradition*. Baltimore: Johns Hopkins University Press, 1957.

Chiarella, Tom. "How It Ends." *Esquire*, September 19, 2011. Accessed December 8, 2012. http://www.esquire.com/.

Clark, Keith. "A Distaff Dream Deferred? Ann Petry and the Art of Subversion." *African American Review* 26, no. 3 (autumn 1992): 495–505. http://www.jstor.org/.

Cohn, Jesse S. "Old Afflictions: Colson Whitehead's *Apex Hides the Hurt* and the 'Post-Soul Condition.'" *Journal of the Midwest Modern Language Association* 42, no. 1 (spring 2009): 15–24.

"The Colossus of New York: A City in Thirteen Parts." *Kirkus Reviews*, July 15, 2003. Accessed July 11, 2014. https://www.kirkusreviews.com/.

"Colson Whitehead: 2013—US and Canada Competition Creative Arts—Fiction Bio." John Guggenheim Memorial Foundation: Fellowships to Assist Research and Artist Creation. Accessed December 31, 2013. http://www.gf.org/.

Cuddon, J. A. "Invective." In *Dictionary of Literary Terms and Literary Theory*, 425–26. New York: Penguin, 1998.

————. "Satire." In *Dictionary of Literary Terms and Literary Theory*, 780–84. New York: Penguin, 1998.

Culler, Jonathan. *Literary Theory: A Very Short Introduction*. Oxford: Oxford University Press, 2011.

d'Arbonne, Jess. "Zombie Book Review: 'Zone One' by Colson Whitehead." *Examiner*, January 16, 2012. Accessed December 8, 2012. http://www.examiner.com/.

Deaton, Clifford D. "Seeing the Specter: A Gothic Metaphor of Subjectivity, Popular Culture, and Consumerism." *Gnovis Journal* 8, no. 2 (spring 2008): 95–108. Accessed December 8, 2012. http://gnovisjournal.org/.

"The Declaration of Independence." *A New World Is at Hand "The Charters of Freedom."* US National Archives and Records Administration. Accessed January 2, 2014. http://www.archives.gov/.

Dickstein, Morris. "Ralph Ellison, Race, and American Culture." In *Ralph Ellison's* Invisible Man*: A Casebook*, edited by John F. Callahan. New York: Oxford University Press, 2004.

Dorson, Richard M. "The Career of 'John Henry.'" *Western Folklore* 24, no. 3 (July 1965): 155–63.

Du Bois, W. E. B. *The Souls of Black Folk*. New York: Barnes & Noble Classics, 2003.

————. "Richard Wright Looks Back: Harsh, Forbidding Memories of Negro Childhood and Youth." In *Richard Wright's Black Boy (American Hunger)*, edited by William L. Andrews and Douglas Taylor, 33–36. New York: Oxford University Press, 2003.

Duncan, Glen. "A Plague of Urban Undead in Lower Manhattan." *New York Times*, October 28, 2011. Accessed December 8, 2011. http://www.nytimes.com/.

Dyson, Michael Eric. Foreword. In *Who's Afraid of Post-Blackness?* New York: Simon & Schuster, 2012.

Eagleton, Terry. *Literary Theory: An Introduction*. Minneapolis: University of Minnesota Press, 2008.

Elam, Michele. "Passing in the Post-Race Era: Danzy Senna, Philip Roth, and Colson Whitehead." *African American Review* 41, no. 4 (2007): 749–68.

Ellison, Charles D. "Define 'Urban Lit' . . ." *Huffington Post*, June 23, 2009. Accessed December 8, 2012. http://www.huffingtonpost.com/.

Ellison, Ralph. "The Novel as a Function of American Democracy." In *Going to the Territory*. New York: Vintage, 1995.

Fassler, Joe. "Colson Whitehead on Zombies, 'Zone One,' and His Love of the VCR." *Atlantic*, October 18, 2011. Accessed December 8, 2012. http://www.theatlantic.com/.

Feurer, Rosemary. "The Elusive Search for the Real John Henry." *Reviews in American History* 35, no. 3 (September 2007): 399–405.

Fishwick, Marshall W. "The Cowboy: America's Contribution to the World's Mythology." *Western Folklore* 11, no. 2 (April 1952): 77–92.

————. "Uncle Remus vs. John Henry: Folk Tension." *Western Folklore* 20, no. 2 (April 1961): 77–85.

Foster, Thomas C. *How to Read Literature Like a Professor*. New York: Harper, 2003.

Franzen, Jonathan. "Freeloading Man," *New York Times*, May 13, 2001. Accessed January 3, 2014. http://www.nytimes.com/.

Freeman, John. "'The Colossus of New York: A City in Thirteen Parts': Poetic Prose Dance to the Many Rhythms of the City." *Pittsburgh Post-Gazette*, December 14, 2003. Accessed July 11, 2014. http://old.post-gazette.com/.

Gates, David. "Name That Town." Review of *Apex Hides the Hurt*, by Colson Whitehead. Sunday Book Review, *New York Times*, April 2, 2006. Accessed December 7, 2014. http://www.nytimes.com/.

Gates, Henry Louis. *The Signifying Monkey: A Theory of African-American Literary Criticism.* New York: Oxford University Press, 1989.

Grausam, Daniel. "After the Post(al)." *American Literary History* 23, no. 3 (fall 2011): 635–36.

Griffin, Farah Jasmine. "Thirty Years of Black American Literature and Literary Studies: A Review." *Journal of Black Studies* 35, no. 2, *Special Issue: Back to the Future of Civilization: Celebrating 30 Years of African American Studies* (November 2004): 165–74.

Hakutani, Yoshinobu. "Creation of the Self in Richard Wright's *Black Boy*." In *Richard Wright's Black Boy (American Hunger)*, edited by William L. Andrews and Douglas Taylor, 131–48. New York: Oxford University Press, 2003.

Handle, Maurice. Introduction. In *Frankenstein*, by Mary Shelley. New York: Penguin, 2003.

Haney, Gladys J. "Paul Bunyan Twenty-Five Years After." *Journal of American Folklore* 55, no. 217 (July–September 1942): 155–68.

Henley, Don. "New York Minute." Metro Lyrics, CBS Interactive, 2013. Accessed July 12, 2014. http://www.metrolyrics.com/.

Hillis Miller, J. "Narrative." In *Critical Terms for Literary Study*, edited by Frank Lentricchia and Thomas McLaughlin, 66–79. Chicago: University of Chicago Press, 1995.

Hodges, John O. "An Apprenticeship to Life and Art: Narrative Design in Wright's *Black Boy*." In *Richard Wright's Black Boy (American Hunger)*, edited by William L. Andrews and Douglas Taylor, 113–30. New York: Oxford University Press, 2003.

Hoffman, Dan G. "Folk Tales of Paul Bunyan: Themes, Structure, Style, Sources." *Western Folklore* 9, no. 4 (October 1950): 302–20.

Holman, C. Hugh. "Satire." In *A Handbook to Literature*, by C. Hugh Holman and William Harmon, 398–99. 4th ed. Indianapolis: Bobbs-Merrill, 1981.

hooks, bell. *Ain't I a Woman: Black Women and Feminism.* Boston: South End Press, 1981.

———. *Writing Beyond Race: Living Theory and Practice.* New York: Routledge, 2013.

Howe, Nicholas. "Bi-coastal Myths." Review of *The Colossus of New York*, by Colson Whitehead. *Dissent* 51, no. 2 (2004): 86–90.

Humanick, Rob. "The Colossus of New York." *Slant*, June 25, 2012. Accessed October 18, 2014. http://www.slantmagazine.com/.

Hunter, J. Paul. Introduction. In *Frankenstein*, by Mary Shelley, edited by Paul Hunter. New York: Norton, 2012.

Inscoe, John C. "Race and Remembrance in West Virginia: John Henry for a Post-Modern Age." *Journal of Appalachian Studies* 10, nos. 1 and 2, *Whiteness and Racialization in Appalachia* (spring/fall 2004): 85–94.

"The Intuitionist." *Publishers Weekly*, December 1, 1998. Accessed January 3, 2014. http://www.publishersweekly.com/.

Jaggi, Maya. "Railroad Blues." *Guardian*, June 22, 2001. Accessed June 30, 2014. http://www.theguardian.com/.

Jay-Z, and Alicia Keys. "Empire State of Mind." Metro Lyrics, CBS Interactive, 2013. Accessed July 13, 2014. http://www.metrolyrics.com/.

"Jay-Z Confirms Great Gatsby Executive Producer Role." BBC Newsbeat, March 15, 2013. Accessed July 13, 2014. http://www.bbc.co.uk/.

Jehlen, Myra. "Gender." In *Critical Terms for Literary Study*, edited by Frank Lentricchia and Thomas McLaughlin, 263–73. Chicago: University of Chicago Press, 1995.

Katz, Jackson. "Memo to Media: Manhood, Not Guns or Mental Illness, Should Be Central in Newtown Shooting." *Huff Post Media*, December 18, 2012. Accessed June 25, 2014. http://m.huffpost.com/.

Keehn, Jeremy. "*Zone One*: Six Questions for Colson Whitehead." *Harper's*, October 17, 2011. Accessed December 8, 2012. http://harpers.org/.

Kirn, Walter. "Books: The Promise of Verticality." *Time*, January 25, 1999. Accessed January 26, 2014. http://content.time.com/.

Kleffel, Rick. "*The Colossus of New York* by Colson Whitehead." Agony Column, October 28, 2003. Accessed July 11, 2014. http://trashotron.com/agony.

Krist, Gary. "The Ascent of Man." *New York Times*, February 7, 1999. Accessed January 3, 2014. http://www.nytimes.com/.

Larimer, Kevin. "Industrial Strength in the Information Age: A Profile of Colson Whitehead." *Poets & Writers*, July/August, 2001, 23.

Lavender, III, Isiah. "Ethnoscapes: Environment and Language in Ismael Reed's *Mumbo Jumbo*, Colson Whitehead's *The Intuitionist*, and Samuel R. Delany's *Babel-17*." *Science Fiction Studies* 34, no. 2 (2007): 187–200.

Leach, MacEdward. "Folklore in American Regional Literature." *Journal of the Folklore Institute* 3, no. 3 (December 1966): 376–97.

Levine, Andrea. "'In His Own Home': Gendering the African American Domestic Sphere in Contemporary Literature." *Women's Studies Quarterly* 39, nos. 1 and 2 (spring/summer 2011): 170–87.

Levy, Jonathan. *Freaks of Fortune: The Emerging World of Capitalism and Risk in America.* Boston: Harvard University Press, 2014.

Liggins, Saundra. "The Urban Gothic Vision of Colson Whitehead's *The Intuitionist* (1999)." *African American Review* 40, no. 2 (summer 2006): 359–70.

Lopate, Phillip. "New York State of Mind." Review of *The Colossus of New York*, by Colson Whitehead. *Nation*, December 1, 2003. Accessed November 9, 2014. http://www.thenation.com/.

Mason, Wyatt. Review of *The Colossus of New York: A City in 13 Parts*, by Colson Whitehead. *New Republic*, December 4, 2003. Accessed October 12, 2014. http://www.powells.com/.

Maus, Derek C. *Understanding Colson Whitehead*. Columbia: University of South Carolina Press, 2014.

McCarthy, Mary. "Portrait of a Typical Negro?" In *Richard Wright's Black Boy (American Hunger)*, edited by William L. Andrews and Douglas Taylor, 41–44. New York: Oxford University Press, 2003.

McLaughlin, Robert L. "After the Revolution: US Postmodernism in the Twenty-First Century." *Narrative* 21, no. 3 (October 2013): 284–95.

Meyer, Michael. Introduction. In *Walden and Civil Disobedience*, by Henry David Thoreau. New York: Penguin, 1986.

Miles, Jonathan. "John Henry Days." *Salon*, May 11, 2001. Accessed June 30, 2014. http://www.salon.com/.

Miller, Claire Cain. "Technology's Man Problem." *New York Times*, April 5, 2014. Accessed June 6, 2014. http://www.nytimes.com/.

Miller, James. Foreword. In *Black No More: Being an Account of the Strange and Wonderful Working of Science in the Land of the Free, A.D. 1933–1940*, by George S. Schuyler. Lebanon, NH: Northeastern University Press, 1989.

Minzesheimer, Bob. "'Intuitionist' Lifts Novelist to New Heights." *USA Today*, December 1999. Accessed December 31, 2013. http://www.usatoday.com/.

Morgan, Thomas L. "Black Naturalism, White Determinism: Paul Laurence Dunbar's Naturalist Strategies." *Studies in American Naturalism* 7, no. 1 (summer 2012): 7–38.

Morris, Vanessa Irvin. *The Readers' Advisory Guide to Street Literature*. Chicago: American Library Association, 2011.

Morrison, Toni. *Playing in the Dark: Whiteness and the Literary Imagination*. New York: Vintage, 1993.

"Movin' on Up." *The Jeffersons* (theme song). YouTube, September 28, 2011. Accessed July 12, 2014. http://www.youtube.com/.

Nelson, Scott Reynolds. *Steel Drivin' Man: John Henry, the Untold Story of an American Legend*. New York: Oxford University Press, 2008.

Nikola-Lisa, W. "John Henry: Then and Now." *African American Review* 32, no. 1 (spring 1998): 51–56.

"No. 1: Trinity School." *Forbes*. Last updated April 29, 2010. Accessed January 2, 2014. http://www.forbes.com/.

"Notable Graduates." Harvard University, 2013. Accessed January 1, 2014. http://www.harvard.edu/.

Otah, Youkie. "Here Is the Colossus of New York." NewYorkBoundBooks.com, June 22, 2013. Accessed July 11, 2014. http://www.newyorkboundbooks.com/.

"Overview." *The Colossus of New York* (1958). Turner Classic Movies, 2014. Accessed October 12, 2014. http://www.tcm.com/.

Parker, Robert Dale. *How to Interpret Literature: Critical Theory for Literary and Cultural Studies*. New York: Oxford University Press, 2011.

Pease, Donald E. "The Author." In *Critical Terms for Literary Study*, edited by Frank Lentricchia and Thomas McLaughlin, 105–18. Chicago: University of Chicago Press, 1995.

Petry, Ann. *The Street*. New York: Houghton Mifflin, 1946.

Poe, Edgar Allan. "The Masque of the Red Death." In *The Complete Tales of Edgar Allan Poe*. New York: Barnes & Noble, 1999.

———. *The Narrative of Arthur Gordon Pym of Nantucket*. In *The Complete Tales of Edgar Allan Poe*. New York: Barnes & Noble, 1999.

"Post-racial." Urban Dictionary, 2014. Accessed January 1, 2014. http://www.urbandictionary.com/.

Poulos, Jennifer H. "'Shouting Curses': The Politics of 'Bad' Language in Richard Wright's *Black Boy*." In *Richard Wright's Black Boy (American Hunger)*, edited by William L. Andrews and Douglas Taylor, 149–70. New York: Oxford University Press, 2003.

Powell, Brent. "Henry David Thoreau, Martin Luther King Jr., and the American Tradition of Protest." *OAH Magazine of History* 9, no. 2, *Taking a Stand in History* (winter 1995): 26–29.

Preston, Rohan. "Colson Whitehead's Zombie Dream." *Star Tribune* Books, October 29, 2011. Accessed January 2, 2014. http://www.startribune.com/.

Ramsey, William. "An End of Southern History: The Down-Home Quests of Toni Morrison and Colson Whitehead." *African American Review* 41, no. 4, *Post-Soul Aesthetic* (winter 2007): 769–85.

Review of *Apex Hides the Hurt*, by Colson Whitehead. *Chicago Reader* Books, April 21, 2006. Accessed December 3, 2014. http://www.chicagoreader.com/.

Review of *Apex Hides the Hurt*, by Colson Whitehead. *Publishers Weekly*. Accessed December 3, 2014. http://www.publishersweekly.com/.

Ribas, Maria. "Q&A with Colson Whitehead." *Collegian*, December 18, 2009. Accessed July 11, 2014. http://thecollegianur.com/.

Rose, Cedric. "Colson Whitehead in the Zombie Zone." *Cincinnati* 45, no. 7 (April 2012): 28–29. Accessed December 8, 2012. http://connection.ebscohost.com/.

Rudin, Michael. "The Forbidden Thought: A Review of *Zone One*, by Colson Whitehead." *Fiction Writers Review*, February 14, 2012. Accessed December 8, 2012. http://fictionwritersreview.com/.

Russell, Alison. "Recalibrating the Past: Colson Whitehead's *The Intuitionist*." *Critique* 49, no. 1 (2007): 46–60.

Saldívar, Ramón. "The Second Elevation of the Novel: Race, Form, and the Postrace Aesthetic in Contemporary Narrative." *Narrative* 21, no. 1 (January 2013): 1–19.

Samuel, Lawrence R. *The American Dream: A Cultural History*. Syracuse, NY: Syracuse University Press, 2012.

Schama, Chloë. "Review of *Apex Hides the Hurt: A Novel*." *New Republic*, July 24, 2006. Accessed December 7, 2014. http://www.newrepublic.com/.

Schuyler, George S. *Black No More: Being an Account of the Strange and Wonderful Working of Science in the Land of the Free, A.D. 1933–1940*. Lebanon, NH: Northeastern University Press, 1989.

———. "The Negro-Art Hokum." In *African American Literary Theory: A Reader*, edited by Winston Napier, 24–27. New York: New York University Press, 2000.

Selzer, Linda. "Instruments More Perfect than Bodies: Romancing Uplift in Colson Whitehead's *The Intuitionist*." *African American Review* 43, no. 4 (winter 2009): 681–98.

———. "New Eclecticism: An Interview with Colson Whitehead." *Callaloo* 31, no. 2 (spring 2008): 393–401.

Sen, Arijit. "Zombie Nation." *Missouri Review*, April 5, 2012. Accessed December 3, 2014. http://www.missourireview.com/.

Shukla, Nikesh. "Colson Whitehead: Each Book an Antidote." *Guernica*, April 24, 2013. Accessed November 22, 2014. https://www.guernicamag.com/.

Sinatra, Frank. "New York, New York." Metro Lyrics, CBS Interactive, 2013. Accessed July 12, 2014. http://www.metrolyrics.com/.

Smethurst, James. "Invented by Horror: The Gothic and African American Literary Ideology in *Native Son*." *African American Review* 35, no. 1 (2001): 29–40.

Sorensen, Leif. "Against the Post-Apocalyptic: Narrative Closure in Colson Whitehead's *Zone One*." *Contemporary Literature* 55, no. 3 (2014): 599–92.

St. Clair, William. "*Frankenstein*'s Impact." *Frankenstein*: A Norton Critical Edition, 2nd edition, ed. J. Paul Hunter (New York: W. W. Norton and Company, 2012.

Sunderman, Eric. "Q&A: Colson Whitehead Talks Gritty New York, Zone One Zombies, and Frank Ocean's Sexuality." *Village Voice*, July 11, 2012. Accessed December 8, 2012. http://www.villagevoice.com/.

Tate, Claudia. "Notes on the Invisible Women in Ralph Ellison's *Invisible Man*." In *Ralph Ellison's* Invisible Man: *A Casebook*, edited by John F. Callahan. New York: Oxford University Press, 2004.

Thoreau, Henry David. *Walden and Civil Disobedience*. New York: Penguin, 1986.

Touré. "Visible Young Man." *New York Times*, May 1, 2009. Accessed November 22, 2014, http://www.nytimes.com/.

———. *Who's Afraid of Post-Blackness?* New York: Simon & Schuster, 2012.

Trachtenberg, Jay. "The Intuitionist." *Austin Chronicle*, March 24, 2000. Accessed January 3, 2014. http://austinchronicle.com/.

Treisman, Deborah. "Fiction: Q&A; Colson Whitehead." *New Yorker*, December 11, 2008. Accessed November 22, 2014. http://www.newyorker.com/.

Trilling, Diana. "Class and Color." *Nation*, 162, no. 10 (March 9, 1946): 290–91. Accessed December 8, 2012. http://search.ebscohost.com/.

Tucker, Jeffrey Allen. "'Verticality Is Such a Risky Enterprise': The Literary and Paraliterary Antecedents of Colson Whitehead's *The Intuitionist*." *A Forum on Fiction* 43, no. 1 (2010): 148–56.

Updike, John. "Tote That Ephemera: An Ambitious New Novel from a Gifted Writer." *New Yorker*, May 7, 2001. Accessed January 1, 2014. http://www.newyorker.com/.

Weinberg, Zoe A. Y. "Raceless Like Me: Students at Harvard Navigate Their Way beyond the Boundaries of Race." *Harvard Crimson*, October 13, 2011. Accessed July 11, 2014. http://www.thecrimson.com/.

Weiss, Bari. "Camille Paglia: A Feminist Defense of Masculine Virtues." *Wall Street Journal*, December 28, 2013. Accessed June 6, 2014. http://online.wsj.com/.

Willard, Charles B. "Our American Folk Tradition: A Unit in American Literature." *English Journal* 42, no. 2 (February 1953): 84–88.

Wise, Tim. *Colorblind: The Rise of Post-Racial Politics and the Retreat from Racial Equity*. San Francisco: City Lights Publisher, 2010.

Wolcott, James. "Men Evolving Badly." *Vanity Fair*, April 21, 2008. Accessed June 22, 2014. http://www.vanityfair.com/.

Woods, Terry. Foreword. In *The Readers' Advisory Guide to Street Literature*, by Vanessa Irvin Morris. Chicago: American Library Association, 2011.

Wright, Richard. *Black Boy*. 1945. New York: Harper Collins, 2006.

———. *Native Son*. 1940. New York: Harper Perennial Modern Classics, 2005.

Young, Elizabeth. "Frankenstein as Historical Metaphor." *Frankenstein*: A Norton Critical Edition, 2nd edition, ed. J. Paul Hunter (New York: W. W. Norton and Company, 2012.

Zalewski, Daniel. "An Interview with Colson Whitehead: Tunnel Vision." *New York Times Book Review*, May 13, 2001. Accessed February 8, 2014. http://www.nytimes.com/.

Zinoman, Jason. "The Critique of Pure Horror." *New York Times*, July 16, 2011. Accessed December 8, 2012. http://www.nytimes.com/.

Index

Africanist, 18, 20

African American(s): African American female, 8; African American heritage, xii, 13, 15, 45, 46, 51–52, 60, 91; African American identity, 27, 34, 46, 117; African American male, 61; Afro-American, 9, 14, 20, 131; artists, xvi, 21, 22, 26, 29, 118, 139; black heritage, xiii, 13, 60, 142; black identity, 29, 32–33, 78, 80, 82, 118, 121, 122–123, 128, 131, 132, 154; black-white conflicts, 119; culture, x, 10, 29, 94; emotional and physical displacement, 34; experience, 14–15, 128, 132, 138; fragmented identity, xviii, 13, 78, 80, 81; hip hop, xv, 93, 115, 118, 138–139, 141, 143; identity crisis, 78, 80, 82; interconnectedness of blacks and whites, 14; literature, xi, xiv, 30, 127; masks, 16, 18–20, 22, 25, 34, 77, 80, 101; miscegenation, 17; mixed background, 14; mixed-raced background, 25, 28; mixed-racial heritage, 25, 28; Negro, 14–15, 21, 27, 32, 46–47, 51, 59, 92, 118, 141; negroid, 32; novels, 9–10; novelists, 20–21, 30, 80; passive resistance or rebellion, 6, 16; stereotypes, 19, 32, 81, 132, 139; stereotypical, 20, 22, 61, 118, 121; trickster, 13, 22, 27, 46. *See also* alienation, social and physical from the

black and/or white society; American(s), white-black relations; American(s), culturally appropriated; black female; black femaleness; black male; black male identity; black militant; black woman; dehumanization; diversity; double consciousness; equality; folklore, African American; Henry, John, black folk legend; Ku Klux Klan; lynchings; minstrel, blackface; mobility; multiracial; nigger; postblack; postblackness; postracial; postsoul; progress; protest novels of African American literature; racial; racism; racist; satire; slavery; uplift; veil, the masking of blackness behind white gazes

African Americanness, 30, 32, 34

African American Review, xi

American(s), xii, xiv–xvi, xvii, 7, 9, 10, 14, 18, 21, 22, 26, 28, 29, 30, 33–34, 39–40, 41, 42–47, 54, 59, 60–61, 62, 63, 69, 71, 74, 75, 78, 80, 88, 91, 93, 98, 102, 106, 118, 121, 122, 123, 128, 129, 133, 137, 140–141, 144, 148, 154; anti-American, 106; aracial, 87, 92, 95n1; aspirational nature of, xvi, xvii, xviii, 34, 39–40, 55, 69; culturally appropriated, 47; culture, x, xiv, xviii, 15, 18, 19, 33, 62, 77, 92, 94, 128, 137;

About the Author

Kimberly Fain, JD, MA, has taught English literature at Texas Southern University (TSU) and Honston Community College (HCC). She has written various articles, essays, or chapters for both legal and literary publishers. Fain's publications specialize in the sociopolitical intersection of race, gender, and class in both classic literature and pop culture. Fain has earned a doctor of jurisprudence degree and master of arts in English from TSU and a bachelor of arts degree in English from Texas A&M University at College Station. She is the associate editor of *World Literary Review* and a freelance editor and book reviewer for various legal, literary, and religious publications. She contributed an essay on Colson Whitehead to the anthology *Street Lit: Representing the Urban Landscape* (Scarecrow, 2014). She is also the author of the upcoming book *Black Hollywood: From Butlers to Superheroes, the Changing Role of African American Men in the Movies* (2015).